Chaucer: An Introduction

Chaucer
An Introduction

S. S. HUSSEY

METHUEN & CO LTD
11 New Fetter Lane, London EC4

First published 1971
by Methuen & Co Ltd
11 New Fetter Lane, London EC4
© *1971 S. S. Hussey*
Printed in Great Britain by
Richard Clay (The Chaucer Press), Ltd
Bungay, Suffolk

SBN 416 14220 6 Hardback
SBN 416 29920 2 Paperback

Distributed in the USA
by Barnes & Noble Inc

Contents

Contents

For David

Foreword

Chaucer rightly holds his place at the centre of the increasing number of courses in Medieval English Literature in universities and colleges. But whereas formerly these courses were accompanied by rigorous investigations of Middle English language and 'background', nowadays the reader is more likely to be well informed about the literature and critical principles of later periods but somewhat at sea when he ventures into the Middle Ages. There seemed to be a need, therefore, for a book which would try to show how and why Chaucer is interesting to *us*, while at the same time suggesting what made him an outstanding poet in his own age.

I am, it goes without saying, greatly indebted to the scholarly and critical writings of numerous Chaucerians. Where I am conscious of the debt I have acknowledged it, but I hope to be pardoned any borrowings I have inadvertently overlooked. The University of Lancaster granted me sabbatical leave during the latter part of 1970 and the University of Edinburgh generously offered me its hospitality: without these kindnesses the writing of this book would have taken far longer than it has. My colleagues, Mr A. J. Gilbert and Mr J. D. Burnley, were good enough to read the first draft of the book. I have tried to profit from their many suggestions, but any inaccuracies or infelicities remaining are mine alone. Messrs Methuen have, as ever, been both efficient and courteous. I should also like to thank Miss Jane Fingland and Miss Jane Lind for typing the manuscript.

I

Poet and Public

For most people English literature still begins with Chaucer.
This is not simply because of the language barrier of Old
English and the (occasionally deceptive) ease of understanding Chaucer's late Middle English, but because we feel
that here is a man who wrote a good deal, with an evident
feeling for style, and who accepted the permanent worth of
what he had written, placing it, with all due modesty, in the
classical tradition:

> Go, litel bok, go litel myn tragedye,
> Ther God thi makere yet, er that he dye,
> So sende myght to make in som comedye!
> But, litel book, no makyng thow n'envie,
> But subgit be to alle poesye;
> And kis the steppes, where as thow seest pace
> Virgile, Ovide, Omer, Lucan, and Stace.[1]

Although tributes to his reputation almost all come from
after his death,[2] there seems little doubt that he was regarded
as a first-class poet by his contemporaries, and that, despite
the occasional assertions of his own inferiority that appear in
his works, he knew that he was a success with them.

Yet he was not a professional poet; probably no one was in
the fourteenth century. It is not surprising therefore, that
we know much more about his life than we know about how
and when he wrote his poems. Medieval audiences, in any

Ther God, may God
make . . . comedye, compose a
comedy (a story with a happy
ending)

no . . . envie, don't compete with
any other poem
pace, pass

case, would seem to have been interested chiefly in the story and less in the personality of its poet. Plagiarism was no sin, and many of Chaucer's stories, like Shakespeare's, are borrowed from other writers. As T. S. Eliot said, one test of a great poet is what he does with his borrowings,[3] and in Chaucer, as again in Shakespeare, much is transformed in the process. Consequently, in medieval poetry, sheer originality is at a much lower premium than it is nowadays, and the sense of tradition is correspondingly strong. That is why Chaucer sees himself in the quotation above as a humble follower of the great classical writers, and why too the approach to his work (especially to *The Canterbury Tales*) is here made primarily through *genre*. In the records we have, then, Chaucer appears as courtier, diplomat and civil servant, but hardly ever as poet.[4]

We do not know exactly when he was born. At a trial in 1386 at which he was a witness, he confessed to being then 'forty years old and more', so that it is usual to put his birth about 1343. He was a Londoner, and his father was a well-to-do wine merchant who enjoyed some minor royal patronage. The family was reasonably prosperous without being gentry, and their fortunes were perhaps in the ascendant – which augured well for young Geoffrey. His education may well have been at St Paul's cathedral school, but this is by no means certain. Wherever it was, it would have involved much learning by heart and dictating from the master's book, for books were expensive and in short supply and there was an almost complete absence of reference books. Chaucer, therefore, had to memorise, but even so his memory was clearly remarkable, and it served him in good stead throughout his poetic career. Unfortunately we have neither a contemporary map nor a detailed description of the London in which Chaucer grew up, although a good deal of information about life in the city can be obtained from the records.[5] As a boy, he probably lived in Upper Thames Street, near the river and wharves, not far either from St Paul's (then a great social as well as a religious centre) or from Lombard Street and the markets of Cheapside. Medieval London was still a place in which it was possible to move about quickly, and it was easy to walk out of the city into the surrounding countryside. Its population in the later fourteenth century may have been between 50,000 and 60,000.

The first mention of Chaucer's name shows him in 1357 in the service of Elizabeth, Countess of Ulster, wife of Prince Lionel, one of the sons of Edward III. The accounts of Elizabeth's household include payments for a short cloak, red and black breeches, a pair of shoes, and twenty shillings 'for necessaries at Christmas'. This suggests that he was a page in Elizabeth's (and later in Lionel's own) service where he would begin to acquire the fashionable code of courtly manners and to further his study of French and Latin. 1359–60 finds him fighting in France, perhaps with Lionel. He was taken prisoner, but the fact that the king contributed to his ransom money might suggest that he had already come under the notice of either Edward or of his famous son, the Black Prince. There follows an annoying gap between 1360 and 1366. Lionel was in Ireland from 1361 to 1366. The records for this expedition are quite full but do not include Chaucer's name, and, if he did indeed go there, Ireland seems to have been the one country he visited which left no mark upon his work. A more probable conjecture is that he was a student at the Inner Temple during those years, but the records for this period have unfortunately disappeared. Although he would have received some legal instruction there, his studies would by no means have been confined to law, since a training of this kind was a natural preparation for a career in public affairs, such as Chaucer's was. In late medieval England, the legal schools were beginning to break the Church's earlier monopoly of education.

In 1366 Chaucer's father died and his mother remarried. Chaucer himself also probably married in this year. We know next to nothing about his married life – a few wry jokes in his works about shrewish wives need not be taken personally – but his wife Philippa was in the queen's service and her sister was first the mistress and then the third wife of John of Gaunt, the most powerful of Edward III's sons, especially after the death of the Black Prince in 1376. Chaucer had clearly made an advantageous marriage, although he may already have been regarded as a coming young man. It may have been his marriage that brought about his transfer to the King's service in which he is described as a valet in 1367 and as a squire in the following year. He may possibly have gone to Spain with the Black Prince in 1366, and more probably to France again in 1369, with Gaunt this time. He was abroad in 1368 and 1370 on diplomatic or commercial business for the King. He surely continued in these years his acquisition of both the code of courtly manners and poetic technique. (We know that he wrote many short poems, some perhaps lost, and several of these are probably early work.) He also made some translations and adaptations from French in the 1360s. His first major poem, *The Book of the Duchess*, can be confidently dated 1369–70. A good comment on these years is the portrait of the Squire on the Canterbury pilgrimage: twenty years old, already with campaign experience, lover, fashionable dresser, good horseman and dancer, composer of songs which he could accompany on the flute, and always courteous and willing to serve – blending (as Blake later put it) 'literature and the arts with his warlike studies'. By 1370, Chaucer had already, in the modern phrase, 'arrived'.

1370–86 were crowded years. He visited Italy twice, in 1372–3 and 1378. It is after *The Book of the Duchess* that the influence of Boccaccio, Dante and Petrarch shows in his poetry, and he may well have first become acquainted with their work in Italy. At home he obtained a rent-free house above Aldgate, in the city of London, in 1374, and he kept it for twelve years. He was appointed Controller of Customs and Subsidies on Wools, Skins and Hides in the Port of London in 1374 – he uncovered a smuggling plot in 1376 and received the whole value of the merchandise as a reward – and Controller of the Petty Customs on wines and merchandise in 1382. In 1385 he became a Justice of the Peace for Kent and in 1386 Knight of the Shire (M.P.) for the same county. But in 1386 he gave up his Aldgate house, both controllerships at the customs, and was not re-elected M.P. in 1387. Perhaps these retirements were connected with the absence from England and the partial eclipse of his patron,

John of Gaunt. Edward III was dead, and the new king, Richard II, was a minor and not yet in control of affairs of state. In London there was opposition, which was to grow stronger later in Richard's reign, to the court party. Father Mathew suggests, but without much evidence, that one of its most prominent members, Robert de Vere, may have been a patron of Chaucer.[6] Two of his acquaintances, Nicholas Bembre and the writer Thomas Usk, were executed in these years. On the other hand, the withdrawal from public service may have been welcome: 1386–7 are the years generally assigned to the *General Prologue* and the drawing up of the scheme of *The Canterbury Tales*. From 1370 to 1386, therefore, Chaucer was a successful diplomat and civil servant, and in his poetry new Italian influences supplemented (but did not replace) the French conventions noticeable from the beginning of his writing.

In 1389 Chaucer was back in public life again – if he had ever been really out of it. Gaunt returned from Spain in 1389, and in the same year Richard announced that he was of age and intended to assume full royal powers. From that year until 1391 Chaucer was Clerk of the King's Works at Westminster, the Tower of London, Eltham and Sheen (the latter two palaces he mentions in *The Legend of Good Women*) and other royal residences, eight in all. His duties also included supervising the survey of walls, sewers, ditches and bridges along the Thames and the construction of seating for tournaments. (In *The Knight's Tale* he describes a magnificent amphitheatre for a tournament which seems, like those in London, to have been a considerable social event.) In 1391 he was appointed sub-forester of the royal forest of North Petherton in Somerset – which may or may not have been a sinecure – and the appointment was renewed in 1398. This is the last regular office he is known to have held. From 1395 onwards he may have been enjoying the favour of John of Gaunt's son, Henry, Earl of Derby, who became Henry IV in 1399. But Chaucer may not have been altogether happy during these years. We find him borrowing money from the Exchequer. In his occasional poems he complains he is getting old and that his scribe will not copy accurately, but these may be no more than half-humorous remarks. In 1399 he leased a house in the garden of Westminster Abbey, but did not live long to enjoy it, for he died in October 1400, not yet sixty. He is buried in the Abbey, but as a resident in the precincts, not as a poet.

It is an impressive public career under three kings. They were stirring years, too, with first the brilliant success and then the gradual failure of English expeditions in France; the greatest medieval outburst of plague, the Black Death, in 1349 (which reappeared in 1361 and 1362 and which killed John of Gaunt's first wife, Blanche the Duchess, in 1369); John Wyclif's attacks on the ecclesiastical system between 1378 and 1381; the papal schism, with rival popes in Rome and Avignon, beginning in 1378; the discontent over economic and social conditions culminating in the Peasants' Revolt in 1381 (during which John of Gaunt's London palace, the Savoy, was sacked); the abdication of Richard II and his murder soon afterwards. Yet about all this Chaucer's poetry has practically nothing to say, unlike his fellow-Londoner Gower who was terrified by the Revolt, and unlike his other contemporary, Langland, who was passionately concerned about economic conditions and spiritual decay. We can only speculate about Chaucer's silences. He may well have been more tolerant and urbane than Gower and Langland. The city gate at Aldgate was opened to the rebels of the Peasants' Revolt. If Chaucer was at home, he fails to mention it. All he does is to compare jokingly a farmyard chase of a fox (in *The Nun's Priest's Tale*) to the insurgents chasing Flemings whom they suspected of taking away their livelihood. Perhaps Chaucer's royal patronage had something to do with it. Perhaps he simply did not regard political or religious events as fit subjects for his kind of poetry. The interactions of his public and poetic career are more intangible. He must have met a great variety of people and apparently got on well with most of them. His poetry testifies to his remarkable knowledge of human nature, and the descriptions of some of his Canterbury pilgrims may contain details of people well known to his audience. His reading – which was considerable – and his writing must have been done in what spare time he could snatch from a busy life. The Eagle in *The House of Fame* taunts the Dreamer in that poem (called Geoffrey) with knowing nothing about his neighbours, but instead going home from his *rekeninges* (perhaps at the Custom House; the dates fit) and poring over yet another book until his look becomes stupefied (*daswed*). In his early poems Chaucer often speaks of his bedside reading, and in one of them, *The Parliament of Fowls*, he tells how darkness

> Berafte me my bok for lak of lyght 87

and how, at the end of the same poem,

> I wok, and othere bokes tok me to,
> To reede upon, and yit I rede alwey. 695–6

He knows other authors (besides Boccaccio, his source) who have written about Criseyde (*Troilus and Criseyde* v, 816, 1044, 1095). One of his great achievements is in making us share so much of the interest and excitement of his reading.

But if we had to rely on Chaucer's works alone we would get a very different view of their author. He would emerge, from his own picture of himself, as a middling poet at best, writing as well as he is able but quite unequal to the complexities of the highest poetry, glad of any ear dropped by far better reapers of the poetic field, a pilgrim whose own *Tale of Sir Thopas* – the *beste rym I kan* – is angrily interrupted by the Host who cannot stand any more of such *verray lewednesse* (downright stupidity) and *drasty rymyng*. (*The Tale of Melibeus*, the *litel thyng in prose* which he offers as a second try certainly meets Harry Bailey's request for *doctryne* (instruction), though hardly for the *murthe* which that worthy suggested as an alternative.) He is naïve, dim even, since it takes him a long time to see what has been evident to everyone much earlier; inexpert in love, since all he knows about that art has come from books; easily impressed by the pilgrims around him, siding with the 'sensible' view of the Monk and captivated by the Prioress.[7]

rekeninges, accounts
Berafte . . . bok, Prevented me from (reading) my book

tok me, devoted myself
yit . . . alwey, I'm still always reading

All this is clearly a poetic pose, perhaps originating in one of the conventions of medieval rhetoric which advocated initial modesty as a simple and easy way of endearing the poet to his audience and, by implication, of winning delighted acclaim when he wrote better than he had promised. It may also have had something to do with Chaucer's bourgeois origins and his position as a court poet seeking to please his social superiors. But we must not take it too far. In recent years this poetic *persona* has loomed larger and larger in the study of Chaucer, so that what began as biographical dichotomy has ended up as critical schizophrenia. It is surely much better to interpret Chaucer's picture of himself as comprising a few rather obvious jokes meant for an audience who were listening to his poems and not reading them quietly as we do now.

For this is how most medieval poetry first saw the light of day. Literacy was not widespread outside the church and the court, and not even universal within the church (especially among parish priests). Even people who could read perfectly well evidently liked, on occasion, to have things read to them. Pandarus surprises a group of Criseyde and her ladies listening to one of their number reading aloud from a 'romance'. A manuscript of *Troilus and Criseyde*, now at Corpus Christi College, Cambridge, has a frontispiece showing Chaucer reading his poetry to what looks like a courtly audience.[8] In any case, Chaucer lived a century before printing was introduced into England. Books, copied by hand, were expensive, especially if illustrated. Chaucer's Clerk would have preferred (*was levere have*) twenty books of philosophy handsomely bound to rich robes or musical instruments; he is unlikely to have *possessed* half as many. Outside a few large private collections and the libraries of institutions such as monasteries, few people owned many books. Where did Chaucer get the books he read? Were they all his? We simply do not know. From the thirteenth century onwards there was much gathering of existing knowledge into encyclopaedias or anthologies. This makes it difficult for us to be sure of first-hand borrowing. If a poem was successful on its first reading, the author might be asked for further copies, and if it was very successful there might well be copies of those copies. This means, however, that the copies go out of the author's hands. He cannot correct the mistakes that inevitably creep in, and if he attempts a revision of his work there is no guarantee that it will supersede the original. The modern editor, including the editor of Chaucer, has therefore to do his best to work back towards the original (which is itself seldom extant), selecting the best manuscript, resolving textual cruxes and interpreting as he goes. The modern punctuation of our present-day medieval texts, including paragraphing and capitalisation, while it makes our reading easier, is inevitably a form of interpretation. The task of establishing what the medieval author wrote is capable of a rather more exact final solution where, as in the case of Chaucer, several manuscripts of his work are still extant; for the eighth-century *Beowulf* and the fourteenth-century *Sir Gawain and the Green Knight*, two of the greatest of our early poems, we now have just one manuscript each.

It is easy to check on the oral transmission, and, equally important, the poet's expectation of such oral transmission, by taking a long poem such as *The Knight's Tale*. At its beginning Chaucer is rapidly summarising the relevant section of Boccaccio's *Teseida*. He has no time to do more than outline the campaign in question and must move on:

> And thus with victorie and with melodye
> Lete I this noble duc to Atthenes ryde,
> And al his hoost in armes hym bisyde.　　872–4

But not too quickly; a few more names, perhaps, before returning to

> This duc, of whom I make mencioun　　893

and his homecoming, because the lament of certain ladies he meets leads to the sack of Thebes and the discovery and imprisonment of two young knights, Palamon and Arcite, found lying wounded among the slain. From their prison they see Emily, Theseus's young sister-in-law, walking in the garden below, and immediately both fall in love with her. It is obvious that the plot will revolve around who wins the girl, and we have already met the four main characters, Palamon, Arcite, Theseus and Emily – although Emily has little to do except look desirable. A lot of ground has been covered quite quickly, but this is going to be a long story (the two young men have to get out of prison, and they are sworn brothers which introduces complications), and when it is recited there can be no quotation marks, nor can the audience turn back a page or two, as the reader can. It is therefore necessary for the author to make completely clear who it is that is speaking at any moment. Consequently we are always coming across narrative directions (e.g. 1092, 1123, 1152, 1334–6, 1449–50, 1488, 1661–2) which signal a change of scene or else say, in effect, 'X has finished speaking and Y begins'. Important facts have to be fixed in the listeners' minds:

> The grete tour, that was so thikke and stroong,
> Which of the castel was the chief dongeoun,
> (Ther as the knyghtes weren in prisoun
> Of which I tolde yow and tellen shal) . . .
>
> 1056–9

their appetite can be whetted:

> Duc Theseus hym leet out of prisoun
> Frely to goon wher that hym liste over al,
> In swich a gyse as I you tellen shal.   1206–8⁹

they (or at least one section of them) can be appealed to:

> Yow loveres axe I now this questioun:
> Who hath the worse, Arcite or Palamoun?
> That oon may seen his lady day by day,
> But in prison he moot dwelle alway;
> That oother wher hym list may ride or go,
> But seen his lady shal he nevere mo.
> Now demeth as yow liste, ye that kan,
> For I wol telle forth as I bigan.   1347–54

Ther as, Where
wher . . . over al, anywhere he pleased
gyse, manner
moot, must

wher hym list, wherever he pleases
Now . . . kan, Now you experts (in *fine amour*) judge as you please

These same lovers can be gently mocked:

> Into a studie he fil sodeynly,
> As doon thise loveres in hir queynte geres,
> Now in the crope, now doun in the breres,
> Now up, now doun, as boket in a welle.

1530-3

but so can the narrator:

> Who koude ryme in Englyssh proprely
> His martirdom? for sothe it am nat I;
> Therefore I passe as lightly as I may.

1459-61

who cannot bear to pass over promising material (which he *can* manage):

> Why sholde I noght as wel eek telle yow al
> The portreiture that was upon the wal
> Withinne the temple of myghty Mars the rede?

1967-9

The invention of printing limited participation at the same time as it widened the audience. In poetry meant for oral delivery, on the other hand, the poet is one of themselves as he gradually unfolds his tale to his listeners. They become part of it, and there is all the time in the world.

Although the rapport between author and audience, with the poet becoming part actor as well as narrator, is evident in much of Chaucer's work, private reading is not excluded. The bookworm of *The House of Fame* and *The Parliament of Fowls* is unlikely to have been the only silent reader in fourteenth-century London, although he probably did more private reading for pleasure than did most of his educated contemporaries. Occasionally in *The Canterbury Tales* the fiction of pilgrims telling tales to each other is forgotten:

studie, reverie
queynte geres, strange goings-on
crope, heights (literally, 'top of the tree')

passe as lightly, pass on as quickly
eek, also

And therefore, whoso list it nat yheere,
Turne over the leef and chese another tale.
                              Miller's Prologue, 3176–7

When some interesting but irrelevant material crops up in
The Knight's Tale, Chaucer remarks:

But of that storie list me nat to *write*   1201

He again says it is *inpossible me to wryte* of the joy and relief of
Dorigen and Arveragus at the close of *The Franklin's Tale*
(1549), and the Second Nun appeals to *yow that reden that*
(what) *I write* (78). In *Troilus and Criseyde*, v 270, he addresses
Thow, redere, and speaks of the poem as being *red . . . or elles
songe* (recited) at v 1797. In any event, if the number of
extant manuscripts is any guide, by the time of *The Canterbury Tales* and *Troilus* Chaucer may have been writing for a
wider public. Three manuscripts each of both *The Book of the
Duchess* and of *The House of Fame* and fourteen of *The Parliament of Fowls* suggest primarily a court audience; over
seventy of *The Canterbury Tales* and the variety of stories
within that work does not exclude a court public but would
seem to include other kinds of readers too.

The second half of the fourteenth century is the high-water
mark of medieval English literature, and this is, in part,
a reflection of what had been happening to the English
language. In the first half of the medieval period the English
language had been in eclipse, following the establishment in
England of a Norman–French aristocracy after the Conquest.
During the thirteenth and fourteenth centuries, however,
English had gradually grown in importance as the links
between England and France grew weaker. As English
nobles more and more settled at home (instead of holding
lands in both countries) so they more and more spoke and
read English, although, even in the earlier period, there was
almost certainly more bilingualism than is usually allowed.
Early fourteenth-century books in English are still sometimes
self-conscious, as if they were admitting to being poor

whoso . . . yheere, whoever doesn't   *list me nat*, I don't want to
  want to listen to it

relations of French, as indeed in technique and sophistication they often were. By Chaucer's time this is over and done with, but there was still no great tradition of English literature for him to draw on. Consequently the court where he grew up as a squire spoke English but often *read* French or Latin. To speak of a man as 'literate' might still mean that he read and understood Latin. Educated men were in fact trilingual: Gower's three major works are written, one in English, one in French and one in Latin. By the late fourteenth century, although most of the great magnates seem to have been bilingual in English and French,[10] we may suppose that they were often better at reading or understanding French than at speaking it. It is just at this period, when English is flexing its muscles to deal with subjects which for long had been the province of French and Latin, that most French words enter the language, either because they filled a need or because writers had simply forgotten the English equivalent. J. A. Sheard analysed the vocabulary of the *General Prologue*[11] and found nearly five hundred French-derived words in its 858 lines; some (*vileynye, chivalrye, daliaunce*) are recognisably French, but others (*pees, honeste, moneye*) seem already by Chaucer's time to have become completely English.

There was no standard English in the modern sense. Men wrote as well as spoke their own dialect, although naturally they were expected to write more formally than they spoke. Chaucer was well aware of the variety of dialects and the possibility of copyists substituting different dialectal forms and corrupting his metre:

> And for ther is so gret diversite
> In Englissh and in writyng of oure tonge,
> So prey I God that non myswrite the,
> Ne the mysmetre for defaute of tonge.
> And red wherso thow be, or elles songe,
> That thow be understonde, God I bieche!
>
> *Troilus and Criseyde* v 1793–8

myswrite, miscopy
mysmetre, get the metre wrong

defaute of tonge, mistake in the dialect

It would be a great mistake, however, to regard dialectal literature as in any way 'provincial' (*Sir Gawain and the Green Knight*, from the North-West Midlands, is among the most courtly of Middle English romances and much fifteenth-century Scottish literature is full of aureate terms). Chaucer's London dialect has, however, one great advantage for us. It was on the basis of this dialect that a written standard English grew up in the fifteenth and sixteenth centuries. The choice of the dialect of London and the South-East Midlands for this standard was not due to Chaucer's literary pre-eminence, although that may have helped; more important factors were the political, social and economic importance of the capital. Professor Barbara Strang has recently pointed out that the opportunities at the close of the Middle Ages for corporate life for young men – at universities, inns of court, as pages in great houses or members of religious communities – must have led to considerable linguistic mixture, and that this, where it involved migration to the capital and its environs, would have assisted the growth of a London-based standard language.[12] As a result we find Chaucer easier to read than many of his contemporaries, although we should beware of too readily giving their modern equivalents to some of his words, like *gentilesse, sad, sentence* and *daunger*.[13]

We may end this introductory chapter by listing the canon of Chaucer's major works. Their order is more impor-tant than their dates which can usually be only approxi-mate.

before 1369–70	translation of (part of) the *Roman de la Rose*, composed in French *c.* 1237–*c.* 1280
	The A.B.C. to the Virgin
1369–70	*The Book of the Duchess*
? late 1370s	*The House of Fame*
? *c.* 1382	*The Parliament of Fowls*
? 1382–5	translation of Boethius, *De Consolatione Philosophiae*, composed in Latin, early sixth century
c. 1385	*Troilus and Criseyde*

c. 1386	*The Legend of Good Women*
1386–7 onwards	*The Canterbury Tales* (incorporating earlier material)
1391–2	*The Astrolabe*
1392	? *The Equatorie of the Planetis*

II
Dreams and their Dreamers

'Grant translateur, noble Geoffrey Chaucier!' exclaims Eustache Deschamps in a *ballade*, possibly composed in 1386 and sent to Chaucer as a gift, together with other poems, by the hand of Sir Lewis Clifford, one of Chaucer's friends at court. It is a laudatory, even an extravagant work,[1] and it is a tribute to Chaucer's standing among contemporary French writers. At the beginning of the second stanza, Chaucer is called 'an earthly God of Love in Albion' (i.e. England) and praised for having translated 'the Book of the Rose' into 'good English'. These two attributes are of special importance and interest in the consideration of Chaucer's early poetry.

The *Roman de la Rose* was a long love poem in French, begun by Guillaume de Lorris about 1237. A translation of some 7700 lines of the whole poem into late fourteenth-century English exists in three fragments, and fragment A (the first 1700 lines) is almost certainly by Chaucer. De Lorris had been responsible for the first 4000-odd lines of the original, and 18,000 more were added, about forty years later, by Jean de Meun (or Jean Clopinel – 'club-foot' – as he is sometimes called). But, however much or little he himself translated, Chaucer obviously knew the whole poem intimately, and its influence can be seen throughout his work.

The poem is set in the form of a dream, and its opening lines discuss the interpretation of dreams. In this particular vision the Dreamer wanders by a river-side, early one May morning, when the earth has recovered from its winter torpor, the birds are singing, the flowers springing up, and the air clear and warm – in fact, the traditional season for loving, for men and animals alike to choose their mates. We are told that the book which relates the dream is 'the Romaunce of the Rose/In which al the art of love I close'.² The Dreamer comes upon a garden enclosed by a wall on the outside of which are painted various disagreeable (allegorical) characters such as Vilanye (Ill-breeding), Covetousness and Elde (Old Age). A maiden called Idleness (Leisure) opens a wicket gate and lets the Dreamer into the garden. Inside he finds more springlike delights, such as birds and small animals, flowers, luxuriant trees and music and dancing, the latter led by Mirth and his retinue who are *pleasant* allegorical figures, unlike those on the wall outside. In the clear water of the well of Narcissus (whose story is told) the Dreamer sees reflected all the delights of the garden, and in particular a rose-bush, covered with fragrant blooms, but surrounded by a hedge. He fixes his eye on one especially beautiful bud. (Fragment A ends here.) The Dreamer, however, has been followed at a distance by Cupid, the God of Love, pictured, as often in medieval literature, not as a blind boy but as a handsome young man. As he leans towards the bud, the God of Love wounds him with arrows from his bow: the Dreamer has become a Lover. He agrees to be the servant of Cupid and is given the latter's commandments ('For now the Romance bigynneth to amende', says the translator) and plenty of good advice about loving. Some of this is astonishingly practical:

> Thyn hondis wassh, thy teeth make white,
> And let no filthe upon thee bee.
> Thy nailes blak if thou maist see,
> Voide it awey delyverly,
> And kembe thyn heed right jolily.   2280–4

and shows the civilising aspect of the aristocratic code of love (*fine amour*) which is Guillaume de Lorris's real subject. Next the Dreamer/Lover meets the young knight Bialacoil ('Fair Welcome', an ally in his quest for the Rose) and the thug

close, include
Voide . . . delyverly, clean it away
  quickly

heed, hair
jolily, nicely

Daunger ('Disdain', the guardian of the rose-bush and clearly an enemy). He rejects Reason's advice to give up his love, and with the help of Bialacoil and Venus even kisses the bud, but at this presumption the defenders rally. Bialacoil is imprisoned in a tower, the defences around the rose-bush are strengthened and the Lover is banished from the garden. At this point Guillaume de Lorris ends.

Jean de Meun, the continuator, was as different from Guillaume de Lorris as chalk from cheese. Jean was primarily an encyclopaedist,[3] and had no lasting interest in Guillaume's story. But although his interests were wide-ranging – from fashion to friars and from alchemy to sleep-walking – he was a successful encyclopaedist: he knew the educational pill had to be sugar-coated. There is a great deal of excellent poetry in the second and longer part of the *Roman de la Rose*, but it occurs in a series of very long speeches, and only the thread of Guillaume's story is precariously retained. These speeches are nearly impossible to summarise adequately, except by a list of the main speakers. Reason reappears and expounds the varieties and contrarieties of love, the use of riches and (especially) the vicissitudes of Fortune, with ancient and modern examples. The Lover is provided with a confidant, Amis (Friend), who gives him a good deal of cynical and worldly-wise advice on women and marriage. (Whereas Guillaume de Lorris had idealised woman, Jean de Meun is most apt to satirise her.) Love reappears, and summons his barons to attack the castle in which Bialacoil is imprisoned. Fals-Semblant (False-Seeming, Hypocrisy) and Abstinaunce break into the castle and bring Bialacoil a gift from the Lover (but not before a long confession by Fals-Semblant which deals largely with hypocrisy in religion, especially on the part of the friars). Bialacoil's jailer is an old crone, the Vekke or Duenna, whose literary successors include the Wife of Bath and the Nurse in *Romeo and Juliet*. She knows all the 'old dance' of love and gives plenty of advice to women on how to get their man – even when almost on the shelf themselves. The Lover is reunited with Bialacoil, makes a further attempt upon the Rose, is once more repulsed and Bialacoil reimprisoned. Love and his barons attack the castle which is defended by Daunger and his followers; there is a long battle, fought with both real and allegorical weapons. Nature (the vicar, or deputy, of God) and her priest Genius now appear. There is much about the marvels of Nature, but she confesses to Genius that of all her creatures man alone will not obey her. Genius visits the host attacking the castle and addresses them. His speech is, among other things, an exhortation to fecundity as a natural part of Nature's scheme, and he therefore gives support to Love against chastity. He promises to his adherents an eternal paradise immeasurably more beautiful than the garden at the beginning of the poem. Venus directs the final attack on the tower, which falls, allowing the Lover to win the Rose. The poem ends with the story of Pygmalion.

This has been a lengthy summary, but it is almost impossible to over-estimate the influence of this poem on Chaucer. Not that all the influence was necessarily at first hand. If Chaucer was translating the *Roman* in the 1360s, Guillaume de Lorris had been writing over a hundred years before. No one imitated the *Roman de la Rose* in the sense of using it as a model, but its influence is everywhere apparent in French love poetry between it and Chaucer, especially in the poems of Machaut, Deschamps (already mentioned), Froissart and Graunson. Chaucer probably knew all these men, certainly the two latter who spent some time in England. Chaucer's early poems, and also *Troilus and Criseyde*, are particularly indebted to the early part of the *Roman* and its French successors. Like them, Chaucer writes about love (remember Deschamps's praise of him as a love poet) and especially about that refined, aristocratic form of love called *fine amour* or sometimes (especially by earlier critics) *amour courtois* (courtly love). This love is often illustrated by imagery either religious (a god of love with his saints, martyrs, commandments and prayers) or feudal (the lady's power and the man's homage as her servant). The language of religion can be clearly seen in Troilus's submission to the God of Love who, after his early and misplaced scorn of lovers, has ensnared him with a glimpse of Criseyde:

Right thus to Love he gan hym for to pleyne:
He seyde, 'Lord, have routhe upon my peyne,
Al have I ben rebell in myn entente;
Now, *mea culpa*, lord, I me repente!

O God, that at thi disposicioun
Ledest the fyn, by juste purveiaunce,
Of every wight, my lowe confessioun
Accepte in gree, and sende me swich penaunce
As liketh the, but from disesperaunce,
That may my goost departe awey fro the,
Thow be my sheld, for thi benignite.'   ii 522-32

The lover is allowed a single confidant (like Amis) and he
cannot sleep or eat for thinking of his beloved; he becomes
pale and thin and lives on hope alone. The poems are cast
in the form of a dream and usually have a Maytime setting
similar to that of the *Roman*.

In one important respect, however, Chaucer's early poetry
differs from the *Roman de la Rose*: it is hardly ever peopled by
allegorical abstractions (some do occur in *The Parliament of
Fowls*, but there they are decorative only). In the *Roman* the
courtship of the Rose – which is a symbol of the Lady's love
rather than the Lady herself who never appears in the poem
– is seen as an encounter with the Lady's varying moods
which are personified. Some of these, such as Bialacoil,
Franchise ('generosity') and Pite (feeling 'sorry' for him) are
encouraging, but others, such as Daunger, Jelousie and
Shame – even, quite often, Reason, whose function is to curb
wille (desire) – are equally clearly off-putting. This is no bad
pre-Freudian way of representing the conflicts in a girl's
mind as she falls in love: her natural inclination to be 'nice'
to a personable young man, but another feeling that she

gan . . . pleyne, began to make
   his complaint
routhe, mercy
entente, intention
Ledest . . . wight, directs every
   creature's end by (thy) just
   provision

lowe, humble
in gree, favourably
disesperaunce, despair
may . . . departe, may turn away
   my spirit
benignite, graciousness

perhaps ought not to be, or at least not too quickly. It is natural, with this kind of representation, that love should often be pictured as a battle:

> This is the stryf, and eke the affray,
> And the batell that lastith ay. 2549–50

and the final scene of the poem as an assault on the castle to win the Rose. It might even be possible to re-write some of *Troilus and Criseyde* in such terms, especially Book II where Criseyde hesitates before accepting Troilus's love. Only Chaucer chose not to use this method – or hardly ever, and then simply as a kind of top-dressing:

> Peraunter thynkestow: though it be so
> That Kynde wolde don hire to bygynne
> To have a manere routhe upon my woo,
> Seyth Daunger, 'Nay, thow shalt me nevere wynne!'
> So reulith hire hir hertes gost withinne.
>
> *Troilus and Criseyde* II 1373–7

> Tho was I war of Plesaunce anon-ryght,
> And of Aray, and Lust, and Curteysie,
> And of the Craft that can and hath the myght
> To don by force a wyght to don folye –
> Disfigurat was she, I nyl nat lye;
> And by hymself, under an ok, I gesse,
> Saw I Delyt, that stod with Gentilesse.
>
> *Parliament of Fowls* 218–24

The real and lasting quality of Guillaume de Lorris's poetry is its ingenuousness, in the older and better sense of that word, the re-creation of the beauty and vulnerability of young love. Some of this spontaneity had been lost by fourteenth-century England, and the secondary rules of the game of love had assumed a disproportionate importance. But enough

eke, also
ay, for ever
Peraunter thynkestow, Perhaps you may think
Kynde, Nature
don, cause

a manere routhe, some pity
gost, spirit
anon-ryght, straightaway
can . . . myght, has the skill and power
nyl nat, will not

remains to show why the poem was so immediately attractive and why Chaucer and his contemporaries thought so highly of it.

Chaucer's first three long poems, *The Book of the Duchess*, *The House of Fame* and *The Parliament of Fowls*, are all, like the *Roman de la Rose*, in the form of a dream. The dream set its dreamer at some little distance from his listening audience. He is, yet is not quite, Geoffrey Chaucer. What happens to him will certainly be unforeseen and may not be entirely in character. Yet the dream begins and ends in the 'real', comfortable world, and, by so doing, respects the medieval wish for some hold on reality and the apparent unwillingness to adopt a wholly fictive stance (as in later novels) where the first-person narrator need bear no relationship to the author. In another important feature these three poems again resemble the *Roman de la Rose*: their concern with *fine amour*. The major part of *The Book of the Duchess* deals with the courtship and eventual marriage of John of Gaunt, Duke of Lancaster, and his first wife Blanche. *The Parliament of Fowls*, as I shall suggest, consists of a critical examination of different kinds of love, including *fine amour*. Just what *The House of Fame* is about is hard to say, especially as Chaucer left it unfinished, but its Dreamer is more than once promised 'tidings' of love.

Fine amour appears first as a code of behaviour in eleventh-century Provence, although there have been attempts to trace its origins further back, especially in Arabic literature. It later spread to Central and Northern France and so to England. Whether it was ever practised in aristocratic circles is open to doubt. There may have been courts of love, pronouncing on particularly difficult questions, in the France of the twelfth century, but since most of the evidence we have is literary, it seems best to regard *fine amour* as a sophisticated literary game. Its theories were partly drawn from a medieval reading of Ovid's *Art of Love* (*Ars Amatoria*) and *Cure for Love* (*Remedia Amoris*) which seriously underestimated the elements of parody and satire in those works. Its own contemporary theorist was Andreas Capellanus ('the chaplain') whose *De Arte Honeste Amandi* (*The Art of Proper*

Loving) consists largely of a series of dialogues between lovers of differing social ranks.[4] Andreas may have been describing conditions at the court of Eleanor of Aquitaine in the early 1170s, although the book may well have been written later under the patronage of Marie of Champagne, Eleanor's daughter. It is, in some respects, a baffling book. Its dialogues usually conclude with remarkably little encouragement to the man, although he professes himself satisfied with such crumbs of hope. It ends with a curious third section in which Andreas says that, having acceded to the 'simple and youthful' request of Walter (the young man for whom he writes and who has never been identified) to set down all the art of love, he now adds, 'of our own accord', 'something about the rejection of love'. This 'something' is very much in the clerical antifeminist tradition which advocated the avoidance of love of women ('there is not a criminal excess that does not follow from this same love') in order that the soul, traditionally thought of as feminine, should be ready for its heavenly Bridegroom. Such rejections (or palinodes) are not uncommon. Ovid had written one; Genius, near the close of the *Roman*, seems to use the promise of eternal paradise to outbid the attractions of the garden of love; and we shall find Chaucer making a somewhat similar 'retraction' at the close of both *Troilus and Criseyde* and *The Canterbury Tales*. Despite their exaggerated language, it is better to view these palinodes as a final restoration of the correct perspective: *fine amour* had much about it that was good, but, in the last resort, it could not compare with the love of Christ.

C. S. Lewis remarks that *fine amour* contains the beginnings of many of our notions of 'romantic' love and is very different from the normal representations in classical epic of love as either divine madness (Dido) or useful domesticity (Penelope). Its most important feature was the idealisation of the lady. The man adores her, but from a distance. He cannot bear being out of her sight, but even if he does summon up enough courage to blurt out his love for her instead of merely composing songs about his lady, he is at first tongue-tied, as John of Gaunt is in *The Book of the Duchess*:

With sorweful herte, and woundes dede,
Softe and quakynge for pure drede
And shame, and styntynge in my tale
For ferde, and myn hewe al pale,
Ful ofte I wex bothe pale and red.
Bowynge to hir, I heng the hed;
I durst nat ones loke hir on,
For wit, maner, and al was goon.
I seyde 'mercy!' and no more.
Hyt nas no game, hyt sat me sore.   1211–20

The lady, for her part, has three possible courses of action. She can turn her lover down flat, as Blanche at first does (*she sayde 'nay'/Al outerly*, 1243–4).[6] She can encourage him, but not too far or too soon, since she must exercise her *daunger*; if she decides to like him in return, it is because of her *pite, mercy* or *routhe* at seeing so fine a young man wasting away for love of her. But once she has agreed to love him she must remain faithful; Criseyde's sin was to desert Troilus for Diomede. Thirdly, she may postpone her decision, as the female eagle does for a year at the end of *The Parliament of Fowls*. A postponement may take the form of a series of tests so that the man can prove himself worthy of her love, and adventures in such a noble cause provided the plot for several medieval romances.

Next in importance to the idealisation of the lady comes secrecy: *qui non celat, amare non potest*. This is not, as used to be thought, because *fine amour* necessarily involved adultery and the husband must at all costs not find out what was going on. The *Roman de la Rose* does not say whether or not the girl is married. Andreas Capellanus assumes adultery, and sometimes it is built into the story (Lancelot and Guinevere deceiving Arthur, and Tristram and Isolde cheating Mark), but in Chaucer, and in Middle English literature generally, *fine amour* is apt to lead naturally to marriage, as it does in

dede, mortal
softe, gently
drede, fear
styntynge, halting
wex, turned

maner, composure
hyt . . . sore, It was no game, it made me suffer
Al outerly, utterly and completely

both *The Book of the Duchess* and *The Knight's Tale*. In *The Franklin's Tale* the hero and heroine are married from the beginning, and it is the squire who contemplates an adulterous relationship with his master's wife. (So does another squire in *The Merchant's Tale*.) The Franklin goes to a good deal of trouble to point out the advantages of wedded bliss, in which the man can be both husband and good courtly lover at one and the same time:

> Heere may men seen an humble, wys accord;
> Thus hath she take hir servant and hir Lord, –
> Servant in love, and lord in mariage.   791–3

and his heroine, Dorigen, seems to be completely unaware of adultery as a likely concomitant of a love-affair:

> What deyntee sholde a man han in his lyf
> For to go love another mannes wyf,
> That hath hir body whan so that hym liketh?
>   1003–5

The wife in *The Manciple's Tale* summons her *lemman* (lover) while her husband is away. The Manciple at once scornfully demolishes any romantic and aristocratic associations of the word *lady*, as opposed to *lemman*:

> Ther nys no difference, trewely,
> Bitwixe a wyf that is of heigh degree,
> If of hir body dishonest she bee,
> And a povre wenche, oother than this –
> If it so be they werke bothe amys –
> But that the gentile, in estaat above,
> She shal be cleped his lady, as in love;
> And for that oother is a povre womman,
> She shal be cleped his wenche or his lemman.

accord, harmony	*dishonest,* dishonourable
deyntee, pleasure	*povre,* poor
in his lyf, ever	*werke bothe amys,* misbehave
hym liketh, he pleases	*gentile . . . above,* gentlewoman,
Bitwixe, between	of higher rank
degree, rank	*cleped,* called

> And, God it woot, myn owene deere brother,
> Men leyn that oon as lowe as lith that oother.

212–22

So much for fashionable adultery.

In *Troilus and Criseyde* the question simply does not arise, for Troilus is a bachelor and Criseyde a widow. The secrecy, in addition to giving spice to the liaison, preserved the lady's reputation from gossips and talebearers. The man was to be discreet (*secre*) and never a boaster (*avauntour*) about his love:

> And if that I to hyre be founde untrewe,
> Disobeysaunt, or wilful necligent,
> Avauntour, or in proces love a newe,
> I preye to yow this be my jugement,
> That with these foules I be al torent.

Parliament of Fowls 428–31

Or again, in *Troilus and Criseyde*:

> And I to ben youre verray, humble, trewe,
> Secret, and in my paynes pacient,
> And evere mo desiren fresshly newe
> To serve, and ben ay ylike diligent,
> And with good herte al holly youre talent
> Receyven wel, how sore that me smerte, –
> Lo, this mene I, myn owen swete herte.

iii 141–6

He was, in fact, allowed one confidant to whom he could pour out his hopes, and his even greater fear that his love would never be returned. Amis (Friend) occupies this position somewhat imperfectly in the *Roman de la Rose* and Pandarus to much better effect in *Troilus and Criseyde*. Pandarus also acts as the go-between for the lovers and arranges their secret meetings.

woot, knows	*verray*, loyal
leyn, lay	*Secret*, discreet
lith, lies	*paynes*, torments
in proces, in the course of time	*newe*, anew
jugement, sentence	*ay ylike*, ever equally
foules, birds	*talent*, wish
al torent, torn to pieces	*me smerte*, I suffer

Much of this material, as will have become evident, can be found in the *Roman de la Rose*, and it is there also in Chrétien de Troyes who, like Andreas, was writing in the later twelfth century. It was Chrétien who combined in a single narrative *fine amour*, allegory (for the psychology) and the Arthurian legend, so that Camelot became the home of courtly love: as C. S. Lewis neatly expresses it, 'What was theory for his own age had been practice for the knights of Britain'.[7] The essentials of *fine amour* had therefore frequently been demonstrated in literature before Chaucer began to write, and he can, if he wishes, assume their existence rather than illustrate them at length. He can also criticise them, as he seems to in *The Parliament of Fowls*. The secondary rules are also to be seen everywhere in Chaucer. True loving was an aristocratic pastime, but the love of the lady ennobled the man even more, as it does Troilus who was a king's son to begin with.[8] Her beauty entered his heart via the eyes – literally, 'love at first sight' – and Cupid's arrows inflict a wound which can be healed only by the beloved as the physician (*leche*). It goes without saying that the lover must be brave, polite, generous, loyal. All these refined manners (it was, after all, *fine amour*) are best summed up in the single quality of *trouthe* ('integrity') which is what attracted Criseyde to Troilus[9] and which is given pride of place in *The Franklin's Tale*:

Trouthe is the hyeste thyng that man may kepe.

Inevitably, in setting out the 'rules' of *fine amour*, I have appeared to represent it as a code or a system to be adopted or rejected in its entirety. In fact, this was not so. An author may accept it as the morality of one poem and use it for ironic purposes in another. Adultery, especially, is only an occasional factor, necessitated by a particular plot such as the Arthurian legend. 'Courtly' love is simply the love proper to persons of courtly rank, and is therefore suitably expressed in the highest and most rhetorical of the three medieval levels of style.[10] It is a matter of decorum, a branch of *gentilesse* (nobility). Hence Andreas's preoccupation with the *rank* of his pairs of lovers and his attempts to modify the lover's approach to different classes of beloved, although he recognises (as did Chaucer) that virtuous character (true *gentilesse*) may sometimes compensate for lowly birth. Similar variations in manner and style occur with the different birds in Chaucer's *Parliament of Fowls*.

The setting for these love poems is frequently an open space, such as the garden in the *Roman*, the woodland grove in which the Dreamer of *The Book of the Duchess* meets the Black Knight and the park of *The Parliament of Fowls*. May had long been the appropriate time for loving, and Pandarus starts out to visit Criseyde and tell her of Troilus's love for her on 3 May:

> In May, that moder is of monthes glade,
> That fresshe floures, blew and white and rede,
> Ben quike agayn, that wynter dede made,
> And ful of bawme is fletyng every mede;
> Whan Phebus doth his bryghte bemes sprede,
> Right in the white Bole, it so bitidde,
> As I shal synge, on Mayes day the thrydde . . .
>
> *Troilus and Criseyde* ii 50–6

Yet, however much the lady may seem to be placed on a pedestal, for the man loving is neither a simple nor always a wholly pleasurable business. From Andreas's opening sentence (my italics):

> Love is a certain inborn *suffering* derived from the sight of and excessive *meditation* upon the beauty of the opposite sex.

to the first lines of *The Parliament of Fowls*:

> The lyf so short, the craft so long to lerne,
> Th'assay so hard, so sharp the conquerynge,

moder . . . glade, the beginning (mother) of the pleasant months	*mede*, meadow
	Phebus, the Sun
	white Bole, Taurus
Ben quike, come alive	*bitidde*, befell
bawme, balm	*assay*, attempt
fletyng, abounding	

> The dredful joye, alwey that slit so yerne;
> Al this mene I by Love . . .

and Criseyde's fear:

> That love is thyng ay ful of bisy drede.   iv 1645

we are made aware of the complexities and possible pitfalls before the delightful outcome. But in these lies the material for a great poet who chooses to dream about love.

THE BOOK OF THE DUCHESS

The Book of the Duchess is an elegy for Blanche, the first wife of John of Gaunt and mother of Henry of Lancaster, the future Henry IV. Blanche died of the plague in September 1369. Gaunt had been nineteen when he married her and she had brought a valuable dowry to add to his own possessions. He had become Duke of Lancaster in 1362 and for the rest of the century (he died in 1399) was a considerable force in politics. It is likely, therefore, that *The Book of the Duchess* was a young poet's tribute to the wife of his patron. It was probably composed soon after Blanche's death; Gaunt remarried in 1371, so that an elegy for his first wife would scarcely have been tactful then or afterwards. Blanche was beautiful and accomplished, and the poem stresses her gaiety and sociability as well.

The poem, however, does not begin with Blanche, or even with John of Gaunt who is not identified with the Knight in Black until the last few lines (1318–19). It opens with the poet's sleeplessness which is leading to melancholy and near-exhaustion. His bedside reading is the story, from Ovid's *Metamorphoses* xi, of the shipwrecked Ceyx and his queen Alcione who prays to Juno for news of him. The drowned Ceyx is made to appear to Alcione in a dream and tell her of his death:

dredful, fearful
alwey . . . yerne, that always slips away so quickly

ay, constantly
bisy drede, anxious fear

And called hir ryght as she het
By name, and sayde, 'My swete wyf,
Awake! let be your sorwful lyf!
For in your sorwe there lyth no red.
For, certes, swete, I nam but ded;
Ye shul me never on lyve yse.

.   .   .   .   .

And farewel, swete, my worldes blysse!
I praye God youre sorwe lysse.
To lytel while oure blysse lasteth!'

                                    200–5, 209–11

and Alcione herself dies two days later. Chaucer provides a
good summary of Ovid, avoiding much of the latter's rhetoric, such as the description of the shipwreck, Alcione's
lament on hearing the news and the final Ovidian meta-
morphosis of the pair into birds. But the Narrator is impressed by gods who can induce sleep – this is just what he
needs – so the description of the underworld cave in which
the gods vie with each other who can sleep soundest is kept.
He finally falls asleep over his Ovid, and sleep 'that knits up
the ravell'd sleave of care' proves a remedy for his grief. He
dreams that he has been wakened on a May morning by the
birds singing outside his window. He hears a horn blow
outside and goes to join the hunt, but is led away by a puppy
down a flower-strewn path into a wood. In a clearing he
comes upon a young knight, pale and distraught, leaning
against an oak. The Dreamer diffidently tries to engage him
in conversation with a view to learning the cause of his
sorrow.

It has taken a long time, 443 lines, almost a third of the
poem, to reach John of Gaunt, but from now on attention is
concentrated unremittingly on his devotion to love as a young
man (*fine amour* supposed an aristocratic upbringing and
plenty of leisure: it was Idleness in the *Roman* who opened
the gate into the garden); his courtship of Blanche, strictly

ryght . . . name, by her own
   name
lyth no red, is no remedy
nam but ded, am dead and gone

on lyve yse, see alive
lysse, relieve
while, time

according to the rules of *fine amour*; their happiness in marriage; and his loss of her. But what has preceded the meeting of Dreamer and Knight is far from mere decoration. The idyllic spring-like setting is very much in the manner of the *Roman de la Rose* and its successors. In *The Book of the Duchess* Chaucer seems to be drawing most often on Machaut, and, in particular, on his *Jugement dou Roy de Behaingne*, a debate over the relative sorrows of a lady who is lamenting her dead lover and a knight who tells of his own unrequited love. French dream poetry between the *Roman de la Rose* and Chaucer had become far less consistently allegorical and more personal – or at least more topical. Chaucer carries this development further still in *The Book of the Duchess* by making his dialogue, as well as his characters, more realistic.[11] Here the framework is, in the first place, an indication that this is to be a poem about love, although we do not yet know that the purpose of recounting the love-affair is to provide an elegy on Blanche, or that the Dreamer is to be an observer and not himself a lover. Perhaps we may also be meant to contrast the bright springtime setting with Blanche's death in the autumn and with the knight dressed in black who pays no attention to the joyful sounds of the hunt around him. The story from Ovid (which Machaut had used too in his *Dit de la Fonteinne Amoureuse*, but with a different aim) is for Chaucer a mirror image of Gaunt's own case, for in Ovid a man had died and his wife mourned him. But the connection, although almost certainly intentional, is not made explicit. To view a poem as the sum of its parts, which may themselves be different in kind, has recently been suggested as a principle of late medieval aesthetics, just as a Gothic cathedral, however many accretions it may have, possesses a unity in diversity. It is our task to perceive this unity.[12] This is different in kind from the classical, 'organic' unity which has usually been the implicit criterion for judging the artistic success of medieval literature. Two additional factors may influence our view of which kind Chaucer intended. The first is simply one of size: it is far easier to achieve an innate unity in a short work, like *The Parliament of Fowls*, than it is in a long one, like *The Canterbury*

Tales, Beowulf, Piers Plowman or Malory's *Morte D'Arthur*.
The second is the fact of oral delivery, which imposes
limits on the degree of unity apparent to a group of listeners.
One might retort, to this last argument, that the author, in
composing his work, will conceive of it as a unity and do his
best to make that unity intelligible to a reading if not to a
listening audience. But if we are prepared to accept more
implicit connection between the parts of *The Book of the
Duchess* than criticism has previously allowed, we might well
argue, for instance, that the Dreamer's own sadness at the
opening of the poem makes him a sympathetic listener to the
Black Knight's own sorrow.

The grief of the Knight is presented in very rhetorical
fashion. Nowadays we are apt to view rhetoric as being very
often a deliberate attempt to conceal a basic weakness of
material or to persuade us to adopt a view we are initially
disinclined to take. In the Middle Ages rhetoric was a
perfectly proper way of embellishing one's source, for poetry
was seldom regarded as inspirational and a poet was
assumed to be building with other men's materials.[13] From
what has been said about oral transmission in chapter I and
from the summary of the *Roman de la Rose* in this chapter, it
will have been seen that medieval narrative poetry was
seldom in a hurry. The digressions, often lengthy, were
intended to point up the beauty or the truth of the subject.
Allegory, if employed, was also a means of directing the
listener to the *sentence* ('theme', 'significance') of the work.
As the fourteenth-century chancellor and bibliophile,
Richard de Bury, expressed it:

> Where the material is feigned but a virtuous doctrine
> is implied, a natural or historical truth is enclosed
> beneath the figurative eloquence of fiction.[14]

There were books about how to write poetry which therefore
assumed that this was something that could be learned (in a
curious way we have returned to this view with university
courses on 'creative writing'). Such books – and Chaucer
knew some of them – gave lists of figures of speech (*colours*
of rhetoric they were called) with illustrative examples,

frequently from classical authors. This may seem to us an excessively mechanical approach to poetry, when, far from the style being the man, a man changed his style as the subject or genre dictated. Where the rhetorical figure is a simple one, such as metaphor or antithesis, I cannot believe that any writer worth his salt needed a text-book to guide him, but where it is lengthy, deliberate or artificial, such as *occupatio* (a pretended refusal to describe while in effect doing so by giving a series of headings, e.g. *Knight's Tale* 2919–66) or *apostrophe* (a highly mannered list of exclamations, e.g. *Troilus and Criseyde* v 540–50), it appears likely that it had to be consciously learned. The guiding principle is that the 'high' style (epic or tragedy or deliberately impressive poetry) contains several rhetorical colours, the middle style correspondingly fewer and the 'low' style (such as that of fabliaux, like *The Miller's Tale* and *The Reeve's Tale*, where the joke will not wait) very few indeed.

In *The Book of the Duchess* the Dreamer's manner is self-conscious and conciliatory as he tries to elicit the reason for the Knight's grief. The Knight's own tone is, appropriately for a knight, much more courtly and formal, and therefore contains several figures of rhetoric. He starts with successive examples of oxymoron (599–649) several of which quite cleverly refer to the hypocritical nature of Fortune. Fortune is then pictured in an elaborate *enigma*, as a deceitful chess-player who has captured the Knight's queen (*fers*). In one of his rare interruptions the Dreamer produces a list of *exempla* (illustrations of a point being made). When the Knight describes his Lady it is in the approved rhetorical fashion, top to toe (855–960). The Squire, in his *Tale*, confesses his inability to describe a beautiful princess:

> But for to telle yow al hir beautee,
> It lyth nat in my tonge, n'yn my konnyng;
> I dar nat undertake so heigh a thyng.
> Myn Englissh eek is insufficient.
> It moste been a *rethor* excellent.

It . . . konnyng, I have neither the eloquence nor the skill

eek, besides
rethor, expert in rhetoric

That koude his *colours* longynge for that art,
If he sholde hire discryven *every part*.   34–40

The Knight's description of Blanche is a good blend of both her physical and moral qualities, not, as often happened with medieval poets, description first followed by a list of the lady's virtues. Her beauty is evidently much more than skin deep. Later in *The Book of the Duchess* more *exempla* occur (1056–87, 1115–25, 1160–70). But the Dreamer, however well-meaning, is at heart a simple-minded fellow. He cannot penetrate all this rhetoric: he fails to understand the *enigma* of the *fers* capturing the knight (which is, in fact, quite apt):

> But there is no man alyve her
> Wolde for a fers make this woo!   740–1

The sixteenth-century critic, J. C. Scalinger, calls *enigma* 'an obscure passage which arrives at a known fact indirectly'. Chaucer is being deliberately tactful by referring to the Knight's (Gaunt's) bereavement thus ambiguously. The Dreamer's query both draws attention to the rhetorical elegance of the riddle and, by its naturalism, makes sure that the audience can interpret it. Despite having overheard, at the very beginning of their meeting, the Black Knight lamenting his wife's death (479–83), he cannot perceive what is the real nature of the 'loss' to which the Knight refers, and he has to have it spelled out for him:

> 'Bethenke how I seyde here-beforn,
> "Thou wost ful lytel what thow menest;
> I have lost more than thow wenest" –
> God wot, allas! ryght that was she!'
>   'Allas, sir, how? what may that be?'
>   'She ys ded!' 'Nay!' 'Yis, be my trouthe!'
> 'Is that youre los? Be God, hyt ys routhe!'
>
>   1304–10

That . . . art, who knew all the figures of speech appropriate to that art
Bethenke, remember
wenest, imagine
wot, knows
Yis . . . trouthe, Yes indeed, on my word
routhe, a pity

The reason for this has been much debated. If, as seems clear, Chaucer's Dreamer is deliberately made so much more obtuse than his creator, why should this be? One might say that medieval dreamers are usually very literal-minded and their function is to ask the sort of question that the least-instructed member of the audience might ask. Or that, had the Dreamer understood immediately, the story would have ended before it had really begun. Or again, that in *fine amour* the 'loss' of a lady was perhaps more likely to mean unrequited love than death. Whether unrequited love or loss by death was the worse, had been, in fact, the subject of Machaut's poem, and *sorwe of deeth* or *los of love* are the two causes of a woeful *gentil herte* in *The Squire's Tale*:

> 'What is the cause, if it be for to telle,
> That ye be in this furial pyne of helle?'
> Quod Canacee unto this hauk above.
> 'Is this for sorwe of deeth or los of love?
> For, as I trowe, thise been causes two
> That causen moost a gentil herte wo.'   447–52

The second of these at once springs to the mind of the Dreamer in *The Book of the Duchess*:

> 'What los ys that?' quod I thoo;
> 'Nyl she not love yow? ys hyt soo?
> Or have ye oght doon amys,
> That she hath left yow? ys hyt this?'
>
> 1139–42

A persuasive argument is Professor Lawlor's,[15] that the function of the Dreamer is gradually to draw out the Knight, to console him by leading him to recall the charm of his Lady and the happiness of their marriage. The elegy thus avoids the danger of morbidity. Certainly, the progress of the recall is the more natural in that it is not chronological: the account of their first meeting comes some time after the full description of Blanche, and the real bitterness of his loss hits the

furial, dreadful
trowe, believe
gentil, noble

thoo, then
Nyl she not, Will she not
oght, in any way

Knight only at the end of the story. This is exactly the way in which Alcione had learned the real truth about Ceyx:

> For in your sorwe there lyth no red.
> For, certes, swete, I nam but ded;
> Ye shul me never on lyve yse.   203–5

I nam but ded: 'I am only dead' or 'I am dead, and that is all there is to be said'? Either way, John of Gaunt did not, like Alcione, die *within the thridde morwe*. Life, as Chaucer was to show later, cannot be like literature. As Professor Lawlor says, the poem itself points out that long continuance of grief is unnatural (*against kynde*). Yet we do not know whether the Black Knight is, in fact, consoled. Interestingly, none of the Dreamer's arguments for consolation has a religious basis. What he offers is less consolation than sympathy. It is no part of his business to do more. The poet has been deferential and understanding: let the patron be consoled – if he can.

THE HOUSE OF FAME

If we come to *The House of Fame* immediately after the *Roman de la Rose* and *The Book of the Duchess*, first impressions are reassuring. Book I opens with a Proem which discusses dreams in the manner of the opening of the *Roman de la Rose*: what causes them, and how do you tell which really foretell the future and which are deceitful? This is followed by an Invocation to the same Morpheus, god of sleep in his underworld cave, that we have met in *The Book of the Duchess*. If we look ahead, we find that Book II has a Proem and Book III an Invocation, so that this would appear to be a well-organised poem, proceeding along familiar lines. There may be some momentary disquiet when we discover that the Dreamer goes to bed on 10 December (surely this is the wrong season?) and that he falls asleep *wonder sone*, without any bedside reading, but when, in his dream, he enters the temple of Venus, on the wall of which there is written the story of Virgil's *Aeneid*, we begin to feel that things are not so very different after all. This may well prove a love poem, and we suspect that the summary of the *Aeneid* may bear some kind of relationship to the poem proper, as did the legend of Ceyx and Alcione in *The Book of the Duchess*. In his summary of the *Aeneid*, Chaucer devotes most time to the episode (in Book IV) of the desertion of Dido by Aeneas who is shown to be a cad and a traitor to his beloved. The point is rubbed home by a list of other men who have promised everything but sailed away in the morning, and Virgil's explanation – that it was Aeneas's destiny to found a new empire in Italy, and that therefore his stay in Carthage could be, at best, only a delightful episode – is added, almost as an afterthought, as something which 'the book' provides *to excusen Eneas*. The Dreamer wanders out of the temple and finds himself in a sandy waste; this seems some way from the Maytime garden of the *Roman de la Rose* and the wood of *The Book of the Duchess*. As he looks up, a huge eagle comes swooping down from the sky.

In Book II the Eagle picks up 'Geoffrey' in his claws and carries him ever upwards through the heavens. He explains to the astonished Dreamer that he has been sent by Jupiter to carry him to the House of Fame as a reward for his poetical devotion to Love and Love's servants, since the Dreamer's preoccupation, with *rekenynges* (at the Custom House?) and afterwards at home with his books, has not allowed him time to get to know even his neighbours. The 'tidings' he will hear in the House of Fame will be principally about *Loves folke*. Fame is so far clearly equivalent to the *fama* of Virgil's *Aeneid* iv and Ovid's *Metamorphoses* xii, i.e. Rumour. On their way there, the Eagle treats Geoffrey to a lecture on gravitation and sound waves, all to prove that sound (which is air) naturally finds its way to Fame's house which is situated midway between earth, air and sea. In doing this, the Eagle is popularising knowledge, as Jean de Meun had done before him. There was evidently a demand for straightforward abridgements of difficult technical matter:

> Telle me this now feythfully,
> Have y not preved thus symply,

rekenynges, accounts

Withoute any subtilite
Of speche, or gret prolixite
Of termes of philosophie,
Of figures of poetrie,
Or colours of rethorike?
Pardee, hit oughte the to lyke!
For hard langage and hard matere
Ys encombrous for to here
Attones; wost thou not wel this?   853–63

As Clemen puts it:

> Such readers will not have looked to Chaucer for any
> specific exhaustive or systematic instruction. He does,
> however, meet a rather different need felt by his readers;
> this was the unscholarly yet expert recognition and
> enjoyment of the store of learning gleaned from past
> centuries. Confined within a well-turned, attractive
> poem, this educational material was bound to forfeit
> some of its gravity.[16]

After more about the wonders of the heavens, the pair arrive
at the House of Fame where the Eagle leaves the Dreamer.
  So far, so good. The starting point in Book I had been
earth. Book II soared upwards; there were parallels for such
a heavenly journey in both religious and secular literature,
but hardly in the company of such a talkative guide. Book III
ought to describe and explain the destination. But it is in
This lytel laste bok (1093) that the proportions somehow go
wrong, so that most readers feel the *The House of Fame*
promises more than it performs, that somewhere the poet
loses his way, that tidings about love become submerged in
the account of a Fame whose significance changes from
Rumour to Reputation. This is, however, to anticipate, for
Book III is almost as long as Books I and II together. The
house stands on a rock of ice; some of the names inscribed

colours of rethorike, stylistic   *matere*, subject-matter
  ornaments   *encombrous*, difficult
Pardee . . . lyke, Goodness, you
  ought to be pleased

on it have almost melted in the sun while others, on the shady side, have been preserved. (Fame is now clearly Reputation.) The dwelling is elaborately gothic in design and inhabited by a bewildering crowd of musicians, magicians and story-tellers:

> And eke in ech of the pynacles
> Weren sondry habitacles,
> In which stoden, al withoute –
> Ful the castel, al aboute –
> Of alle maner of mynstralles,
> And gestiours, that tellen tales
> Both of wepinge and of game,
> Of al that longeth unto Fame.
>
> 1193–1200

so that the poet is unable to describe all the marvels inside. At first Fame seems a tiny creature, but spreads out to span both earth and heaven (like Virgil's Rumour). By line 1406, however, her twofold significance is established when she is addressed as 'Goddess of Renown or of Fame'. On the pillars of her house stand those great writers who have handed on the records of past ages and great men. Nine companies of petitioners then approach Fame in turn; she rewards them capriciously, without any concern for the justice of their requests:

> And somme of hem she graunted sone,
> And somme she werned wel and faire,
> And some she graunted the contraire
> Of her axyng outterly.   1538–41

and Aeolus, god of the winds, trumpets their reputations to all quarters of the earth. In this Fame comes close to the medieval view of the instability and deceitfulness of Fortune,

eke, in addition
habitacles, niches
al withoute, (and) outside as well
gestiours, story-tellers
game, mirth
longeth unto, pertains to

sone, immediately
werned . . . faire, well and truly refused
her axyng, their requests
outterly, utterly

who, we learn a few lines later, is her sister. The Dreamer is now asked why he is there: is he too seeking Fame? He replies that he is in search of *Tydynges . . . of love, or suche thynges glade*, but that, so far, he hasn't seen what he is looking for:

> For certeynly, he that me made
> To comen hyder, seyde me,
> Y shulde bothe here and se,
> In this place, wonder thynges;
> But these be no suche tydynges
> As I mene of.   1890–5

He has always known about Fame, although not where she lives. So he is taken to the House of Twigs which continually whirls about. It has entrances on all sides and is full of people whispering *tydynges* to each other. The Eagle reappears briefly and takes the Dreamer inside, as Jove has commanded:

> But sith that Joves, of his grace,
> As I have seyde, wol the solace
> Fynally with these thinges,
> Unkouthe syghtes and tydynges,
> To passe with thyn hevynesse,
> Such routhe hath he of thy distresse.
>
>   2007–12

These *tydynges* do not appear to be quite those which the Eagle had originally promised (644 ff.). They fly back to Fame who decides what is to happen to them. If Chaucer is here saying that Rumour is subordinate to Fame and that reputation is based largely on rumour, it would be an acceptable conclusion which would fit well with the earlier symbolism of the fragile glass temple of Venus, the House of Fame built on ice and the House of Rumour constructed of

wonder, marvellous
sith that, since
wol the solace, wants to cheer you up

Unkouthe, strange
To . . . hevynesse, to get rid of your grief
routhe, sadness

twigs. The only trouble is that the meaning is not made explicit. The Dreamer makes his way to a corner of the building where men are talking of *love-tydynges* (the original object of the journey). He sees a man of 'great authority' whom he cannot name, and the poem breaks off, unfinished.

What are we to make of all this? It is pointless to speculate who the man of great authority was or what he would have said. Because the poem is unfinished, we are likewise unable to see whether Chaucer is continuing the technique of *The Book of the Duchess* (and of *The Parliament of Fowls*) which juxtaposes sections of the poem, but without explicit comment. The relationship between Fame and Fortune is made clear, but not that between Fame and Love. Part of the difficulty lies in the twofold significance of Fame as Rumour and Reputation. Both meanings were current in the fourteenth century, as the *Middle English Dictionary* shows:

fame 1 Reputation (whether good or bad) as to character or behavior.
2 (Wide-spread) reputation, celebrity, renown.
3 Any report, rumour, or widely circulated opinion; also, a tiding or rumour.

The sheer accumulation of both people and description in Book III is perhaps necessary to show Fame's power and her diversity of interests, but it is almost impossible for us to appreciate in any detail. Far from being impressive, Fame becomes grotesque, sometimes almost comic. Chaucer has let his imagination run riot. The invention is simply too extravagant and the interests too diverse. If, as has been suggested, he was searching for subject-matter beyond the conventional *fine amour*, and that therefore *The House of Fame* represents an advance in his poetic progress, the search is disorganised. His reading, too, has spilled over into his poem in a way that was never again to happen. Virgil, Ovid, Dante, Boethius all contribute, not to mention such writers as Martianus Capella and Alan of Lille (985–90). The Eagle, his first great comic creation, dominates Book II with his loquaciousness, but, from another point of view, almost wrecks the proportions of the poem. He appears to be derived from two different eagles in Dante, and perhaps from Virgil, Dante's guide in the *Divine Comedy*. But, as Muscatine remarks,[17] the original seriousness of the Dante material is swallowed up in the comedy that follows. The function of the Dreamer in *The House of Fame* is, too, less obvious than that of his counterpart in *The Book of the Duchess*. The latter, by his sympathetic questions, led the Knight in Black to recall past happiness as well as present sorrow. In *The Parliament of Fowls* the Dreamer establishes a hierarchy among the assembly of birds as he does not among the denizens of Fame's palace. If indeed *I wot myself best how y stonde* (1878), he does not confide in us. The trouble with *The House of Fame* is neither the rhetoric, which is often less gratuitous than in *The Book of the Duchess*, nor the octosyllabics which hurry us along without obtruding themselves, but the apparent incoherence of the final book, an incoherence which cannot have been a wholly deliberate representation of the variety and uncertainty of Fame. Book III could have benefited by a little of the triumphant discipline of the Eagle:

> 'A ha!' quod he, 'lo, so I can
> Lewedly to a lewed man
> Speke, and shewe hym swyche skiles
> That he may shake hem be the biles,
> So palpable they shulden be.' 865–9

THE PARLIAMENT OF FOWLS

The Parliament of Fowls, like Caesar's Gaul, divides naturally into three parts. The poet – and we have come to expect this by now – does not know love *in dede*, but only from books. One of the books he reads is 'Tullyus of the Drem of Scipioun', that is, the *Somnium Scipionis* in Book VI of Cicero's *De Republica*, but known to the Middle Ages as part of Macrobius's longer commentary on it (*c.* 400 A.D.). Chaucer's summary, the *grete*, of this stresses two things: the importance

wot, know	*biles*, bill(s)
Lewedly, straightforwardly	*palpable*, obvious
skiles, arguments	

of working for the general good (*commune profyt*, 47, 75) and
the insignificance of life here on earth in comparison with
life in heaven. Tired out by his day-long study of the
Somnium, the poet falls asleep – quickly this time, with no
formal invocation to Morpheus – and, naturally enough,
dreams of Scipio. Scipio wishes to reward the Dreamer for
his devotion to *myn olde bok totorn* (shades of that other guide,
the Eagle in *The House of Fame*!) and leads him to a walled
park where he stands puzzling over the inscriptions above
the two halves of the gate. One suggests the road to the
welle of grace and *al good aventure*, but the other speaks forbid-
dingly of the *mortal strokes of the spere* and implies aridity and
imprisonment. But, with the remark that these inscriptions
do not apply to the Dreamer but to 'Love's servants',
Africanus leads him into the garden.

It is no surprise to find that part two of the poem, the
description of the garden, is very like the setting of the
Roman de la Rose. The flowers, trees, rivulets, birds, small
docile creatures, Cupid and his train, all make their appearance, but this time (as at the close of the *Roman* rather than
at the beginning) there are hints of a paradisal garden:

> Th'air of that place so attempre was
> That nevere was ther grevaunce of hot ne cold;
> There wex ek every holsom spice and gras;
> No man may there waxe sek ne old;
> Yit was there joye more a thousandfold
> Than man can telle; ne nevere wolde it nyghte,
> But ay cler day to any manes syghte.   204–10

As he wanders through the garden, the Dreamer finds a
temple of Venus, and here Chaucer is indebted to an
episode from Boccaccio's *Teseida* (the source for *The Knight's
Tale* too). Inside the temple Venus lies languorously on a
couch, and the atmosphere is fragrant and sensuous. In
Chaucer she does not quite dominate the scene as she does
in Boccaccio: in the former she is discovered *in a prive corner*,

totorn, tattered	*grevaunce*, extreme
aventure, fortune	*wex*, grew
attempre, gentle	*ay*, always

but in the latter we are directed to 'a more secret part of the temple . . . through that door'. The Dreamer is fascinated by the appearance of Venus, but nevertheless is somewhat relieved to get outside afterwards into the good fresh air of the garden. He soon comes upon the noble goddess Nature, sitting in a clearing upon a hill of flowers and presiding over the birds who have come to choose their mates on St Valentine's Day. The ensuing assembly of the birds (*parlement of foules*) and their debate form part three of the poem.

These three sections are formally linked, since Scipio Africanus, the chief character of the *Somnium*, acts as the Dreamer's guide to the garden, and Nature, who appears in the garden, presides over the debate. But they are written in different styles.[18] The first part is expository. Its tone is philosophical and somewhat austere, and its style does not draw attention to itself. Part two (the garden) moves comparatively slowly, especially in the description of Venus's temple; its syntax is more involved and, as might be expected, its diction more poetic. It is a rather literary presentation of 'romantic' love, and the abstract allegorical characters are more decorative, in the manner of Boccaccio and the Renaissance, than functional, in the manner of the *Roman de la Rose*. The language of the debate varies according to the speaker, from the courtly vocabulary of the eagles to the colloquialisms of the lower-class birds.

Yet within the garden setting we are clearly meant to contrast Venus and Nature. Venus obviously personifies love, but here it is an illicit and corrupted love of which we are intended to disapprove. The lovers in her temple are unhappy, and the wall paintings of the great classical figures show not only *al here love* but also *in what plyt they dyde*. Nature is somewhat more complex. Chaucer says (line 316) that she appears as described by Alanus de Insulis (Alan of Lille) in the late twelfth-century *De Planctu Naturae*, but in fact he borrows very little detail from Alan's wildly rhetorical description. She is much more like her namesake in the second part of the *Roman de la Rose* (which, to be sure, had itself borrowed from the *De Planctu Naturae*) where she is also described as God's deputy (*vicaire*, *Parliament*, 379, and compare the phrase *ful of grace*, 319, used here of Nature but usually of the Virgin Mary).

Nature, in her green open-air surroundings, is to be admired, as Venus, in the hothouse atmosphere of the temple, is to be distrusted. She personifies the creative, reproductive force, and also represents the order and harmony manifest in God's scheme of creation (380–1). She is eternal, yet renews herself each year. As Dr Brewer points out,[19] Chaucer is probably remembering Jean de Meun's Reason who (unlike Guillaume's Reason) advocates a good and useful love concerned with begetting offspring, but condemns mere sensual pleasure. The substitution of Nature for the god or goddess of love who presided over the usual *demande d'amour* of French poetry indicates that the concerns of the *Parliament* are wider than those of the typical love vision. It may be that Nature and Venus elaborate the contrasting inscriptions over the twin halves of the gate into the garden which were mentioned earlier. Nature might represent the *welle of grace* and Venus the sad end of a life dominated by *Disdayn* and *Daunger*. This would appear to make better sense than interpreting the inscriptions in terms of the 'practical' and 'courtly' attitudes to love in the debate between the birds. To this assembly, which gives the poem its title, we must now turn.

Ostensibly the debate is concerned with which of three male (*tercel*) eagles is most suitable for the hand of the female (*formel*) eagle who perches on Nature's wrist. For this is St Valentine's Day, when the birds have come together to choose their mates. If the poem does indeed reflect some fashionable game at court where 'partners' for the ensuing year were chosen, it is likely that it was begun in 1382 (an astrological reference at line 117 suggests this as a possible date) for reading at court in February 1383.[20] In any event, birds debating in the manner of men were by no means unknown to medieval literature. The tercels state their case in turn before Nature who presides, and all the other birds crowd around. The speech of the first and 'royal' eagle – who seems the favourite candidate and who clearly has Nature's support (632–3) – is a compendium of all the approved attitudes of *fine amour*, both positive and negative. He addresses himself to his *soverayn lady*, vows unremitting devotion to attract her *mercy* and *grace*, will never be disloyal, cruel or boastful. The second eagle stresses the length of his devotion to the formel and the third the intensity of his, but they are not far behind the first as devotees of an extreme *fine amour*. The Dreamer is greatly impressed by these three speeches, but not so the lower-class birds, for things have gone on too long and they are impatient to choose their mates and be away. After an initial period of confusion, Nature resumes control and suggests that one member of each class of birds shall put a representative view. The falcon votes for the first eagle; the goose says bluntly 'if she won't love him, let him love someone else'; the turtle-dove argues for everlasting constancy to the lady, but the duck shouts this down as being pointless unless the love is returned; the cuckoo, typically selfish, simply does not care about the eagles so long as *he* gets his mate. When the formel is invited by Nature to make her choice, she asks for a postponement of a year in order to make up her mind. The mass of birds are delighted to agree, and fly away joyfully with their mates, rousing the Dreamer with the noise they make. This debate, with its crowd of birds jostling round Nature, could easily have got out of hand, like the third book of *The House of Fame*. The *Parliament* is a good deal shorter than either of its predecessors, and the choice of a seven-line stanza with decasyllabic lines instead of the earlier octosyllabics may have imposed more control. The birds are not simply seeking something for themselves (like Fame's petitioners) but are, to some extent, rivals, although we must not exaggerate any conflict between the noble eagles and the *lewed* duck or goose. This is not the class struggle, and there are positions (such as the falcon's or the turtle-dove's) between the extremes. Like the occasional use in the poem of the language of the national parliament,[21] the overtones of *gentil* and *cherl* make the debate more dramatic. And Nature proves a much better chairman than Fame.

In origin the debate is a fashionable *demande d'amour* where

lewed, ignorant

the audience is invited to decide between different but apparently equal claims. But after the falcon's reply, interest shifts from the respective merits of the three eagles to a consideration of the practicality of *fine amour*. Has it any place in real life? Does it *work*? Would mutual agreement rather than the lady's fiat not be better? We have come a long way from the confections (the word is Muscatine's) of Machaut and his contemporaries. Yet this is still a philosophical discussion, no matter how tempers rise, and the decision is not made but postponed. In *Troilus and Criseyde* events in the Trojan War force the lovers to test the worth of *fine amour* in a real-life situation. What Chaucer would appear to be doing in *The Parliament of Fowls* is employing his old technique of placing differing views side by side to reveal the strength and weakness of each by juxtaposition. It has often been remarked too how much use the style of this poem makes of the rhetorical figure of *contentio* or contrast. The subject, once more, is love. We see in turn love of one's fellow men, that is, Scipio's (and perhaps Nature's) 'common profit'; the illicit, corrupted love represented by Venus; and the ultra-courtly approach of the three eagles which, if self-important, is no less selfish and over-simplified than the superficially better sense spoken by some of the lower-class birds. The 'courtly' and the 'commonsense' views, at least, are complementary,[22] and all kinds of love are perhaps to be judged in the light of their contribution to the 'common profit'. To adapt a phrase used by Muscatine of the *Roman de la Rose*, the *Parliament* can be seen as a kind of 'symposium on love'. And the Dreamer who has closely followed all this? Whatever he was looking for in the *Somnium Scipionis*, he had not found it:

> For bothe I hadde thyng which that I nolde,
> And ek I nadde that thyng that I wolde. 90–1

At the end of the poem he is apparently no nearer a final solution:

For . . . wolde, For I both had something which I did not want, and also I did not have the thing I did want.

And with the shoutyng, whan the song was do
That foules maden at here flyght awey,
I wok, and othere bokes tok me to,
To reede upon, and yit I rede alwey,
I hope, ywis, to rede so som day
That I shal mete som thyng for to fare
The bet, and thus to rede I nyl nat spare.   693-9

So he goes back to his books. It is only with the story of the 'double sorrow' of Troilus, that the observer – now no longer a dreamer but a narrator – finds himself taking sides.

THE LEGEND OF GOOD WOMEN

Recipe. Begin with a *sententia*, or wise old saying. Add one narrator, none too bright, who knows a good deal about books but not much about life or love. Find a revered figure – the God of Love will do – and flavour with a few well-preserved *auctores*. Use a May morning for setting. Bake the whole in the shape of a dream, and, if you have followed these simple and well-tried directions correctly, you will have the Prologue to *The Legend of Good Women*. You can, in fact, produce two versions: a longer and more poetical one (called B or F by modern editors) or a revised, somewhat better integrated one (A or G). Either, however, is rather simpler than the recipe you may have found in earlier books, for a few ingredients have been omitted, There is no preliminary bedside reading, and no guide is provided for the dreamer.

Had the Prologue to *The Legend of Good Women* been composed just after *The Book of the Duchess*, we should hardly have been surprised. In fact, since it mentions Chaucer's *Troilus and Criseyde*, it must have been written after that poem, and the fact that G omits a command in F to present the finished work to the Queen at Eltham or Sheen has been held to refer to Richard's decision to destroy the royal palace at Sheen following Anne's death in 1394. In other words,

do, finished	*ywis*, truly
tok me to, devoted myself to	*mete*, discover
yit . . . alwey, I'm still for ever reading	*spare*, stop

Chaucer was probably at work on *The Legend of Good Women* at the same time as he was writing some of *The Canterbury Tales*. With our attention nowadays directed to character, verisimilitude and tension in literature,[24] *The Legend of Good Women* may seem a partial regression in Chaucer's poetic career, but it did not to those fifteenth-century readers who, valuing him for his eloquence and 'morality', would scarcely underrate a poem like this. In one way *The Legend of Good Women* looks forward, not back: it is written in decasyllabic couplets, the metre employed for most of *The Canterbury Tales*, and this was perhaps the first time that this metre had been used in English. The Prologue begins in the now familiar way, with the tribute to books as the poet's most familiar friends and the repositories of all useful knowledge:

> And yf that olde bokes were aweye,
> Yloren were of remembraunce the keye.   25-6

The only thing that will draw him away from his books is his devotion to the daisy which, in May, he would gladly watch all day. This is no simple Wordsworthian adoration, for its background is literary. There was a contemporary rivalry between the devotees of the flower and the leaf, probably an aristocratic cult of a similar artificiality to that of St Valentine in *The Parliament of Fowls*. Chaucer does little more than mention the contest itself, but he is consciously using the same kind of setting. Yet when the poet, like the flower, goes to rest at the setting of the sun, there is, as in Wordsworth, something to be learned from the initial description, some emotion recollected in tranquillity, for he sees, in his dream, the God of Love and his queen, Alcestis, followed by a great procession of women. (In this poem the natural description *precedes* and gives rise to the dream; it is not contained within the dream, as in *The Book of the Duchess* and *The Parliament of Fowls*.) The God is angry that the Dreamer should be worshipping his flower, for, by translating the *Roman de la Rose* and composing *Troilus and Criseyde*, he has shown himself a heretic against love: why couldn't he have written about *good* women? This charge does not seem altogether justified.

aweye, gone   *Yloren were*, would be lost

Although Criseyde, by deserting Troilus for Diomede, sinned against the morality of *fine amour*, the satire against women comes in the second part of the *Roman de la Rose* which, so far as we know, Chaucer did not translate. But, as Professor Lawlor reminds us,[25] there had been some pointed remarks about predatory men in the closing stanzas of *Troilus and Criseyde*, and this would fit well with the scheme of the *Legend*.

Fortunately Alcestis is ready to defend the Dreamer. Being *nyce* (foolish), he might not have realised the malice in what he did. Or perhaps he was commanded to write and dared not refuse. Has he not also written *The House of Fame*, *The Book of the Duchess*, *The Parliament of Fowls* – and a further list of unexceptionable works (some since lost)? In any case, a god should show mercy as well as justice. And so he does, handing over the Dreamer to Alcestis for sentence. The penance she imposes is:

> Thow shalt, while that thou lyvest, yer by yere,
> The moste partye of thy tyme spende
> In makyng of a glorious legende
> Of goode wymmen, maydenes and wyves,
> That weren trewe in lovyng al hire lyves;
> And telle of false men that hem bytraien,
> That al hir lyf ne do nat but assayen
> How many women they may doon a shame;
> For in youre world that is now holde a game.
>
> F 481–9

This queen is the Alcestis who, according to legend, died for her husband and is therefore the exemplar of true love:

> And wost so wel that kalender ys shee
> To any woman that wol lover bee.
> For she taught al the craft of fyn lovynge,
> And namely of wyfhod the lyvynge,
> And al the boundes that she oghte kepe.
>
> F 542–6

moste partye, greatest part
hire, their
ne . . . assayen, do nothing but try

kalender, model
of . . . lyvynge, the way to be a perfect wife

The Legend of Good Women says that this paragon of *fyn lovynge* (i.e. *fine amour*) was later turned into a daisy, which is Ovidian enough in manner but is not in any source that we know. However, it does form a link with the poet's own devotion to this flower which is also worshipped by all the ladies who serve Alcestis. These women are all 'good' according to the 'religion' of love for which many of them suffered martyrdom. Chaucer elsewhere refers to his poem as *The Seintes Legende of Cupyde* and *The Book of the XIX Ladies*. The Man of Law, who speaks of this poem as one of Chaucer's earlier compositions, calls it a large volume.[26] But eight heroines he mentions do not appear in *The Legend of Good Women*, and he does not mention Cleopatra and Philomela whose stories do appear there. Do his remarks refer to Chaucer's *plan* for the poem, or did Chaucer compose further stories, since lost?

Perhaps the series was meant to end with the story of Alcestis, but in fact we have only nine legends, and the ninth is unfinished. Dido we have met before in *The House of Fame* as an example of the woman who loved not wisely but too well and was deserted by her man. One or two choices, like Cleopatra or Medea, may cause the modern reader to raise an eyebrow, but all the stories conform to the same pattern:

> Lo! this is he, that with his flaterye
> Bytraised hath and don hire vilenye
> That was his trewe love in thought and dede!
>
> 2540–2

The ladies are always willing, like Hypsipyle, to help men in distress:

> Of hire goodnesse adoun she sendeth blythe
> To wyten if that any straunge wight
> With tempest thider were yblowe a-nyght,
> To don him socour, as was hire usaunce

Bytraised, deceived	*were . . . a-nyght*, had been
don hire vilenye, wronged her	driven in the night
blythe, quickly	*usaunce*, custom
wyten, know	

> To fortheren every wight, and don pleasaunce
> Of verrey bounte and of curteysye.   1473–8

Like Phyllis, they are good listeners to tales of hardship at sea, and, like Dido, offer all the comforts of their palace to the shipwrecked sailor. If he is in prison, like Theseus, Ariadne will find a means to get him out. But see how they are rewarded! Jason, after worming his way into Hypsipyle's affection with the willing help of Hercules, marries her, has two children, appropriates a good share of her possessions,

> And drogh his sayl, and saw hir nevere mo.
>
>   1563

He leaves two more children with Medea before later marrying for a third time. Philomela is ravished and has her tongue cut out. Theseus sails off with Ariadne's sister (although, it must be admitted, Ariadne herself had shown an eye for the main chance, 2126–35). Lucrece commits suicide rather than live with the shame of her violation by Tarquin, and Cleopatra ends by jumping into a pit full of snakes (apparently only in Chaucer and Gower who also tells the story). No dye is too deep for these villains: the only true one of the bunch is Pyramus, and Chaucer apologises for him. Aeneas is as excellent a courtly lover as Sir Lancelot himself, but it is all pretence. Theseus grovels for his life and promises to serve Ariadne as a page:

> But what is that that men nyl don for drede?
>
>   2095

Jason, perhaps, is the supreme philanderer:

> > Thow rote of false lovers, Duc Jasoun,
> > Thow sly devourere and confusioun
> > Of gentil wemen, tendre creatures,

fortheren, assist	*nevere mo*, never again
and . . . curteysye, do good out of (her) utter charitableness and courtesy	*nyl . . . drede*, won't do for fear
	rote, prime example
drogh, struck	*gentil*, noble

Thow madest thy recleymyng and thy lures
To ladyes of thy statly aparaunce.
And of thy wordes, farced with plesaunce,
And of thy feyned trouthe and thy manere,
With thyn obeysaunce and humble cheere,
And with thy contrefeted peyne and wo.
There othere falsen oon, thow falsest two!

1368–77

Most of this subject-matter is not new, of course. Chaucer seems to have used a variety of sources in *The Legend of Good Women*: Ovid (*Heroides*, *Metamorphoses* and *Fasti*), Virgil, Guido delle Colonne and Boccaccio. And these sources are compared in a manner characteristic rather of his later poetry than of his earlier:

Al be this nat rehersed of Guido,
Yit seyth Ovyde in his Epistels so. 1464–5

But Chaucer's frequent references to his sources throw a different light on the poem. It is as if he were most anxious not to get things wrong, to demonstrate how carefully he was adhering to the commands of Alcestis. Every opportunity is taken to point the moral.[27] Three times over we are reminded how deceitful Demophon was: his father was Theseus, and he is clearly his father's son. Three times the deceit of Aeneas's departure from Dido is emphasised:

For on a nyght, slepynge, he let hire lye,
And *stal awey* unto his companye,
And as a traytour forth he gan to sayle
Toward the large contre of Ytayle.
Thus he hath left Dido in wo and pyne,
And wedded ther a lady, hyghte Lavyne.

recleymyng and thy lures, entice-   *contrefeted*, pretended
  ments and your baits (both   *There*, Where
  from hawking)   *falsen*, deceived
statly aparaunce, noble looks   *rehersed of*, recounted by
farced, stuffed   *pyne*, torment
obeysaunce . . . cheere, deference   *hyghte*, called
  and humble expression

> A cloth he lafte, and ek his swerd stondynge,
> Whan he from Dido *stal* in hire slepynge,
> Ryght at hire beddes hed, so gan he hie,
> Whan that he *stal awey* to his navye.   1326–35

Almost from the beginning there are signs of hastiness. He cannot stop to describe the wedding feast of Antony and Cleopatra:

> And forthy to th'effect thanne wol I skyppe,
> And al the remenaunt, I wol lete it slippe.
>
>   622–3

This is scarcely rhetorical language. Tereus's return to Progne is covered at top speed:

> This Tereus is to his wif ycome,
> And in his armes hath his wif ynome,
> And pitously he wep, and shok his hed,
> And swor hir that he fond hir sister ded;
> For which this sely Progne hath swich wo
> That nygh hire sorweful herte brak a-two.
> And thus in terys lete I Progne dwelle,
> And of hire sister forth I wol yow telle.
>
>   2342–9

Casualness seems to have turned into *ennui*:

> But, shortly of this story for to passe,
> For I am wery of hym for to telle.   2257–8

Chaucer seems to have lost interest in the story of Phyllis, a good deal of which is simply padding, where for the one and only time he includes a lengthy extract from the letter in *Heroides*. In this same legend (the last before the unfinished *Hypermnestra*) the whole task seems to have become a *penance* indeed:

ek, also
so . . . hie, in such a hurry was he
forthy, therefore
effect, point
ycome, come
vnome, took

wep, wept
sely, poor
nygh, almost
brak a-two, broke in two
lete, leave
passe, pass over

But, for I am agroted herebyforn
To wryte of hem that ben in love forsworn,
And ek to haste me in my legende,
(Which to performe God me grace sende!)
Therefore I passe shortly in this wyse.   2454–8

We must not be unfair. The legends are short, and we
naturally do not become as interested in the fate of these
ladies as we did in that of Criseyde. The fatal fascination of
Cleopatra can be stated (599–606) but hardly demonstrated;
she is, in any case, here rather the aristocratic beauty with a
strawberries-and-cream complexion (*fayr as is the rose in May*)
than the lass unparalleled with a tawny front. So we are left
with a few memorable details: the violence and speed of the
battle of Actium; the gossiping neighbours through whom
Pyramus and Thisbe learn of each other's existence; how
Lucrece's husband conceives the idea of a visit home on
impulse and how thereafter Tarquin cannot get Lucrece out
of his mind; Lucrece herself awakened by the weight of
Tarquin, with drawn sword, pressing down on her bed;
Ariadne, in another bed, groping in the dawn to find
Theseus gone. These are the signs of a true *narrative* poet.

am agroted, have had enough of   *haste me*, hurry up
ek, besides

III

Troilus and Criseyde

What could be simpler than the opening of *Troilus and Criseyde*?

> The double sorwe of Troilus to tellen,
> That was the kyng Priamus sone of Troye,
> In lovynge, how his aventures fellen
> Fro wo to wele, and after out of joie,
> My purpos is, er that I parte fro ye.

It is a love story, and its author, 'the servant of the servants of the God of Love', begs the lovers in his audience to remember the bitter-sweet nature of their own passion and how sorrow and hardship preceded happiness. But this story has no happy ending, for it tells of the love of a faithful man for a women who ultimately proved faithless:

> For now wil I gon streght to my matere,
> In which ye may the double sorwes here
> Of Troilus in lovynge of Criseyde,
> And how that she forsook hym er she deyde.
>
> i 53–6

We know *what* happens, therefore, from the beginning. Our interest is in *how* and *why* it happens, and this involves a greater complexity, for we are likely to want to take sides, to blame one lover or excuse the other. And which side we take will, in turn, depend on the author's own presentation of his story.

the . . . Troye, King Priam of
  Troy's son
aventures, fortunes

wele, happiness
er that, before
matere, subject

The setting is the Troy of the Trojan War. For us this means Homer, but not for the Middle Ages, since Homer was a partisan of the Greeks while the Britons traced their descent from Brutus, the great-grandson of Aeneas. Furthermore, Homer was inaccurate, writing, as he did, a long time after the event, and, in any case, he had foolishly represented the gods fighting like men. As one late fourteenth-century alliterative romance put it:

But som poyetis full prist that put hom therto
With fablis and falshed fayned there speche,
And made more of that mater than hom maister were.
Some lokyt ouer litle, and lympit of the sothe.
Amonges that menye, to myn hym be nome,
Homer was holden haithill of dedis
Qwiles his dayes enduret, derrist of other,
That with the Grekys was gret, and of Grice comyn.
He feynet myche fals was neuer before wroght,
And turnet the truth, trust ye non other.
Of his trifuls to telle I haue no tome nowe,
Ne of his feynit fare that he fore with:
How goddes foght in the filde, folke as thai were![1]

The Destruction of Troy is a free treatment of a thirteenth-century Latin prose text, the *Historia Trojana*, by the Sicilian, Guido delle Colonne. Guido's Latin is itself based on a long twelfth-century French poem, Benoit de Sainte-Maure's

But som . . . thai were, But some very smart poets who took up the story falsified their language with fables and deceptions, and made more of the subject than was their job. Some examined it too superficially, and departed from the truth. Among that company – to recall him by name – Homer was considered famous for his doings for as long as he lived, the most excellent of all those who were renowned among the Greeks and who came from Greece. He invented much that was false and had never been done (written?) before and distorted the truth – you can be sure of that. I have no time now to relate his fairy-tales nor his imaginary materials that he worked with: how gods fought on the battlefield, just as if they had been men!

Roman de Troie, and Benoit himself says that he is following
Dares Phrygius, who *was* in Troy, himself took part in the
battles and kept a diary of what he saw. Benoit refers also,
but less often, to Dictys Cretensis who was in the Greek
camp at the time of the siege. These eyewitnesses were
thought to be far more trustworthy than Homer, although it
can now be shown that the present Latin form of Dares's *De
Excidio Trojae Historia* dates probably from the fifth or sixth
century A.D. and that of Dictys's *Ephemeris Belli Trojani* from
the fourth century A.D. Even if earlier Greek versions of
these texts existed, they can hardly be earlier than the second
century A.D., and, in any event, do not include the Troilus
and Criseyde story. Chaucer links Homer, Dares and Dictys
as background reading for the Trojan War:

> But the Troian gestes, as they felle,
> In Omer, or in Dares, or in Dite,
> Whoso that kan may rede hem as they write.
>
> i 145–7

and again directs his readers to Dares for additional information about Troilus's bravery:

> His worthi dedes, whoso list hem heere,
> Rede Dares, he kan telle hem alle ifeere.
>
> v 1770–1

But Homer is only a name, for few fourteenth-century
Englishmen could read Greek. By Dares Chaucer may have
meant an elaborate paraphrase by Joseph of Exeter at the
end of the twelfth century, from which he took a few details
in Book v. In Book v Chaucer also uses Benoit, whose story
does not begin until that point, with the separation of the
lovers.

The story of Troilus and Criseyde, however, came first to
completeness in Boccaccio's *Il Filostrato* ('the one stricken by
love'), composed *c.* 1338. Boccaccio provided a beginning to

gestes, stories   *whoso . . . heere*, whoever wants
felle, occurred   to listen to them
     ifeere, together

complement and explain Benoit's conclusion. His Troilo sees and falls in love with Criseida whom Boccaccio makes a widow, perhaps believing that such a combination of freedom and experience resulted in the ideal mistress. After a period of intense happiness the lovers are separated (as in Benoit) when Criseida is involved in an exchange of prisoners with the Greeks, and in the Greek camp she subsequently deserts Troilo for Diomede, a Greek warrior. Boccaccio also adds to the story the considerable figure of Pandaro. *Il Filostrato* is Chaucer's real source, although it has been suggested that he also used a contemporary French prose translation of the Italian.[2] Yet Chaucer never refers to Boccaccio in his poem. There are two possible reasons for this. The manuscript he used may simply not have mentioned Boccaccio at all, for it was by no means axiomatic for a medieval text to include its author's name. Or Boccaccio may not have seemed ancient and respectable enough for an 'authority' on an episode in the Trojan war. Book ii of *Troilus and Criseyde* is dedicated to Cleo, the muse of history (thus claiming truth for the narrative) and its proem, or prologue, says that the story is taken from Latin. Elsewhere this Latin source is called Lollius (i 394), an ascription which may have resulted from a misreading of one of Horace's epistles to produce a 'Lollius, greatest of writers on the Trojan war'. In *The House of Fame* (1468) Lollius is mentioned in conjunction with Dares and Dictys. Whatever the explanation, the story of Troilus and Criseyde is in all essentials that of *Il Filostrato*. What is different, as we shall see, is Chaucer's characterisation and the expansion of the setting, both of which result in a slowing down of the action. About one-third of Boccaccio's poem is translated directly, but much more often a line in Boccaccio sets Chaucer off and he adds the rest of the stanza, or sometimes two or three stanzas. The most extensive additions occur in Book ii, the winning of Criseyde, and in Book iv, the philosophical arguments of Troilus. In all probability, Troilus and Criseyde was composed in, or soon after, 1385, for the planetary situation which in iii 624 ff. produces the storm which keeps Criseyde in Pandarus's house overnight occurred in Britain in May 1385 for the first time in over six hundred years. If so, *Troilus and Criseyde* would follow *The Parliament of Fowls* (depending, in part, on another work of Boccaccio, the *Teseida*) and precede *The Legend of Good Women* in which the poem is mentioned for the first time. More important, the influence of Boethius's *Consolation of Philosophy*, which Chaucer had translated into prose in the early 1380s, provides a depth to the poem which is lacking in Boccaccio.

In Chaucer we are made more aware than in *Il Filostrato* of the background of a leisured society. In both, of course, the war and the desertion of Criseyde's father Calchas to the Greeks are introduced at the beginning of the poem, and in both the war then recedes into the background until it re-emerges much later as the reason for the separation of the lovers. But with Chaucer, life, as well as war, goes on in Troy. Priam's other sons appear: Hector, who is always chivalrous to Criseyde and who votes against the plan to exchange her for Antenor; Deiphebus, who seems especially close to Troilus; and Paris who is seen little but whose 'wife' Helen takes her place among the Trojan ladies. The friends of Poliphete, Criseyde's adversary, are the future traitors to the city, Antenor and Aeneas (ii 1474–5). Pandarus surprises Criseyde and her ladies listening to an account of the siege of Thebes *withinne a paved parlour* (ii 82), and after he has left she reads Troilus's letter in private. We see her with her nieces and ladies in waiting walking in the garden of a suspiciously medieval-looking town house:

> Adown the steyre anonright tho she wente
> Into the garden, with hire neces thre,
> And up and down ther made many a wente,
> Flexippe, she, Tharbe, and Antigone,
> To pleyen, that it joye was to see;
> And other of hire wommen, a gret route,
> Hire folowede in the garden al abowte.

steyre, stair	*wente*, turn
anonright, straightaway	*To pleyen*, enjoying themselves
tho, then	*route*, company

This yerd was large, and rayled alle th'aleyes,
And shadowed wel with blosmy bowes grene,
And benched newe, and sonded alle the weyes,
In which she walketh arm in arm bitwene.

ii 813–23[3]

from the window-seat of which – with Criseyde perched on
a cushion decorated with gold – Pandarus and Criseyde
glimpse Troilus riding back from battle. At the time of the
exchange of prisoners Pandarus cannot be with Troilus, for
there are other things going on in Troy:

This Pandare, that of al the day biforn
Ne myghte han comen Troilus to se,
Although he on his hed it hadde sworn,
For with the kyng Priam alday was he,
So that it lay nought in his libertee
Nowher to gon – but on the morwe he wente
To Troilus, whan that he for hym sente.

v 281–7

In Book v the walls of Troy are wide enough to walk along.
They have gates (through one of which Criseyde leaves for
the Greek camp) which are shut at night by a watchman,
as in a medieval city.

This actualisation, in which the frequently colloquial
language of the dialogue plays its part, is accompanied by a
'medievalisation' of Boccaccio's story. Despite the respective
dates of Boccaccio and Chaucer, Boccaccio's characters
show a cynicism and calculation which seems to us typical
of Renaissance Italy but foreign to their counterparts in
Chaucer. The society of *Troilus and Criseyde* is that of an
aristocracy which practises *fine amour*. Boccaccio's Troilo
shows, as it were, symptoms of the disease, but his actions
are not explicitly ascribed to it. The *fine amour* is, as C. S.

yerd, garden
aleyes, paths
blosmy, flowering
benched newe, freshly provided
   with (turf) benches

weyes, paths
on his hed, deeply
on the morwe, the next morning

Lewis showed,[4] mostly Chaucer's addition to his source. In *Troilus and Criseyde* Chaucer has, in fact, taken the three central figures of the code as presented in the *Roman de la Rose*, the Lady, the Lover and the Friend (confidant), and has given them their correct characteristics, but, at the same time, he has made them credible human beings. It follows that Criseyde's fault is not that she accepts Troilus's love without marriage – Chaucer never condemns the affair for its immorality, and adultery is not in question since Troilus is a bachelor and Criseyde a widow – but that, once having accepted Troilus as her love, she deserts him for Diomede. The conventions of *fine amour* also explain Troilus's inability to help Criseyde when she has to leave Troy to return to the Greek camp under the terms of the truce. He can't negotiate, can't complain to his father Priam, can't flee with Criseyde, because any one of these would reveal their love and endanger not only Criseyde's reputation but perhaps her life:

> 'Whi nyl I make atones riche and pore
> To have inough to doone, er that she go?
> Why nyl I brynge al Troie upon a roore?
> Whi nyl I slen this Diomede also?
> Why nyl I rather with a man or two
> Stele hire away? Whi wol I this endure?
> Why nyl I helpen to myn owen cure?'

> But why he nolde don so fel a dede,
> That shal I seyn, and whi hym liste it spare:
> He hadde in herte alweyes a manere drede
> Leste that Criseyde, in rumour of this fare,
> Sholde han ben slayn; lo, this was al his care.

v 43-54

riche and pore, one and all	*hym . . . spare*, he wanted to avoid it
inough to doone, plenty to occupy them	*manere drede*, kind of fear
upon a roore, in an uproar	*in . . . fare*, once this deed was reported
fel, cruel	*care*, worry

He does actually propose flight together at the end of Book
iv, but Criseyde refuses; later she wishes she had accepted.
But *qui non celat amare non potest* is a hard rule. It provides a
wall of defence against gossips in the earlier stages of a love
affair, but it is a wall which can pen you in as well as keeping
your opponents out. Troilus is thus not free to act within the
morality of the poem, and after the beginning of Book iv is increasingly acted upon.

Spring, as we have seen often enough, is the traditional
season for loving. The feast of Palladion, at which Troilus
first catches sight of Criseyde standing in the temple, is the
time

> Of Aperil, whan clothed is the mede
> With newe grene, of lusty Veer the pryme,
> And swote smellen floures white and rede.

> i 156–8

Pandarus sets off to visit his niece to acquaint her with
Troilus's love for her on the third of May (ii 50–6). He tells
her that he first became aware of Troilus's love for her in a
garden, near a fountain (ii 508). On learning from Pandarus
that the news from Criseyde is encouraging, Troilus revives
like woods and hedges in May after the cold of winter. Much
later, Diomede, *as fressh as braunche in May*, visits Criseyde in
her tent. In a work which comes so late in the courtly
tradition as this, it is only necessary to indicate these things
to a sophisticated audience whose memory of May mornings and delightful gardens will supply the necessary atmosphere. The courtship of Criseyde, similarly, proceeds
according to the dictates of *fine amour*. She promises at first
only to *maken hym good chere* ('be nice to him'), to *plese* him –
so long as her reputation is safeguarded – and no more than
this. His *good servyse*, as the Narrator is careful to remind us,
is still to be demonstrated:

> For I sey nought that she so sodeynly
> Yaf hym hire love, but that she gan enclyne

qui . . . potest, he who cannot
conceal, is not fit for love

of . . . pryme, the beginning of
the joyful springtime
Yaf, gave

> To like hym first, and I have told yow whi;
> And after that, his manhod and his pyne
> Made love withinne hire herte for to myne,
> For which, by proces and by good servyse,
> He gat hire love, and in no sodeyn wyse.
>
> ii 673–9

Yet, as with all these courtly heroines, *pite* (feeling 'sorry' for him) is the weak chink in the Lady's armour:

> But moost hir favour was, for his distresse
> Was al for hire, and thoughte it was a routhe
> To sleen swich oon, if that he mente trouthe.
>
> ii 663–5

Pandarus, old campaigner that he is, knows this, and has already used the argument to encourage Troilus:

> And also thynk, and therwith glade the,
> That sith thy lady vertuous is al,
> So foloweth it that there is som pitee
> Amonges alle thise other in general.
>
> i 897–900

The later episode with Diomede takes exactly the same course, with Criseyde's initial promise of 'friendship', but in this case the sheer speed of the affaire drains the courtship of all romance.[5] Much of the attraction of Chaucer's poem lies in his charting of the gradual progress of the love between Troilus and Criseyde. Fulfilment, when it comes, seems all the more marvellous because of the time and ingenuity it has taken to overcome the obstacles which *fine amour* itself and a naturally hesitant pair of lovers have created.[6] In this Chaucer is again deliberately slowing down the pace of Boccaccio's story. The most obvious instance is Criseyde's

pyne, torment
myne, mine its way
by proces, in the course of time
routhe, pity
swich oon, such a one

mente trouthe, his intentions were honourable
glade the, cheer yourself
sith, since
other, other (qualities)

alternation in Book ii between happiness and fear, but the later hurried meetings between the pair, Troilus's impatience that he cannot see her often enough, and his final utter helplessness without Criseyde as he moons around Troy, associating particular spots in the city with particular happy memories of their love (v 561–81) and wondering who is with her now in the Greek tents, all contribute to our 'modern' feeling that this is what it is really like to be in love, as well as being completely in character with the 'medieval' convention of *fine amour*. For much of *fine amour* is permanent rather than medieval, and in *Troilus and Criseyde*, perhaps because of the virtual absence of allegory, we find it no longer inhibiting.

Chaucer, however, is not here dealing with figures in a dream, but with credible people. Troilus, Criseyde and Pandarus are real in a sense that the Man in Black never was, even though he may have represented John of Gaunt. We must be careful, though, of talking about medieval characters as if they appeared in a modern novel. Very often a medieval author will use his characters mainly to illustrate a pattern of behaviour, his *sentence*. There is little development of character in the sense of change – they seldom act completely unexpectedly or 'out of character' – but, naturally enough, a long work will gradually reveal more about their nature. Even so, their end is in their beginning, and we are not given more than the plot requires us to know. We do not need to be told about Criseyde's marriage or, in Chaucer (who stops at how she 'forsook' Troilus), about her final degredation as a prostitute and a leper, just as we are not invited to speculate about the girlhood of Shakespeare's heroines or the number of children born to Lady Macbeth. But, with these reservations, it is undeniable that Chaucer conceives his characters as more complex personalities than Boccaccio's. The pattern of *Il Filostrato* is simple: Troilo, the gay young man about town; Criseida, the willing but ultimately faithless mistress, who also represents Boccaccio's unresponsive lady-love, Maria d'Aquino; and Pandaro, Criseida's cousin and not her uncle, another gay young spark like Troilo. Boccaccio's prologue explains how and why he came to tell the story. His lady absent, he is brought close to death, but

> I found the surest augury of future happiness. And the way was this: that, in the person of somebody stricken with love as I was and am, I should tell my sufferings in song. And so with zealous care I fell to turning over old stories in my mind to find one which I could fitly use as a cloak for the secret grief of my love . . . And if you chance to read them [these words addressed to his lady], as often as you find Troilus weeping and lamenting the departure of Criseida, you will be able to understand and know my very words, tears, sighs, and agonies; and whenever you find portrayed the beauty of Criseida, her manners, and any other excellent qualities in a woman, you can understand that it is spoken of you.

Boccaccio, therefore, is personally involved, and not only at the beginning of the story. When Criseida leaves Troy under the terms of the truce, for instance, he says that he can well describe Troilo's grief since he too is parted from his lady. Boccaccio's is a good story, but slight, and although Professor Howard goes somewhat too far in calling it 'the stuff of Italian opera and *la dolce vita*',[7] we can see well enough what he means. Chaucer, in any case, was far better fitted to appreciate the deeper significance (serious, philosophical, and even humorous) of his material. Boccaccio was twenty-five when he wrote his poem; when he wrote his Chaucer was over forty and had, in addition, translated Boethius.

THE CHARACTERS

In all essentials Troilus is as in Boccaccio, except that he is more considerate, as befits a courtly lover. Troilo has been in love before, but hitherto has always believed that the advantages were outweighed by the worry. Troilus is an innocent in love; his early jokes against 'these lovers' are the result of ignorance and inexperience, and his own love, when it comes, is likely to prove both all-demanding and fraught with difficulties which stem from his character as well as from the more easily recognisable obstacles of *fine amour*. In the early part of the poem his sensitivity, even awkwardness, is often discernible behind the feelings and gestures of the conventional lover, yet by Book iii he has grown both more serious and somewhat more assured – 'grown up', in fact.[8] This, too, is fully in accordance with *fine amour*, for the act of loving further ennobles a man already noble:

> In alle nedes, for the townes werre,
> He was, and ay, the first in armes dyght,
> And certeynly, but if that bokes erre,
> Save Ector most ydred of any wight;
> And this encrees of hardynesse and myght
> Com hym of love, his ladies thank to wynne,
> That altered his spirit so withinne.   iii 1772–8

In Book iv, although initially Troilus goes to pieces at the news of the exchange of prisoners, imagines himself dead and rails against Fortune, the final decision to refrain from action when Criseyde leaves Troy is his and not Pandarus's. By this time he is able to expose the shallowness of his friend:

> Thow biddest me I shulde love another
> Al fresshly newe, and lat Criseyde go!
> It lith nat in my power, leeve brother;
> And though I myght, I wolde nat do so.
> But kanstow playen raket, to and fro,
> Nettle in, dok out, now this, now that, Pandare?
> Now foule falle hire for thi wo that care!
>   iv 456–62

ay, always
dyght, arrayed
but if that, unless
ydred, feared
thank, favour
lith, lies
leeve, dear

raket, tennis
Nettle ... out, first one thing, then another (from rubbing stings with dock leaves)
Now ... care, Now may misfortune befall her who feels pity for *your* grief

The monologues on predestination in this book (their content taken almost wholly from Boethius, but without Boethius's conclusion) are a philosophical exposition of his dilemma, yet these questionings about free will and destiny also arise naturally from the longing for death of the typical unhappy lover. In this, as in much else, Chaucer has seen the possibilities of *fine amour* as a morality for his story. Professor Robertson has acutely remarked that the Troilus of Book v appeals to our own generation:

> . . . the frustrated, neurotic and maladjusted hero of modern fiction, an existentialist for whom Being itself, which he has concentrated in his own person, becomes dubious.[9]

Yet this is a 'medieval' Troilus too, for when Pandarus tells Troilus 'Delyte nat in wo thi wo to seche' (i 704), he is criticising him not for acting out of character but for failing to see that there can be a solution to his problem. In Malory too, just as the characters shake with huge gusts of laughter, so everyone (men as well as women) appears to burst out crying at the slightest opportunity. What looks like gross exaggeration to us, seemed merely appropriate to the Middle Ages: great grief demanded suitable expression. Troilus is no fool. He really knows that he has lost Criseyde long before he admits it, and the final evidence of the brooch pinned to Diomede's tunic (which he sees at v 1660, but which is mentioned earlier, at line 1040, as an indication of Criseyde's faithlessness) only forces him to realise the truth of what he has tried to hide from himself. Yet he cannot stop loving Criseyde, and because, like Malory's Lancelot, he is a 'true lover', he is allowed finally to see earthly and heavenly love in proper perspective. But the *wrecched world* and *blynde lust* of the poem are fallible and impermanent only in comparison with Heaven itself.

In Boccaccio Criseida throws off her last remaining garment as the lovers melt into each other's arms. In Chaucer Pandarus has to tear off Troilus's clothes and throw him into the bed of a Criseyde who quakes like an aspen leaf. For Criseida the necessary secrecy of the affair simply adds spice to it. Once she has agreed that Troilo shall visit her, it is she, not Pandaro, who makes the arrangements. Pandaro therefore has no need of a Horaste or a Poliphete. When Criseida turns to Diomede for consolation, there is less surprise, and accordingly far less need of the excuses which Chaucer feels compelled to make for her.

As far as direct description goes, Criseyde has all the virtues but few individual traits. There are only two of the latter: her joined eyebrows (a slight blemish to Chaucer but a mark of beauty in the classical sources) and the fact that she is *slydynge of corage* (v 825), a point to which I shall return. Otherwise she is of medium height, slender, fair-haired, of fresh complexion, bright-eyed, demure, yet self-possessed and with a proper share of social finesse, with a love of well doing (whatever that may mean, it *sounds* right), above all *wommanly*, Chaucer's highest term of praise. It could be the ideal beauty of a hundred medieval lyrics,[10] or the Duchess Blanche, except that we see and hear more of Criseyde than we do of them. This is important, because we are allowed, at any time before Book v, to enter fully into Criseyde's thoughts. What we see, and what of course Troilus does not see, is, as Professor Donaldson says,[11] usually encouraging but occasionally disturbing too. Book ii, especially, is Criseyde's book, for she does not speak at all in Book i and Troilus does not speak in Book ii before line 945. In this book we see Criseyde making up her mind whether or not to return Troilus's love, a process which takes far longer in Chaucer than it had in Boccaccio. Pandarus's view is simply that all personable young women are made for loving:

> And for to speke of hire in specyal,
> Hire beaute to bithynken and hire youthe,
> It sit hire naught to ben celestial
> As yet, though that hire liste bothe and kowthe;

to bithynken, considering	*though . . . kowthe*, though she
sit, suits	could, and might want to

> But trewely, it sate hire wel right nowthe
> A worthi knyght to loven and cherice,
> And but she do, I holde it for a vice.　　i 981-7

Initially, Criseyde is quite against this:

> 'I? God forbede!' quod she, 'be ye mad?
> Is that a widewes lif, so God yow save?
> By God, ye maken me ryght soore adrad!
> Ye ben so wylde, it semeth as ye rave.
> It sate me wel bet ay in a cave
> To bidde and rede on holy seyntes lyves;
> Lat maydens gon to daunce, and yonge wyves.'
> ii 113-19

When she reflects to herself, however, after Pandarus has gone, we see another side to Criseyde. She knows she is as beautiful as any woman in Troy – at least, she's heard people say so – so it can be no wonder if Troilus is attracted. She has no family responsibilities. So why should she not fall in love if she wants to? But immediately Danger and his forces rush to repel such forward thoughts. In fact there are no allegorical characters, but the arguments are the same: loss of liberty in return for – what, love's torments?; gossips always at hand; men are fickle and their love doesn't last. As a widow she has a certain freedom of decision, apparently based on relative economic security. What she might well lose by loving Troilus is the independence and tranquillity she at present enjoys in Troy, but which she regards as somewhat precarious following her father's desertion to the Greeks. In the end she makes up her mind, as she always does, as a result of outside influences: Antigone's song, which stresses the happiness in love; the nightingale singing outside her bedroom window; her dream of the eagle; a glimpse of Troilus riding past her house; and, of course, all the arguments of Pandarus ranging from gentle persuasion to downright hectoring. Her decision, naturally, is for caution, not

sate, would befit
nowthe, now
but she do, unless she does
soore adrad, deeply afraid

rave, are going mad
wel bet, much better
bidde, pray

to meet him yet, as Pandarus had wanted, but not to discourage him either:

> And whi, for shame; and it were ek to soone
> To graunten hym so gret a libertee.
> For pleynly hire entente, as seyde she,
> Was for to love hym unwist, if she myghte,
> And guerdon hym with nothing but with sighte.
>
> ii 1291–5

But the leaven of *pite* has begun to work. Thereafter, although it still needs Pandarus to push both lovers further and faster than they are quite ready to go, the culmination of their love in Book iii follows naturally. Pandarus sees to it that events put Criseyde in an impossible position:

> This accident so pitous was to here,
> And ek so like a sooth, at prime face,
> And Troilus hire knyght to hir so deere,
> His prive comyng, and the siker place,
> That, though that she did hym as thanne a grace,
> Considered alle thynges as they stoode,
> No wonder is, syn she did al for goode.   iii 918–24

but she knows that she has in reality yielded long since:

> This Troilus in armes gan hire streyne,
> And seyde, 'O swete, as evere mot I gon,
> Now be ye kaught, now is ther but we tweyne!
> Now yeldeth yow, for other bote is non!'
> To that Criseyde answerede thus anon,
> 'Ne hadde I er now, my swete herte deere,
> Ben yold, ywis, I were now nought heere!'
>
> iii 1205–11

it . . . soone, it would be too soon
pleynly hire entente, her full intention
unwist, secretly
guerdon, reward
accident, incident
at prime face, at first sight
prive, secret
siker, safe

did hym . . . a grace, gave him her favour
streyne, press
as . . gon, as I live and breathe
tweyne, two
bote, alternative
anon, straightaway
Ne hadde I . . . ben yold, if I had not yielded

At first all the talk in Book iv is about how Criseyde can be prevented from leaving Troy, and the lovers assume, fatalistically, that she must be exchanged for Antenor as the Trojan parliament has decreed. It is Pandarus who first raises the notion of Criseyde's possible *return* to Troy (iv 935), and she mentions it to Troilus at iv 1272. Having mentioned the idea, Criseyde proceeds to embroider it: they should not expect love to be all happiness; it isn't *far*, only half a morning's ride; they have been apart for ten days often enough before; all her friends and property are in Troy, which will draw her back; peace is on the way; her greedy father will allow her to go to and fro and carry valuables with her – she can easily manage *him*, in any case. She believes desperately that something will turn up, that love will find a way. Perhaps she is convincing herself of the rightness of this plan. Troilus is far less certain that it will work, but she persuades him that it is far better for both of them than flight together from Troy.

It is not until the very beginning of Book v that Criseyde actually leaves Troy and Chaucer's job of explaining the desertion to Diomede really begins. He realises what he has to do at the beginning of Book iv. He cannot explain it *away*, for Criseyde is clearly guilty, but he can minimise her guilt as much as possible:

> For how Criseyde Troilus forsook,
> *Or at the leeste, how that she was unkynde,*[12]
> Moot hennesforth ben matere of my book,
> As writen folk thorugh which it is in mynde,
> Allas! that they sholde evere cause fynde
> To speke hire harm, and if they on hire lye,
> Iwis, hemself sholde han the vilanye.   iv 15–21

In the first place he stops short at the desertion, and then passes to Troilus's death, omitting what comes between. From the very beginning of Book v circumstances throw Diomede and Criseyde together as they had not Troilus and

matere, subject   *Iwis*, truly
in mynde, transmitted   *vilanye*, blame

Criseyde. Diomede escorts her back to the Greek camp. He is affable and courteous, offers his services and even his love.[13] This last might seem a little premature, but Diomede is *sodeyn* and far too smooth an operator to miss a chance like this with the two of them together:

> Thus seyde I nevere er now to womman born;
> For, God myn herte as wisly glade so,
> I loved never womman here-biforn
> As paramours, ne nevere shal no mo.
> And, for the love of God, beth nat my fo,
> Al kan I naught to yow, my lady deere,
> Compleyne aright, for I am yet to leere.
>
> v 155–61

This is the first time. This is for real. (This is what they all say.) Criseyde is so overwhelmed with grief that she hears only part of it all, but thanks Diomede politely and says she will remember his offer of friendship.

There follows the long passage in which Troilus tries to fill the ten days as best he can. It is that very tenth day (v 842) that Diomede goes to visit Criseyde, whereas Boccaccio had put the visit 'not four days' after she left Troy. She has had long enough to realise the plight she is in 'With wommen fewe among the Grekis stronge'; with no sympathy from her father; missing the good times in Troy; and with no one to confide in. Stealing back across no-man's-land to Troy looks infinitely harder from the Greek lines than it had when first imagined in Troy:

> And if that I me putte in jupartie,
> To stele awey by nyght, and it bifalle
> That I be kaught, I shal be holde a spie;
> Or elles – lo, this drede I moost of alle –
> If in the hondes of som wrecche I falle,

wisly, surely
As paramours, truly
mo, others

Compleyne . . . leere, make a proper lament, for I am still to be instructed
holde, thought

I nam but lost, al be myn herte trewe.
Now, myghty God, thow on my sorwe rewe!

v 701–7

Nevertheless, her resolve seems firmer than it does in Boccaccio: she will go *to-morwe at nyght* (751) and concludes *To Troie I wole* (765), which is better than Boccaccio's 'I shall do all I can . . .'

All this, however, is no match against Diomede, who, unlike Troilus, has no need of an intermediary. He assumes, he says, that she loves *som Troian*, but what use is that, for Troy's days are numbered? Calkas himself has foreseen it, unless he is misleading us all with *ambages* (and these seem far less likely to be realised than the gods' *amphibologies* at iv 1406). Come on, dry those pretty eyes; why, I'll be your servant myself! Then comes the carefully prepared blush:

> And with that word he gan to waxen red,
> And in his speche a litel wight he quok,
> And caste asyde a little wight his hed,
> And stynte a while; and afterward he wok,
> And sobreliche on hire he threw his lok,
> And seyde, 'I am, al be it yow no joie,
> As gentil man as any wight in Troie.'

v 925–31

This is enough for one day, though, and he offers to return the next:

> Ye wol me graunte that I may to-morwe,
> At bettre leyser, tellen yow my sorwe.   v 944–5

Criseyde cannot manage a lover like this one. She makes the only reference she ever does to her dead husband as her one and only love, and, by omitting any mention of Troilus,

---

I . . . lost, it will be all up with
   me
rewe, take pity
ambages, ambiguities
amphibologies, riddles
a . . . quok, he trembled a bit

caste, turned
stynte, paused
wok, came to
al, although
gentil, noble
bettre, more

takes the first step along the slippery path of deceit. When
the Greeks have won Troy (which she regards as impossible,
like Dorigen's condition of the removal of the black rocks)
will be time enough to return Diomede's love. If she ever
encourages any Greek, it will be Diomede. Once again, she
does not want to be rushed:

> I say nat therefore that I wol yow love,
> N'y say nat nay; but in conclusioun,
> I mene wel, by God that sit above! v 1002-4

Diomede, after taking a glove as a favour, and chalking this
up as a good day's work (1013), leaves her. And she goes
to bed, but not to sleep, just as in Book ii:

> Retornyng in hire soule ay up and down
> The wordes of this sodeyn Diomede,
> His grete estat, and perel of the town,
> And that she was allone and hadde nede
> Of frendes help; and thus bygan to brede
> The cause whi, the sothe for to telle,
> That she took fully purpos for to dwelle,
>
> v 1023-9

Diomede is back the very next day, but no more is really
necessary. Direct speech can give way to narrative, and, if
the narrator is an historian, he must make his testimony
with proper caution. For the 'stories' (i.e. Benoit) say that
Criseyde gave Diomede a steed, a brooch once given her by
Troilus, a pennant made from her sleeve, and that she
tended his wounds. But they *trewely* (1051) say that she
grieved for Troilus and for her own reputation. And no
source says how long it was between 'falsing' Troilus and
fully accepting Diomede (which is surely as much as to say

N'y . . . nay, and I don't say no   *grete estat*, important position
sit, sits   *brede*, breed
Retornyng, turning over   *took . . . purpos*, made up her mind
soule, mind   *dwelle*, remain
sodeyn, impetuous

that it may well not have been sudden). Finally comes the direct admission:

> Ne me ne list this sely womman chyde
> Forther than the storye wol devyse.
> Hire name, allas! is punysshed so wide,
> That for hire gilt it oughte ynough suffise.
> And if I myghte excuse hire any wise,
> For she so sory was for hire untrouthe,
> Iwis, I wolde excuse hire yet for routhe.
>
> v 1093–9

Criseyde is no Tess, but the President of the Immortals has scarcely been on her side.

Chaucer cannot change the story, nor does he ever make any attempt to do so, but, as I have tried to show, he minimises Criseyde's guilt in every way possible. Boccaccio's conclusion, 'may love grant you grace to love so wisely that in the end you die not for a worthless woman', is far from Chaucer's. In the description of Criseyde, one of the three 'portraits' somewhat oddly introduced into the middle of Book v, occurs the line:

> Tendre-herted, *slydynge of corage*,　　　v 825

Most of the description is general and unexceptionable enough, yet this phrase seems to suggest some individuality. But what does it mean? 'unstable in affection', as *MED* 1 (a), or 'lacking in strength of mind', as *MED* 3 (a)? If the phrase is Benoit's, as it very well may be ('Fickle and infirm, her feelings were very soon changed; very weak and inconstant was her heart.'), or if the interpretation is that of the *Laud Troy Book*, dependent on Guido delle Colonne:

> She hoped neuere of him [Troilus] mariage
> She changed her wil and corage:
> Doghti Troyle sche gan forsake,
> To Diomedes sche gan hir take.　　　13555–8

Ne me ne list, I don't want to　　*any wise*, in any way
sely, poor　　　　　　　　　　　*Iwis*, truly
devyse, suggest　　　　　　　　　*routhe*, pity
punysshed, disgraced

the former would seem likely. One of Chaucer's rare uses of *slydynge* is to describe Fortune in his translation of Boethius, where it glosses *lubrica* (slippery, fickle).[14] But the latter idea fits better with the general air of praise in Chaucer's 'portrait', and Criseyde sees clearly what the consequences of her deceit will be:

> Allas! of me, unto the worldes ende,
> Shal neyther ben ywriten nor ysonge
> No good word, for thise bokes wol me shende.
> O, rolled shal I ben on many a tonge!
> Thorughout the world my belle shal be ronge!
> And wommen moost wol haten me of alle.
> Allas, that swich a cas me sholde falle!
>
> v 1058–64

Is Chaucer's final judgment on Criseyde that her tragedy was to see clearly enough where her actions were leading her, but that she was not strong-minded enough to overcome events?

Later authors gave Criseyde much harsher treatment. Robert Henryson begins his *Testament of Cresseid* (*c.* 1490) with the situation in Chaucer's Book v. He then takes up *ane vther quair* (61)[15] in which he finds that Criseyde too, according to the tragic formula, *endit wretchitlie*. For Diomede tired of Cresseid, and (*sum men sayis*) she became a prostitute. Yet Henryson's narrator, like his master Chaucer, would partly excuse Cresseid because of her harsh treatment by Fortune:

> ȝit neuertheles, quhat euer men deme or say
> In scornefull langage of thy brukkilnes,
> I sall excuse als far furth as I may
> Thy womanheid, thy wisdome and fairnes,
> The quhilk Fortoun hes put to sic distres
> As hir pleisit, and nathing throw the gilt
> Of the – throw wickit langage to be spilt! 85–91

shende, disgrace	*deme*, think
rolled, discussed	*brukkilnes*, frailty
my . . . ronge, my reputation will spread everywhere	*quhilk*, which
	sic, such
quhat, what	*spilt*, ruined

Cresseid, in Henryson, is no sentimentalist. She explains simply to her father:

> Fra Diomeid had gottin his desyre
> He wox werie and wald of me no moir.   101–2

It is only when, in her prayers, she blasphemes against Venus and Cupid that the gods exact a fearful retribution by inflicting her with leprosy and consequent expulsion from society. Even so, we may feel that her real punishment comes at the end of the poem when Troilus rides past the crowd of lepers, does not recognise her (although some quirk of memory recalls Cresseid to his mind at just that instant), and throws her a purse.

Henryson, through Cresseid's lament, warns his audience against the mutability, not only of the pleasures of the flesh, but of life itself. In the hundred-odd years between Henryson and Shakespeare's *Troilus and Cressida* blame for Criseyde had largely succeeded pity. Shakespeare doubtless thought Henryson's poem to be a sequel by Chaucer, for all sixteenth-century editions of Chaucer include it as his. Several translations of the *Iliad* (notably Chapman's), Lydgate's *Troy Book* and Caxton's *Recuyell of the Historyes of Troye* were available to Shakespeare as background for the Trojan war, as they had not been to Chaucer. For the first half of the play Shakespeare is infinitely more concerned with war than with love, and the play also ends on the battlefield in a flurry of destruction. The love-affair is good when it comes, but there is all too little of it. We cannot really gauge the seriousness of the love of Troilus and Cressida before we see them together in Act III, scene ii.[16] Then, in the very next scene, Diomede sets out to bring Cressida back to the Greek camp. Troilus and Cressida are never allowed to develop as characters, and Pandarus stage-manages everything from the start in a far more cold-blooded manner than in Chaucer: his reputation too had deteriorated drastically. There can be no doubt about the guilt of Cressida. Ulysses's speech is uncompromising:

Fra, When	*wald . . . moir*, wanted nothing
wox, grew	more to do with me

There's language in her eye, her cheek, her lip,
Nay her foot speaks, her wanton spirits look out
At every joint and motive of her body.
O these encounterers, so glib of tongue,
That give a coasting welcome ere it comes,
And wide unclasp the tables of their thoughts
To every ticklish reader; set them down
For sluttish spoils of opportunity,
And daughters of the game.   IV v 55–63

and, as if to confirm it, we are allowed, with Troilus, to
eavesdrop on Diomede and Criseyde talking together. Her
function in Shakespeare is to force Troilus to distinguish
between appearance and reality and 'to raise doubts in our
minds about the value of romantic love, as Achilles raises
doubts about epic heroism'.[17] The really memorable lines
in the play are therefore those which show Troilus's con-
frontation with the truth about Cressida's duplicity:

This she? No, this is Diomed's Cressida.
If beauty have a soul, this is not she;
If souls guide vows, if vows be sanctimonies,
If sanctimony be the gods' delight;
If there be rule in unity itself,
This is not she. O madness of discourse,
That cause sets up with and against itself!
Bi-fold authority, where reason can revolt
Without perdition, and loss assume all reason
Without revolt. This is, and is not, Cressid.
                                    V ii 137–46

But finally he does believe she is false, and he turns against
her, unlike Chaucer's Troilus who can never find it in his
heart to *unloven* Criseyde. Shakespeare is not interested in
Cressida's ultimate fate, and she drops out of the play when
she has fulfilled her task. If, as seems possible, the play was
originally written for a cultured audience – perhaps at the
Inns of Court – priding itself on its unshockable 'realism',[18]
this mixture of noble deeds and cynicism becomes more
intelligible.

With Pandarus we return to Chaucer, since his function in Shakespeare is all too plain. But we should make the journey via Boccaccio, for it was Boccaccio who first added Pandaro to the story, making him a contemporary of Troilo and with no illusions about Criseida: 'My cousin is a widow and desirous: and if she were to deny it I should not believe her.' Chaucer makes Pandarus *seem* older; there is no evidence of his age in the poem, but he is uncle to Criseyde (not cousin, as in Boccaccio) and the impression he gives is that of a cultured and worldly-wise courtier, not nearly so dazzled by Criseyde as Troilus is. Chaucer's change of relationship complicates matters, for Pandarus has responsibilities both to Troilus, his closest friend and confidant, and to his niece Criseyde whose guardian he has been in Troy since her father Calchas deserted to the Greeks. And Pandarus realises these responsibilities. His pose towards Criseyde is that of the uncle who is willing to play the fool to amuse his niece:

> Therewith she lough, and seyde, 'Go we dyne.'
> And he gan at hymself to jape faste,
> And seyde, 'Nece, I have so gret a pyne
> For love, that everich other day I faste – '
> And gan his beste japes forth to caste,
> And made hire so to laughe at his folye,
> That she for laughter wende for to dye.
>
> ii 1163–9 (cf. iii 554–5)

but he is well aware of what he is really doing:

> For the [Troilus] have I bigonne a gamen pleye,
> Which that I nevere do shal eft for other.
> Although he were a thousand fold my brother.
>
> That is to seye, for the am I bicomen,
> Bitwixen game and ernest, swich a meene

Therewith, At that	*fold*, times
lough, laughed	*Bitwixen . . . ernest*, With one
jape, make fun of	thing and another
wende, imagined	*swich*, such
eft, again	

As maken wommen unto men to comen;
Al sey I nought, thow wost wel what I meene.
For the have I my nece, of vices cleene,
So fully maad thi gentilesse triste,
That al shal ben right as thiselven liste.   iii 250–9

Following this, however, he goes on to talk in the language of
fine amour, so that the idea of the bawd is obscured by the
need for secrecy and for not boasting. Troilus replies that
Pandarus is not acting for money but out of friendship and
gentilesse. As an excuse this is of no use at all, and, in any
case, is achieved only by a wilful semantic misunderstanding
on Troilus's part. It must, as Mrs Gordon says,[19] qualify
our hitherto high opinion of Troilus, but, at the same time,
it is difficult to see how Chaucer could have avoided this
feature of the story.

Pandarus twice tricks Criseyde into seeing Troilus, first on
the pretence that he is sick and that if she wants his support
against Poliphete she must visit his bedside, and later when
he brings Troilus to Criseyde's room on the night of the
storm. On this second occasion his excuse is that Troilus has
been told that Criseyde loves Horaste (Pandarus is excellent
at inventing plausible-sounding adversaries) and will not be
comforted until he has heard her deny it with her own lips.
When Troilus proves none too expert in his part and swoons
in Criseyde's bedroom, it is Pandarus who pushes him into
bed.

The success of Pandarus as a character is his general air of
managing things. He is by nature a 'fixer' and always offering
his services:

Yef me this labour and this bisynesse,
And of my spede be thyn al that swetnesse.
                                                i 1042–3

Al . . . nought, Although I won't   *gentilesse*, honour
   name it   *liste*, would wish
wost, know   *Yef*, Give
cleene, innocent   *spede*, success

And, by youre leve, I wol but in right sterte
And do yow wyte, and that anon, iwys,
If that he slepe, or wol ought here of this.

ii 1634–6

He is always ready to keep the love-affair moving (ii 1460,
iii 484), and he knows that in order to do this careful planning is necessary (i 1062–71). He actually prods Criseyde
when she comes to visit Troilus whom she believes to be sick
(iii 116), but hurries her away quickly when he hears people
coming (iii 190). Similar detailed plotting is necessary to
bring the lovers together in circumstances where they may
consummate their love. He foresees the storm, secretes
Troilus, persuades Criseyde to stay overnight, apparently
surrounding her with women and with himself as guardian
in the outer room (iii 659–86). Then he leads the trembling
Troilus – for whom he thoughtfully provides a fur cloak –
into Criseyde's bedroom by means of a secret door.
Throughout the bedroom scene, as Mrs Gordon remarks,[20]
Pandarus's presence is a reminder of the 'game' that is
being played, at the same time as the Narrator celebrates
the lovers' joy. He knows every step of the *olde daunce*,
and moreover has the ability to perceive what others are
thinking: he is one who 'so wel koude feele/In every thyng'
(iii 960–1).

His greatest achievement in this vein is the long scene in
Book ii where he convinces Criseyde that Troilus is in love
with her and that she ought to return his love. Most of this
is original with Chaucer, and it will pay us to examine the
passage (ii 78–497) in some detail. Pandarus greets his niece
politely and affects to be interested in the book being read.
He tells her that she ought to enjoy herself more, at which
she pretends to be scandalised; she reminds him that she is,
after all, a widow. He then spends some time impressing on
her what a piece of good fortune has befallen her, and how
she must on no account fail to grasp the opportunity; yet he

in right sterte, just look in
do yow wyte, let you know
anon, straightaway

iwys, for certain
wol . . . this, wants to hear any-
    thing about this

deliberately omits to say what the good fortune is. Nevertheless, he gradually introduces Troilus into the conversation, at first coupling him with Hector (*the townes wal and Grekes yerde*); what is true of one is equally true of the other. After this he prepares to go, but stays when Criseyde says that she has business to discuss with him. When they have finished he again starts to leave, but adds, apparently as an afterthought, that she can enjoy herself now this good fortune has happened. Again he refuses to tell her what it is: the matter requires leisure and he would not want to hurt her if she took it amiss. Yet again he adds that she ought to seize such an opportunity. By this time Criseyde's curiosity is fully aroused, although she is almost equally afraid of what the news will prove to be:

> For both I am agast what ye wol seye,
> And ek me longeth it to wite, ywys.
>
> ii 311–12

Only now does Pandarus tell her that Troilus is in love with her, and before Criseyde can get her breath he is threatening her with Troilus's death – and his own too – if she does not show him *frendly cheere*. In fact, unless she shows some *pite*, she would be better off dead as well, and the threat is made even more frightening by the deliberate rhetoric:

> Wo worth the faire gemme vertulees!
> Wo worth that herbe also that dooth no boote!
> Wo worth that beaute that is routheeles!
> Wo worth that wight that tret ech undir foote!
> And ye, that ben of beaute crop and roote,
> If therwithal in yow ther be no routhe,
> Than is it harm ye lyven, by my trouthe!
>
> ii 344–50

yerde, scourge	*boote*, remedy
wite, know	*routheeles*, without pity
ywys, certainly	*tret ech*, treads everyone else
Wo worth, Woe befall	*crop and roote*, the very paragon
vertuless, with no power	*therwithal*, with that

Poor Criseyde is not able to compete with this, and after this outburst Pandarus can comfortably relax a little with the air of a man prepared to make concessions: I don't necessarily mean anything very serious; people won't suspect an occasional visit; you're both getting older (Pandarus is careful to address Criseyde the woman). Criseyde, overwhelmed, bursts out weeping, complaining that the uncle who ought to forbid her to love is demanding that she should do that very thing. Once again Pandarus prepares to leave, pretending to take offence at her lack of trust in him and once more blaming her for two deaths, so that Criseyde has to pull him back (447–8). She has constantly been put on the defensive, and is prepared to accept the lesser of two evils; by this time she imagines Troilus dying in her presence (460), a detail even Pandarus had not thought to add. They finally agree that Criseyde will return Troilus's love, but that it is to be an honourable affair on both sides. Pandarus can congratulate himself on a good day's work. In subsequent conversation he almost goes too far (ii 584–90), but this mistake – if it was one, with Pandarus it is sometimes difficult to be sure – is easily enough retrieved, and the love-affair has begun.

This appearance of incessant activity is reinforced by Pandarus's speech and behaviour. He hardly ever walks, he runs or leaps. His conversation is full of emphatic catch-phrases (cf. ii 120–40 where, in the space of twenty lines, he uses *As evere thrive I, as evere mote I thryve, And I youre borugh, as mote I thryve, as blyve* and *as evere have I joye*). Proverbs, which by their air of accumulated wisdom give an impression of plausibility, also bespatter his language. Troilus notices this early on:

> For I have herd thi wordes and thi lore;
> But suffre me my meschief to bywaille,
> For thi proverbes may me naught availle.

> i 754–6

lore, teaching   *meschief*, misfortune

but, unabashed, Pandarus can still think in proverbs at the
height of his friend's grief:

> And to hymself ful sobreliche he seyde,
> 'From haselwode, there joly Robyn pleyde,
> Shal come al that that thow abidest heere.
> Ye fare wel al the snow of ferne yere!' v 1173–6

Although he seems so knowledgeable about love, he is, in
fact, an unsuccessful lover himself. Criseyde teases him about
this, and he jokes about it (rather ruefully) on other occa-
sions. All these features make Pandarus more than the mere
tactician, the manipulator, the 'function of the plot', that
some critics have seen in him.

At first, like Troilus, Pandarus is bowled over by the plan
to exchange Criseyde for Antenor, but after a conventional
remark about the unpredictability and fickleness of Fortune,
he goes to work, in the way he knows so well, to cheer Troilus
up: he too is unhappy in love, there are plenty more fish in
the sea, a new love will soon wipe out memories of the old.
When these arguments fail, he asks Troilus why he does not
carry off Criseyde by force. Pandarus is ready enough to set
aside the rules of *fine amour* when they make things too
difficult. Loving is but *casuel plesaunce* (probably 'due to
fortune', but the secondary meaning 'trivial', 'transitory' is
found in Middle English), just as earlier Criseyde's timidity
and courtly *desdeyn* had become, with him, *nyce shame and
youre folie* (ii 1286). Troilus, however, is so devoted to
Criseyde, and his fidelity and integrity so much the pattern
of *trouthe*, that to elope with her is just what he cannot do.
As Book v progresses, Pandarus knows that things are not
going to come out right. He knows Criseyde will not return.
He keeps up Troilus's spirits for as long as he is able, because
he is essentially kind and because the encouragement of
Troilus has become second nature, but finally there is no
more he can do. Or say: for now, even Pandarus is at a loss
for words:

haselwode, the hazelwood	*Ye*, Yes
there, where	*ferne yere*, yesteryear
abidest, wait for	*nyce*, silly

> This Pandarus, that al thise thynges herde,
> And wiste wel he seyde a soth of this,
> He nought a word ayeyn to hym answerde;
> For sory of his frendes sorwe he is,
> And shamed for his nece hath don amys,
> And stant, astoned of thise causes tweye,
> As still as ston; *a word ne kowde he seye.*   v 1723–9

His final comment, 'I hate Criseyde' is a bitter defeat for him too, and at this point he drops out of the story. He is one of the first complete characters in English literature, in the tradition of the Wife of Bath, of Harry Bailey (as Muscatine says), or of Falstaff. And, like Falstaff, Pandarus is equal to every occasion but the supreme one. In the face of a *tresoun* (v 1738) which he cannot fight, or even fully comprehend, he is as useless to Troilus at the end of the poem as Falstaff is when Henry rejects him at the end of *Henry IV*, Part ii. And as this is a measure of the change in Prince Hal newly become King Henry V, so is it a measure of the tragedy of Troilus.

To these three characters, Troilus, Criseyde and Pandarus, recent criticism has often added a fourth, the Narrator. We have seen that, in Chaucer's early love poems, his narrators frequently adopt poses – of inexperience, impressionability, dullness – which are unlikely to have been true of Chaucer himself. Are we again seeing in *Troilus and Criseyde* a *persona*, deliberately made distinct from the poet and therefore capable of manipulation, or is this simply the case of an author who became very involved in his story? The evidence is most obvious in the proems to the first four books and in the last few stanzas of the poem, the Epilogue as it is often called (although the manuscripts do not distinguish it as such), in which Troilus ascends to the heavens and appears to condemn *fine amour* in comparing it with the divine love of God. Yet the Narrator intervenes frequently in the poem itself, especially in the first three books. One at least of the

wiste, knew
seyde a soth, spoke the truth

stant, stands
astoned of, dumbfounded for

earlier attitudes is repeated in *Troilus and Criseyde*, that the Narrator is no practised lover himself but, as the proem to Book i says, he recounts Troilus's *unsely aventure* as an illustration of the torments that lovers endure. Perhaps this is to be explained by the court poet's feeling of inferiority. He is a man addressing his betters;[21] they are aristocrats, he is bourgeois, and therefore they are more knowledgeable about *fine amour* than he can ever expect to be:

> For myne wordes, heere and every part,
> I speke hem alle under correccioun
> Of yow that felyng han in loves art,
> And putte it al in youre discrecioun
> To encresse or maken dymynucioun
> Of my langage, and that I yow biseche.
>
> iii 1331–6

His Narrator will naturally admire an apparently successful love-affair like the one he is relating.

Yet there are important differences between the early poems and *Troilus*. Since they were much shorter, and could therefore be recited much more easily, any discrepancy between the narrator and the poet before them is readily observable by the audience. In taking leave of his poem the Narrator of *Troilus and Criseyde* speaks of it as being *red . . . or elles songe* (v 1797). The frontispiece of the Corpus manuscript of *Troilus and Criseyde* shows Chaucer reading aloud to a court audience, but it need not represent a performance of this poem, just as the dust-jackets of modern novels frequently repeat critical acclamation of their author's *previous* work. In addition the early poems were *dreams* whose retelling requires the narrator to mediate between their unusual content and their real-life audience. Even so, in *The Parliament of Fowls*, the poem which probably immediately preceded *Troilus and Criseyde*, there is much less direct participation by the narrator (and correspondingly more description) than in either *The Book of the Duchess* or *The House of*

---

unsely aventure, unhappy lot   *encresse . . . Of,* expand or abridge
felyng, perception (experience?)

Fame.[22] In *Troilus and Criseyde* the Narrator is no longer a dreamer but a reader. He is therefore in our own position, with the considerable difference that he already knows the end of the story. Indeed, if we are to believe him, he sees his position as less that of reader than historian, who has consulted more than one source and who desires above all to explain the truth of the matter. But at the same time he is a creative artist, a 'maker' who, while he knows how the story will end, increasingly regrets that it ended in the way it did. I think that the tension between these two attitudes – a historian who knows he ought to be objective but an artist who finds he cannot be – accounts for much of the difficulty we experience with the Narrator of *Troilus and Criseyde*. On the one hand is the occasional fussiness of 'explaining' things we do not really need to know but which are part of the truth of the story, on the other is the overwhelming desire to excuse Criseyde as much as possible by stressing the difficulties she had to contend with. As Professor Donaldson has demonstrated,[23] there is an uncertainty uncharacteristic of Chaucer in the stanzas before the final triumphant solution which, by remembering that Troilus and Criseyde were pagans and by seeing *fine amour* as an example of Boethian 'false felicity', puts earthly love in its proper perspective to heavenly. What the presentation by the Narrator convinces us of, is the attraction of Criseyde for Troilus, how and why he could continue loving her for so long, so that we are almost (although perhaps not quite) persuaded that she was worthy of such a love.

TRAGEDY, FORTUNE AND BOETHIUS

Although Chaucer is using the convention of *fine amour*, *Troilus and Criseyde* is not an occasional poem like *The Book of the Duchess* or *The Parliament of Fowls*; it is a tragedy, as he himself calls it (v 1786). The medieval idea of tragedy was of a man of high rank who enjoyed great success but, because of sudden disaster, fell from this high position to a miserable end. *The Monk's Tale* is a collection of tragedies on this pattern, and *The Monk's Prologue* defines them thus:

> Tragedie is to seyn a certeyn storie,
> As olde bookes maken us memorie,
> Of hym that stood in greet prosperitee,
> And is yfallen out of heigh degree
> Into myserie, and endeth wrecchedly.   1973–7

Or, as a gloss to Chaucer's translation of Boethius puts it:

> Tragedy is to seyn a dite of a prosperite for a tyme that endith in wrecchidness.

Or Dante:

> Tragedy in its beginning is admirable and quiet, in its ending or catastrophe foul and horrible.

(Comedy, by contrast, ended serenely, as Dante's *Divine Comedy* ends in paradise.)

Troilus, a king's son who shows great bravery ('Hector the second') in the war-torn city of Troy, is a fit subject for this kind of tragedy. From the time he fell in love with Criseyde he has deliberately become the servant of the God of Love who rewards him, both with the possession of Criseyde – they are together for more than a year of the three years which the poem spans – and also, as the code of *fine amour* taught, with the spiritual ennoblement of his whole being. Yet the God of Love is not omnipotent. Above him is Fortune, the executor of Destiny who is in turn God's minister, and it is Fortune, as manifested in the capture of Antenor and the subsequent exchange of prisoners in which Criseyde is involved, which causes everything to go wrong. The representation in art and literature of Fortune presiding over a wheel, on which men rose to the highest position and then, as the wheel slowly turned further, fell from the other side, and her inherent fickleness which this figure demonstrated, were medieval commonplaces, and Chaucer had used them already in *The Book of the Duchess*. The Monk identifies Fortune as the agent of man's tragic fall:

maken us memorie, remind us   *dite*, story
heigh degree, high position

> I wol biwaille, in manere of tragedie,
> The harm of hem that stoode in heigh degree,
> And fillen so that ther nas no remedie
> To brynge hem out of hir adversitee.
> For certein, whan that Fortune list to flee,
> Ther may no man the cours of hire withholde.
>
> 1991–8

Fortune, in fact, is shown to be in control of the war right from the beginning of *Troilus*:

> The thynges fellen, as they don of werre,
> Bitwixen hem of Troie and Grekes ofte;
> For som day boughten they of Troie it derre,
> And eft the Grekes founden nothing softe
> The folk of Troie; and thus Fortune on lofte,
> And under eft, gan hem to whielen bothe
> Aftir hir course, ay whil that thei were wrothe.
>
> i 134–40

In Books ii and iii, however, the war slips into the background. There is occasionally talk of battles, and Criseyde catches sight of Troilus riding back from a skirmish with the Greeks, but, for the most part, the setting in these books is a prosperous, leisured one in which *fine amour* can flourish. Action takes place indoors rather than out, for this is the comfortable, close world of romance. Nevertheless, there are ominous references to Fortune towards the close of Book iii, and Fortune's wheel is the motif of the proem to Book iv:

> But al to litel, weylaway the whyle,
> Lasteth swich joie, ythonked be Fortune,

fillen, fell
nas no, was no
hir, their
list, decides
withholde, withstand
fellen, turned out
Bitwixen, between
som, one
boughten . . . derre, the Trojans suffered the more
eft, another

nothing softe, not a bit soft
on lofte, on high
eft, then
whielen, whirl
Aftir, according to
ay . . . wrothe, all the time they were at war
al . . . whyle, alas, all too short a time
ythonked be, thanks to

That semeth trewest whan she wol bygyle,
And kan to fooles so hire song entune,
That she hem hent and blent, traitour comune!
And whan a wight is from hire whiel ythrowe,
Than laugheth she, and maketh hym the mowe.

From Troilus she gan hire brighte face
Awey to writhe, and tok of hym non heede,
But caste hym clene out of his lady grace,
And on hire whiel she sette up Diomede.   iv 1–11

Chaucer saw, however, that although it was Fortune's
wheel that sent Troilus tumbling, he could show the agonis-
ing descent in some detail. For Troilus's gradual loss of hope
and the final realisation that Criseyde has deserted him come
closer to our own idea of tragedy, and this may be one of the
marks of modernity we think we see in *Troilus and Criseyde*.
As Pandarus puts it (prophetically) in Book iii:

For of fortunes sharpe adversitee
The worste kynde of infortune is this,
A man to han ben in prosperitee,
And it remembren, whan it passed is.

iii 1625–8

In Books iv and v (especially in v) the Trojans are less
successful in the war:

Fortune, which that permutacioun
Of thynges hath, as it is hire comitted
Thorugh purveyaunce and disposicioun
Of heighe Jove, as regnes shal be flitted
Fro folk in folk, or when they shal be smytted,

wol bygyle, intends to deceive
entune, attune
hent and blent, seizes and blinds
comune, common to all
the mowe, a mocking face
writhe, turn
grace, favour
infortune, misfortune

which that, who
permutacioun, change
comitted, entrusted
purveyaunce, foresight
regnes, kingdoms
flitted, transferred
smytted, struck down

Gan pulle awey the fetheres brighte of Troie
Fro day to day, til they ben bare of joie.

v 1541-7

and this may provide a parallel – perhaps not deliberate on Chaucer's part – to Troilus's declining fortunes. Sometimes, in medieval tragedies, Fortune works by making the hero submit to a passion unworthy of a great man. This is not the tragedy imposed from without by the gods, as in Greek drama, but – at least partly – from within, an aspect of man's free choice, like Macbeth's ambition or Othello's jealousy. Both Boethius and Gower envisage a Fortune that capitalises on a man's own strength and weakness (Gower indeed comes close to regarding Fortune as our excuse for our own shortcomings):

Fortune ne schal nevere maken that swiche thynges ben thyne that nature of thynges hath maked foreyne fro the. *Boece*, Book ii, Prosa 5

So that the man is overal
His oghne cause of wel and wo.
That we fortune clepe so
Out of the man himself it groweth.

Confessio Amantis, Prol. 546-9

The poem is also written in an appropriate tragic style. The classical and early medieval books of rhetoric distinguished three levels of style – high, middle and low – usually illustrating them by examples from Latin literature, and later writers (Dante and Boccaccio, for example) suggested that the vernacular might be used with the high style provided the subject warranted it. Several of Chaucer's additions to the story increase the 'high style' of *Troilus and Criseyde*. Most prominent are the proems to the first four of the five books, with their invocations and elaborate syntax;

swiche, such
foreyne, alien
overal, in every case

That . . . clepe, What we call Fortune

the formal songs, prayers and letters scattered throughout the poem (e.g. i 400, 659, ii 827, 1065, v 1317, 1590); the classical and astrological allusions; and the occasional stylised expression at important moments, especially in Book v where it demonstrates the intensity of Troilus's grief. He stands in front of Criseyde's empty house in Troy:

> Than seide he thus: 'O paleys desolat,
> O hous of houses whilom best ihight,
> O paleys empty and disconsolat,
> O thow lanterne of which queynt is the light,
> O paleys, whilom day, that now art nyght,
> Wel oughtestow to falle, and I to dye,
> Syn she is went that wont was us to gye!
>
> 'O paleis, whilom crowne of houses alle,
> Enlumyned with sonne of alle blisse!
> O ryng, fro which the ruby is out falle,
> O cause of wo, that cause hast ben of lisse!
> Yet, syn I may no bet, fayn wolde I kisse
> Thy colde dores, dorste I for this route;
> And farwel shryne, of which the seynt is oute!'
>
> v 540–53

Again, the Narrator compares the end of Troilus's earthly love with the infinity of divine love:

> Swich fyn hath, lo, this Troilus for love!
> Swich fyn hath al his grete worthynesse!
> Swich fyn hath his estat real above,
> Swich fyn his lust, swich fyn hath his noblesse!

whilom, formerly
ihight, called
queynt, quenched
Syn . . . gye, since she who was accustomed to guide us has gone
lisse, joy

syn . . . bet, since I can do no better
dorste I, if I dared
route, crowd
Swich fyn, Such an end
estat real above, great royal position
lust, desire

Swich fyn hath false worldes brotelnesse!
And thus bigan his lovyng of Criseyde,
As I have told, and in this wise he deyde.

v 1828–34

Most of the philosophical material in *Troilus and Criseyde*
(which, by universalising the theme, makes the poem more
than a mere story of a love-affair, however tragic) was taken
from Boethius's *Consolation of Philosophy*. This book was
probably much in Chaucer's mind at the time he composed
Troilus, for he had almost certainly translated it from Latin
not long before, in the early 1380s. The original is in 'proses'
and 'metres'. Chaucer's translation is wholly in prose, but
the metres are in a more elaborate and ornate style than the
proses. Boethius, after a successful public life, was exiled and
imprisoned by the Gothic leader Theodoric (who ruled in
Italy after the fall of Rome) on a charge of attempting to
restore the power of the Roman Senate, and was put to
death in 524. In his book the Lady Philosophy, an allegorical
figure, visits Boethius while he is under arrest. In the
dialogue between them she argues that his regret for his
former happiness should be overcome by a recognition that
worldly dignities (possessions, fame, beauty, and their like)
are transitory, and frequently pernicious, and that a truly
wise man will find his happiness in the sovereign God who
alone is good. This demonstration takes up most of the first
three books of the *Consolation*. It is in the last two books that
the question of predestination and free will, the relationship
between God's foreknowledge and man's own actions (a
question in which Chaucer's own century was greatly
interested) is raised. Boethius asks the Lady Philosophy why
God, who is good, apparently rewards men indiscriminately
and often allows evil to triumph. If God is both omnipotent
and omniscient, how can man have any free will? Why, in
fact, should we bother to pursue the good, since events seem
to be wholly removed from our control? Philosophy replies
that God's foreknowledge (*purveaunce*) disposes and orders

brotelnesse, fragility

everything, but that this plan is carried out in detail on earth by God's minister Destiny and her servant Fortune. Because Fortune (being twice removed from God's stability) is changeable and fickle, what men actually *see* happening may seem unjust and unreasonable, but all is truly and finally directed towards man's good by a benevolent deity. On the question of free will, we err if we confuse man's view of past, present and future with God's eternal present. God does not really foresee, but simply sees, and therefore he views our (future) voluntary acts as already chosen by our own free will. God knows when and how our actions may happen, and he allows for our change of purpose, but this foreknowledge does not imply necessity. To illustrate from an example given in Boethius: if you see someone walking, you know he is of necessity walking, but you are not responsible for the walking, for the man chose to walk of his own free will. To you, as a beholder, all this is present at one and the same time, and this is how God's seeing works. Man therefore possesses a measure of free will, but there are certain universal laws he cannot change (such as the daily rising of the sun or the eventual death of every man), and, even though he may have free choice, he cannot always control the results of his choice. Since man's free will does not therefore invalidate God's foreknowledge, man should properly choose virtue.

Troilus is often, especially in Books iv and v, in the position of Boethius. There are, however, two important differences. Boethius was almost certainly a Christian whereas Troilus is a pagan, and, furthermore, he has no Lady Philosophy to answer his questions. But Chaucer and his readers *were* Christians and they, or at least some of them, had read Boethius carefully. The characters of *Troilus and Criseyde* are apt to blame Fortune for their unhappiness, but they have no perception of Fortune's true role in God's scheme. In one of the long passages from Boethius which Chaucer probably added at a late stage in the composition of the poem, Troilus's conclusion is that it really does not matter whether *divine purveyaunce* has predestined his separation from Criseyde or whether predestination itself brings about God's *prescience*. Free will seemingly has no place of any importance, and we inhabit a deterministic universe:

> . . . and thus the bifallyng
> Of thynges that ben wist bifore the tyde
> They mowe nat ben eschued on no syde.
>
> iv 1076–8

Poor Troilus obtains scant consolation from philosophy. Criseyde's advice (echoed by Theseus, another pagan, in *The Knight's Tale*) is to 'make a virtue of necessity' (iv 1586). Troilus's love for Criseyde is natural and good of itself, but it cannot bear the load Troilus imposes on it.[24] He cannot substitute Cupid for God. At the culmination of Book iii, Troilus, in the bliss of love at last satisfied, sings a hymn to the Love which holds the universe together in harmony (1744–71). The source is Boethius, Book ii, metre 8:

> . . . al this accordaunce of thynges is bounde with love, that governeth erthe and see, and hath also comandement to the hevene. And yif this love slakede the bridelis, alle thynges that now loven hem togidres wolden make batayle contynuely, and stryven to fordo the fassoun of this world, the which they now leden in accordable feith by fayre moevynges. This love halt togidres peples joyned with an holy boond, and knytteth sacrement of mariages of chaste loves; and love enditeth lawes to trewe felawes. O weleful were mankynde, yif thilke love that governeth hevene governede yowr corages.

Despite Troilus's single reference to God (1765) and another in the invocation to Venus which forms the proem to Book iii, the God of Love for Troilus is Cupid and not Christ. In

ben . . . tyde, are known before the event
eschued . . . syde, avoided in any way
slakede the bridelis, loosened the reins
togidres, together
fordo the fassoun, ruin the shape
leden . . . moevynges, direct in harmonious belief through the proper motion
halt, holds
knytteth, binds
enditeth, gives
felawes, companions
weleful, happy
thilke, that same
corages, affections

Boethian terms, Troilus's obsession with Criseyde is a form
of false felicity, although Boethius does not mention love for
a woman as a type of deceitful happiness.

As a pagan, Troilus cannot be blamed for confusing the
power of Venus and Cupid with that of the Christian God,
but there was no excuse for the medieval reader. And since
Troilus was a true lover according to his lights, after his
death he too is allowed to see that true happiness comes only
through a rejection of the world, a world which contains the
love of a worthy man like Troilus for a woman as beautiful
and charming as Criseyde. For the frailty of *fine amour* must
fall short of a divine love which is *uncircumscript and al maist
circumscrive*. Muscatine notices that in *The Parliament of
Fowls* the palinode, with Africanus's advice to repudiate the
world, had come first, and the birds' demonstration that
there is more to life than this is subsequent and separate.
In *Troilus and Criseyde* the palinode grows out of the whole
tragic story.[25] The priorities are the same in Malory a
century later:

> But firste reserve the honoure to God, and secundly thy
> quarell must com of thy lady. And such love I calle
> vertuouse love.

It is the tragedy of *Troilus* too, however much Criseyde
may engage our (and Chaucer's) attention. Even when he
is offstage, Criseyde and Pandarus are often talking about
him. It is Troilus, too, who is left there, at the close of the
story proper, looking out over the walls of Troy, hoping
against hope that Criseyde will return. And the poem had
never promised us anything other than a tragedy. The
opening lines say, in effect: Love is a sad business. You
lovers, who have yourselves known sorrow, pray for those in
Troilus's plight 'That Love hem brynge in hevene to solas'.
Which is Troilus's own end, but not before we have seen
the poem and its hero sweep from initial raillery against
lovers, through the anxiety of unsatisfied love, to the utter
heaven of consummation, where Fortune's wheel seems for
a time to stand still, and down again, in the deliberately
long-drawn-out Books iv and v, to the hell of separation and

desertion. But here Chaucer has added a new dimension to the old recipe for medieval tragedy:

> For of fortunes sharpe adversitee
> The worste kynde of infortune is this,
> A man to han ben in prosperitee,
> *And it remembren whan it passed is.*[26]   iii 1625–8

It is this, it seems to me, which makes *Troilus and Criseyde* a piece of sustained narrative which, in high seriousness, Chaucer never surpassed: a success by any standards, medieval or modern.

infortune, misfortune

IV

The Canterbury Tales

[I]

Plan and General Prologue

Not until the end of the seventeenth century did *The Canterbury Tales* assume the importance in the Chaucer canon that
they now have. Hitherto Chaucer had been regarded as the
poet of love and the master of the rhetorical style, with consequent attention to *Troilus and Criseyde* and the earlier poetry.
No one today is likely to underestimate these poems, but
most of us first come to Chaucer via *The Canterbury Tales*,
which, after all, do represent his final poetic achievement.
They have frequently been modernised, a practice which
began with Dryden and at which Pope and Wordsworth also
experimented. In this century several versions have appeared, some keeping the original text but with extensive
glossing,[1] others trying to recapture the spirit of the original
in the language of our own day. Recently they have been
adapted for the stage. Before discussing them, however, even
the *General Prologue*, it may be useful to consider the whole
scheme of the *Tales*.

This is outlined by the Host, whose idea it was, at the end
of the *General Prologue*:

> This is the poynt, to speken short and pleyn,
> That ech of yow, to shorte with oure weye,
> In this viage shal telle tales tweye
> To Caunterbury-ward, I mene it so,

shorte with, shorten   tweye, two
viage, journey

> And homward he shal tellen othere two,
> Of aventures that whilom han bifalle.   790–5

Yet the plan was never fully carried out. In the first place it would have involved one hundred and twenty stories. Twenty-six pilgrims are described in the *General Prologue* (including the five Guildsmen who are treated as a group); to these we must add the second Nun, the Nun's Priest, the Host and finally Chaucer himself who joined the pilgrimage and acted as narrator. In fact, twenty-four tales are told. Seven pilgrims (the five Guildsmen, the Yeoman and the Ploughman) do not tell a tale at all. Chaucer himself tells two stories, but only because his first, the *Tale of Sir Thopas*, is interrupted by the Host. The Canon's Yeoman, who joins the pilgrims near Canterbury and who is therefore not described in the *General Prologue*, also tells a story. Two tales, those of the Squire and the Cook, are left unfinished. The pilgrims do not even quite reach Canterbury, a fact which would in itself reduce the number of tales to two each. But when the Host calls on the Parson to tell a story in his turn, he says:

> For every man, save thou, hath toold *his tale*.
> X 25

and the Parson himself says that his tale is meant

> To knytte up al this feeste, and make an ende.
> X 47

It may be, of course, that Chaucer intended to fit further tales into the series. A few critics have thought that *The Parson's Tale* was meant for a late stage on the homeward journey, but it seems likely that Chaucer had abandoned his original ambitious idea in favour of the more manageable plan of one tale per pilgrim. Even so, we cannot be sure, since the tales as we have them are clearly not in their final arrangement. No one of the more than eighty surviving manuscripts is Chaucer's autograph copy, and even the most reliable of them seem to represent the desire of early fifteenth-

---

whilom, in the past   *feeste*, entertainment
kyntte up, round off

century editors to achieve the best possible order of tales. There are problems of geography and time. In one of the best texts (the Ellesmere manuscript whose arrangement is followed in this book) a reference to Sittingbourne precedes a reference to Rochester, yet Sittingbourne is ten miles nearer Canterbury. The occasional references to time, taken in conjunction with the pilgrims' likely stopping places en route, give a very short second day. What has been said in an earlier chapter about medieval conditions of publication makes it likely that tales or groups of tales circulated separately and that scribes were not above making arrangements of their own. Furthermore, Chaucer almost certainly incorporated earlier material into the scheme. *Melibeus, The Parson's Tale, The Man of Law's Tale, The Manciple's Tale* (but not the links and individual prologues associated with them) and perhaps one or two other stories may represent earlier work. The Prologue to *The Legend of Good Women* refers to 'al the love of Palamon and Arcite/Of Thebes, thogh the storye ys knowen lyte', but whether this was a first draft of *The Knight's Tale* we cannot now say. Some inconsistencies have not been removed; the Second Nun calls herself an 'unworthy son of Eve'; the Shipman, with his references to the *sely housbonde* who must clothe and pay for *us*, speaks as if he were a woman; the beginning of *The Merchant's Tale* looks as if the speaker is a cleric; the Man of Law says *I speke in prose* and immediately begins in verse; the Host calls on the Cook a second time, as if he had not already begun a tale. It is easy to conclude that Chaucer was still revising when he died, or that, like Shakespeare, the published form of his work does not seem to have been his major concern, and sometimes we may think we can retrace the process of revision. For instance, *The Shipman's Tale* is likely to have been meant originally for the Wife of Bath (scarcely for one of the nuns![1]) Its subject, a rich merchant and his menage, hardly suggests a sailor as teller. *The Second Nun's Tale* is assigned to its teller – who is not described in the *General Prologue* – only in rubrics; it may represent an extreme instance of earlier work never satisfactorily integrated into

sely, poor

the plan of *The Canterbury Tales*. We should not suppose that the scheme of *The Canterbury Tales*, as we now have it, necessarily came to Chaucer in a flash. Perhaps he only gradually realised all the possibilities: quarrels between pilgrims (Miller and Reeve, Friar and Summoner, Cook and Manciple), additions to the company (the Canon and his Yeoman), even the 'marriage group'. Some tales, probably composed after the *General Prologue*, are more suitable to their tellers than are others. The fact that when a tale seems to have been removed from its original teller it is given to a pilgrim still without a tale (Man of Law, Shipman), might be the result of a later change to a more limited scheme of one tale per pilgrim.[2] If the *Retraction* at the end of *The Canterbury Tales* is genuine – and most Chaucer scholars believe it is – it may represent, together with the immediately preceding *Parson's Tale*, a change of plan from the proposed final celebration at the Tabard at which the teller of the best story was to have been feted by his fellow-pilgrims.

What we have now, therefore, is an introductory *General Prologue* describing, at varying length, most but not all of the pilgrims. There then follow groups or blocks of tales with connecting 'links' within each group, but the groups are not directly connected to each other (except by the general fiction of a pilgrimage) and are not placed in a final order. Several of the tales have individual prologues in which the teller introduces his story, and sometimes comments on the story which has preceded his. The Ellesmere arrangement is:

Group I (A). *General Prologue, Knight's Tale, Miller's Prologue and Tale, Reeve's Prologue and Tale, Cook's Prologue and Tale*

Group II (B¹). *Man of Law's Prologue and Tale*

Group III (D). *Wife of Bath's Prologue and Tale, Friar's Prologue and Tale, Summoner's Prologue and Tale*

Group IV (E). *Clerk's Prologue and Tale, Merchant's Prologue and Tale*

Group V (F). *Squire's Prologue and Tale, Franklin's Prologue and Tale*

Group VI (C). *Physician's Tale, Pardoner's Prologue and Tale*

Group VII (B²). *Shipman's Tale, Prioress's Prologue and Tale,
Prologue and Tale of Sir Thopas, Melibeus, Monk's Prologue
and Tale, Nun's Priest's Prologue and Tale*
Group VIII (G). *Second Nun's Prologue and Tale, Canon's
Yeoman's Prologue and Tale*
Group IX (H). *Manciple's Prologue and Tale*
Group X (I). *Parson's Prologue and Tale, Retraction.*

(The letters in brackets refer to an alternative arrangement by some modern editors to remove inconsistencies in
the time scheme.) Groups III, IV and V may represent one
longer group, but there is no actual link between them, and
the connection, if there is one, is of subject-matter (see below
for the theory of the 'Marriage Group'). The linkage may be
illustrated from Group I. At the end of the *General Prologue*,
the Knight draws the cut to tell the first tale. The Host
praises the story and calls on the Monk for a second tale,
but the drunken Miller insists on telling his story first. Most
of the pilgrims laugh at *The Miller's Tale* which had been
about a trick played on a carpenter. Only the Reeve, who is
a carpenter himself by trade, is vexed, and he accordingly
tells the next tale about a miller who tried to cheat two
students but is himself finally cheated. The Cook, who is
mightily amused at *The Reeve's Tale*, offers to tell the next,
and the Host agrees, but *The Cook's Tale* breaks off after a
promising beginning of some fifty lines.

There had been several previous collections of tales. In his
love poetry Chaucer had often borrowed from Ovid's
Metamorphoses. Boccaccio had written no less than three
collections, the best known of which is his *Decameron* (1348–
58). In the *Novelle* (*c.* 1385) Boccaccio's fellow-countryman
Sercambi describes a large and varied party journeying
through Italy on horseback, like Chaucer's pilgrims. We do
not know that Chaucer had read either the *Decameron* or the
Novelle, and in these collections there is nothing like the
variety of tellers that is evident in *The Canterbury Tales*;
Sercambi himself tells all his stories. Gower's *Confessio
Amantis* (*c.* 1390) has a similarly inflexible framework, and is,
in any case, too late to have influenced the composition of

the *General Prologue* which can probably be dated 1386–1387. Chaucer's own two earlier collections, *The Monk's Tale* (probably composed before *The Canterbury Tales*) and the *Legend of Good Women* (whose first version, at least, precedes them) each comprises a series on the one subject – the tragic fall of great men and women deceived in love respectively – and each has a single narrator. *The Canterbury Tales*, in fact, may well have been Chaucer's own idea. Pilgrimages were a common feature of medieval life, and the shrine of the martyr St Thomas à Becket at Canterbury was the greatest of English pilgrimages. Chaucer lived at Greenwich, en route to Canterbury, for a time. His pilgrims assemble at the Tabard Inn in Southwark (only a plaque marking the site remains today) at the southern end of London Bridge, the only bridge across the Thames at that time. Such inns as the Tabard acted as assembly points for Canterbury pilgrims; Chaucer mentions (*General Prologue* 28–9) the spaciousness of its rooms and stables. The road to Canterbury lay through Deptford, Greenwich, Rochester, Sittingbourne, Osprey and Broughton. There is no mention of where the travellers stayed overnight, although Dartford was the usual stopping place on the first night. In the whole of *The Canterbury Tales*, in fact, Chaucer mentions remarkably few places north of the Wash, and then in a way which suggests he knew little more than their names. But the south and the east were easily the most populous parts of England, and not until the industrial revolution in the nineteenth century did any sizeable part of the population live in the north. Two Northern undergraduates do appear in *The Reeve's Tale*, and their speech has clear features of the northern dialect, but the tale itself is set near Cambridge. For Europe and the Near East the outposts are represented by the Knight's campaigns and the Wife of Bath's pilgrimages (in each case *possible* for one person, but perhaps hardly likely). Otherwise Chaucer concentrated on those areas of Northern France, Flanders and Italy which he had himself visited. There is mention of horses or riding in the description of several of the pilgrims, but an almost complete lack of scenery in the *General Prologue*. Nor do the travellers meet anyone except the Canon and his Yeoman.

Chaucer is clearly trying to give the illusion of pilgrimage rather than a completely realistic description, and we should not press him too closely in this regard. How could thirty travellers, strung out along the road, *hear* all the stories? If the Miller rides first and the Reeve last, how can they be quarrelling? As well as having a religious objective, pilgrimages also provided a welcome break from the monotony of most people's daily life, and the entertainment they provided must have ranked high in their attraction. The Host assumes that the pilgrims will naturally want to tell stories on the way:

> And wel I woot, as ye goon by the weye,
> Ye shapen yow to talen and to pleye;
> For trewely, confort ne myrthe is noon
> To ride by the weye doumb as a stoon.
>
> I 771–4

The framework of *The Canterbury Tales* – General Prologue, links and individual prologues – was therefore intended to convey verisimilitude, if not realism, in a way that the plots of the tales seldom do, although the dialogue and sometimes the action of the tales is usually convincing enough. With *The Canterbury Tales* Chaucer had moved from early dream poetry, via the history of *Troilus and Criseyde*, to present time, here and in England.[3] It is time for us, too, to turn to the pilgrims themselves.

From the order in which the pilgrims are described in the *General Prologue*, it is possible to detect some groupings, although whether these were deliberate on Chaucer's part it is impossible to decide.[4] He simply says that he has not put the pilgrims in order of rank (*degree*, 744). But he does begin at the top, for the Knight, who is accompanied by his son, the Squire, and his attendant, the Yeoman, form the first group. The Knight is the epitome of chivalry, a code with both social and religious obligations. Consequently he shows good breeding (*curteisie*), but never its opposite *vileynye*. His integrity (*trouthe*) and his generosity (*fredom*) shine

woot, know   *talen*, tell stories
shapen yow, intend

out in all he does. His campaigns, which take up the bulk of the portrait, are in the defence of christendom against the heathen or the barbarian, and in these he has achieved the highest reputation. But, although distinguished, he is prudent; his equipment is good but not ornate. In fact, he is going on pilgrimage immediately after returning from an expedition; he is perhaps one of the few pilgrims in whose mind the religious object of the journey is uppermost. His son, the Squire, is still only twenty. His fighting has therefore been nearer home, and he hopes he has won a reputation of a kind to attract his lady's regard. For it is natural that *fine amour*, for which he shows all the correct accomplishments, should occupy most of the thoughts of a young man like this. But his fashionable dress must not blind us to the final remark about his humility: he realises that he is still serving his apprenticeship in knighthood. The essence of the Yeoman's portrait is discipline and efficiency. His equipment gleams and is ready for use wherever needed. He is probably a kind of bailiff or gamekeeper (*forster*) on the Knight's estate: the modern meaning, 'small landowner' was not much used before the next century. There is little satire in this first group of three.

The second group, also of three,[5] (Prioress, Monk and Friar) are all members of the regular orders, that is, those religious who live in communities according to a rule, as opposed to the seculars – the bishops, priests and deacons, etc – who are involved in the day-to-day administration of the church. The Prioress is head of a convent, and so a person of some consequence. Yet the terms used to describe her: *semely* (three times), *faire and fetisly, wel ytaught, curteisie, of greet desport, plesaunt and amyable, estatlich, digne of reverence, tretys* and *fetys*, are more characteristic of the great lady, even of the romance heroine (like her name Eglentyne, 'sweet briar', her grey eyes and her rosebud mouth) than of the nun she is. Her exquisite manners, her elegant but not completely correct French accent, her sensibility (which

fetisly, elegantly
of greet desport, very sociable
estatlich, dignified

digne, worthy
tretys, well-shaped

with her easily becomes sentimentality towards small
animals) all point in the same direction. Yet to the Narrator
she is clearly the charming representative of high society
that she would love to be. It is only at the end of the description, perhaps, that we remember that its very first line told
us she is a *nun*, who technically should not have been on
pilgrimage at all or keep small dogs, and certainly not feed
them on the best bread. In her defence it might be said that
these infringements of her rule are only minor, and that
nunneries were often the refuge for well-bred daughters for
whom there was no dowry. There is a good deal of ambi-
valence in this portrait, but no really harsh criticism of the
Prioress's fashionable romantic pretensions.

Where the Prioress had been all *conscience and tendre herte*
and a little old-fashioned, the Monk is virile, prosperous-
looking and radical in his views. He is an outrider (like the
monk in the later *Shipman's Tale*) who supervised one of the
celles or outlying dependent houses of a large monastery. By
Chaucer's time many of the monasteries had acquired large
estates, often scattered over a wide area and requiring
efficient management, so that several of the community
might be engaged principally in administration. This monk's
duties would bring him into contact with wealthy landowners
who loved hunting and good living, and regular travelling
must have relaxed regular discipline.[6] But, once again, there
is a marked discrepancy between appearance and profession.
The Monk's plumpness, his shining tonsured crown, his
supple boots, his fine horse, and especially his positive obsession with hunting, all bespeak a gross self-indulgence. And,
as for his progressive views on outdated monastic obser-
vances and his question *How shal the world be served?* – well, a
monk is not meant to serve the world but God. Monks were
expected to remain in their cloisters, unless allowed, by
virtue of their particular office, to journey outside. Friars
were out and about among the people. Their preaching was
popular and successful, and they therefore became involved
in a running quarrel with the parish priests ('possessioners')
whose livelihood they often threatened. The Monk had been
manly and authoritative; the Friar is also sumptuously

clad and imposing (*solempne*). He is also extremely versatile, for we see him successively as limiter (licensed by his order to beg within a certain district), matchmaker, familiar and confessor of the rich, pedlar, entertainer, frequenter of taverns and arbiter in disputes. All this is in complete contrast with his duties. As Professor Hodgson puts it (p. 92):

> The friars were vowed to absolute poverty, dedicated to evangelical lives of active service, to minister and preach, to help the poor, sick and needy, and through their own practice to point the way to heaven.

With the Friar, as with the Monk, Chaucer has allowed his pilgrim to expose himself by his own arguments which follow logically, but only if you grant the premise. A man may be upset, almost contrite, for his sins, yet some men cannot weep. But they *can* give, and so be confessed:

> *Therfore* in stede of wepynge and preyeres
> Men moote yeve silver to the povre freres.
>
> 231–2

(Compare the *Therfore* of line 189.) *The Summoner's Tale* (told against the Friar) is a good comment on the friars' unctuous and flattering manners towards the rich, and also on their quarrel with the parish priests. There can be little excuse for the Friar. The Monk is perhaps a misfit in the religious life; Hubert contemptuously abuses it. He is thoroughly hypocritical, glib and selfish, cynically scorning the neglected members of society, the beggars and the sick, whom he should especially serve. They are to him *poraille*, and there is no future (*it may nat avaunce*) in spending time on *them*. With the Prioress Chaucer had been tolerant; with the Monk satirical but, in part, understanding; with the Friar he shows a complete lack of sympathy.

The third group of pilgrims is more numerous and more difficult to classify as a group. It consists of the Merchant, the Clerk, the Lawyer, the Franklin, the five Guildsmen and their Cook, the Shipman, the Physician and the Wife of Bath. They are all middle-class and are all, to a great extent,

yeve, give   *poraille*, poor folk

characterised by their attitude to material possessions. Fourteenth-century society was becoming more acquisitive, with a notable increase in population and prosperity, often through trade. The really good people on the pilgrimage – Knight, Clerk, Parson and Ploughman – are concerned with things other than money. The first of this third group, the Merchant, wishes to give the impression of responsibility and reliability; hence his formal conversation and his fashionable clothes (to which the portrait in the Ellesmere manuscript does full justice). But he is really an unattractive character, a money-grubber and by no means as financially sound as he suggests:

> This worthy man ful well his wit bisette:
> Ther wiste no wight that he was in dette.
>
> 279–80

The direct satire here is in contrast to the irony with the preceding group. Chaucer was the son of a London wine-merchant and himself had been Controller of the Customs at the Port of London, so that he would certainly know several importers and exporters. This particular portrait may indeed contain hints from a real merchant who had lent Chaucer money. The Clerk, alone in this group, is not interested in worldly possessions, unless they are books. Chaucer stresses his threadbare appearance (in contrast to that of most of the pilgrims) and his devotion to study. He is at the university, in minor orders, and destined almost certainly for a career in the church or (because of the church's virtual monopoly of education) as teacher or administrator. The Lawyer is a man of the highest standing in his profession, but, unlike the Clerk, his considerable knowledge is put to practical use and directed firmly towards his own financial gain. His legal expertise had also enabled him to invest profitably in land on his own account. His manner has something of the Merchant's desire to impress (although his clothes are serviceable and not for show); line 322 suggests that the Lawyer too is not perhaps quite all he seems. His companion is the Franklin, who must have been of some wealth to keep up

---

his wit bisette, used his wits   *wiste,* knew

such a good table as his portrait describes. Nevertheless, this description is a kindly one: as well as stressing the Franklin's hospitality, it mentions his local standing as Justice of the Peace, Member of Parliament (both of which offices Chaucer had held, if only briefly) sheriff and auditor of taxes. The only implicit criticisms of this country gentleman – made not in the *General Prologue* but in the links and in his tale – is that his ideas are somewhat old-fashioned and that he himself is slightly uneasy in important company.

The five Guildsmen (haberdasher, carpenter, weaver, dyer, tapestry maker) are treated as a group and are accompanied by their Cook. None of them tells a tale, although the Cook begins one. They are members of a religious guild – not to be confused with the craft guilds who did much to foster medieval drama in England – and show every sign of rising in civic affairs, egged on by their socially-conscious wives. Their livery and accoutrements are brand-new for the pilgrimage and evidently intended so impress. The Cook here appears competent enough: the only pity (says Chaucer) is the running sore on his shin. Elsewhere the Host accuses him of low standards in hygiene. The Shipman, too, is highly proficient in seamanship, but he is not averse to pilfering from his cargo, or even above a little piracy. Medieval medicine was an odd compound of classical and Arab authorities on the one hand, and on the other a reliance on astrology in casting horoscopes for the patient's birth, the onset of the illness and the best time for administering the cure. Any medicines the Physician prescribed would aim at restoring the balance of the humours or fluids in the body, the proportions of which gave any man his *complexioun* or temperament, a word of considerably wider meaning then than now. This doctor has grown rich from the plague, but he is a cautious man, both financially and in his own diet. Some critics believe that deliberate ambiguities in Chaucer's language imply that the Physician too is guilty of impressive talk and sharp practice. This group of pilgrims (if group it is) is rounded off magnificently by the portrait of the Wife of Bath, easily the most experienced pilgrim of them all. Once again she is associated with commerce, for she is a clothmaker, an expanding fourteenth-century trade. The prologue to her own tale, which relates her life with five husbands, shows her to be a great feminist ('so much her own mistress, so often a wife', as Maurice Hussey succinctly puts it) and the personification of 'sovereignty' and 'mastery', which is brought out here by her love of social precedence at church and still more by her flamboyance in dress and boldness in manner. As she later says, she is a compound of Mars, who gave her her pugnacity, and Venus who bequeathed her an amorous disposition.

The next group contains only two pilgrims: the saintly Parson and his brother the Ploughman. In almost every village the church stood out as the focal point and centre of parish life. Most country priests, however, were non-graduates – some were almost completely ignorant of their offices – and the general level of pastoral work was low. One can see why the much better-educated friars were so successful. In contrast to most of his fellow priests, Chaucer's Parson is *a lerned man, a clerk*. There are few individualising traits, and the account shows him as the exemplar of perfect christian charity. The key to the description is line 514:

He was a shepherde and noght a mercenarie.

He was a shepherd to his flock, not covetous (as so many clerics in the *General Prologue* are seen to be) nor a hireling (Latin *mercenarius*), for he preferred to remain at home and show consideration to them rather than to be an absentee priest with a sinecure elsewhere. The Ploughman is another idealised figure. Like his brother, he loves both God and his neighbour. His short coarse coat and the mare on which he rides indicate his poverty. In some late medieval literature the ploughman is the symbol of the poor and exploited. On the other hand, the portrait may be meant to criticise, by implication, the growing discontent of the labouring classes following the Black Death of 1349; in this case, as with the Parson, we should remember what the Ploughman did *not* do, as well as what he *did*.

Lest the list of pilgrims should seem to be growing too long, Chaucer tells us that there are not many to go:

There was also a Reve, and a Millere,
A Somnour, and a Pardoner also,
A Maunciple, and myself – ther were namo.

542–4

Among this last group of thieves and rascals Chaucer
humorously includes himself. (However, the character of
Chaucer the pilgrim is never described, but is left to emerge
from his reactions to his fellow-travellers.) As his appearance
suggests, the Miller is a lout and a great talker, quarrelsome
too, and later the first to oppose the Host as master of ceremonies. The Reeve, his enemy, is by contrast spare, with-
drawn, efficient and cunning. He terrorises the peasants over
whom, as manorial foreman, he has control, stocks his own
comfortable dwelling while at the same time managing to
keep his accounts straight, and even cheats his own master by
lending him goods which by rights should have been his own.
There are no personal details whatsoever in the description of
the Manciple which comes between those of the Miller and
the Reeve. His essence lies simply in his use of his position as
purchasing officer to cheat a group of men who were
infinitely more learned than he.

The modern reader will need to be told more about the
duties of the last two members of the group, the Summoner
and his companion (*freend and his compeer*) the Pardoner, for
the satire, which becomes increasingly bitter, lies in the per-
version of their offices. In the Middle Ages there were both
secular and ecclesiastical courts of law. The Summoner, as
his name implies, was the bearer of a summons to the latter,
presided over by the archdeacon or the bishop. He also saw
that offenders appeared in court and, even more important,
was an informer, always on the watch for indictable offences.
Laymen were tried in the ecclesiastical courts for offences
against the church (such as non-payment of tithes) and also
for moral offences (such as fornication). The Summoner
therefore had ample opportunities for taking bribes. One of
his methods revealed here was to gain the confidence of the
young people of the diocese and use the information thus

---

namo, no more

gained for blackmail. Other methods are exposed in the later *Friar's Tale* which demonstrates that the only match for a summoner is the devil himself. His appearance is as loathsome physically as his actions are morally. His face is covered with spots and pimples (probably the result of his own lechery) and frightens children. His diet is equally repulsive, and his knowledge a matter of a few Latin tags repeated parrot-fashion. This grotesque figure is capped by the mention of the garland and the buckler-like cake at the end. Pardons were indulgences, remission of part of the temporal punishment (*poena*) for sin which remained after confession and absolution had saved the sinner from eternal damnation by forgiving the guilt (*culpa*). This remission was made possible by drawing on the Treasury of Merit, made up of the superabundant goodness of Christ and his saints. But it was popularly believed that merely buying pardons achieved forgiveness of sins. There were genuine pardoners, licensed to sell indulgences to raise money for the church, but the system easily gave rise to impostors such as this one who sold false relics and so deceived the gullible. Because of such abuses of the system, pardoners were abolished by the Council of Trent in the sixteenth century which dissociated giving alms from obtaining indulgences. The effeminate appearance of Chaucer's Pardoner, with his thin yellow hair lying in strands over his shoulders, his glowing eyes and his exhibitionism in manners and in fashion are all indicative of the physical and spiritual eunuch he is. But he is brilliant in church (best of all at singing the offertory!) and his prologue and tale are in the form of a sermon.

Near the beginning of the *Prologue*, Chaucer says he will describe his fellow-pilgrims under three headings:

> To telle yow al the condicioun
> Of ech of hem, so as it semed me,
> And whiche they weren, and of what degree,
> And eek in what array that they were inne.
>
> 38–41

eek, also

that is, what kind of people they were (*whiche they weren*), of what rank (*degree*) and finally their appearance (*array*). Although these three aspects are usually covered, they hardly ever appear in this order, and frequently items which should logically come together are separated. In the short description of the Squire, for example, we learn (in this order) that he was a lover, he had curly hair, he was twenty years old, well built, had fought abroad in the hope of winning his lady's favour, was dressed fashionably, could do all the things appropriate for a young man in love, was humble and at table carved opposite his father. The apparently random impressions, together with the casual way in which the pilgrims are introduced (*A Knyght ther was . . . , A Yeman hadde he . . . , There was also a Nonne . . .*), may be intended to show how a man would pick individuals out of a crowd, or it may be all that Chaucer the pilgrim (who does his best, but a poor best, as we learn later) is capable of. It is sometimes said that the pilgrims represent a complete cross-section of late fourteenth-century society. This is not strictly true, for those of the very highest rank (above the Knight) would be unlikely to go on a public pilgrimage, and equally the very poor would be unable to go. They are representative however in that, although there are twice as many secular pilgrims as those in some way connected with the church, almost half the space is devoted to the latter. For the church had not only a unique spiritual authority, it was also a powerful central organisation. Since it possessed a virtual monopoly of education and was becoming increasingly wealthy, it frequently found itself cooperating closely with the civil power in government. There could be few people who did not come into frequent contact with some branch of church affairs.

Yet successive generations of readers have found Chaucer's pilgrims realistic. In a few cases (the Merchant, the Reeve, the Host) Chaucer may have been basing his portrait on living people whom his audience would recognise. In many more the details suggest that he pictured them as individuals rather than as types: the Miller's wart, the Cook's ulcer, the Wife of Bath's wide-spaced teeth, the Knight's dirty tunic, the Squire's carving. All this, however, is mostly a matter of physical description (the *array*). In their behaviour (*whiche they weren*) the pilgrims usually represent their profession as it would appear to a general audience, and it is easy to parallel the criticism made in the *General Prologue* both in contemporary literature (Langland, Gower or the earlier *Roman de la Rose*) and in contemporary moralists (Wyclif or collections of sermons). The Friar's habit of giving easy penance to the rich, the Monk who was infinitely happier outside his monastery than inside, the mercenary Lawyer, the ideal Ploughman: all these are stock figures.[7] (In a few cases, such as the Monk and the Friar, Chaucer increases the realism by making the characters condemn themselves out of their own mouths.) Even some of the details are borrowed, but two only, both from the description of the Prioress, must suffice by way of illustration. The beautiful table manners of the Prioress is one of the first things to capture the Narrator's attention. But the lines are taken almost bodily from a passage in the second part of the *Roman de la Rose*. More than this, they are there spoken by the Duenna (La Vieille), the old woman who acts as guardian to the imprisoned Bialacoil. She is vastly experienced in love, and in her old age ready to give advice on the subject to the young and even to the not so young. The Duenna is early in a line which stretches out to include not only the Wife of Bath but Juliet's Nurse, and the incongruity of this material being included in the description of a *prioress* does much to convey Chaucer's ironic blend of nun and would-be romantic heroine. The Prioress's affection for her small dogs is at first sight attractive but – should they have been her first concern? The Dominican preacher John Bromyard is more direct in his condemnation of wealthy women who

> provide for their dogs more readily than for the poor, more abundantly and more delicately too; so that, where the poor are so famished that they would greedily devour bran-bread, dogs are squeamish at the sight of wafer-bread and spurn what is offered them, trampling it under their feet.[8]

Other details, however, are, so far as we know, Chaucer's own, although they are usually in accordance with general contemporary opinion. The Wife of Bath, we are told, is an experienced pilgrim:

> She koude muchel of wandrynge by the weye.
>
> 467

But *wandrynge by the weye* could also refer to some of the extra-marital affairs she hints at in her own Prologue, and the very next line beginning *Gat-tothed was she* continues the ambiguity, for this feature was held to indicate not only a love of travel but also a propensity to boldness and lasciviousness. (The mention of *Gat-toothed* and *seinte Venus seel* in successive lines of her *Prologue*, III 603-4, would seem to clinch the matter.) The Reeve enjoys a standard of living somewhat above his station:

> His wonyng was ful faire upon an heeth;
> With grene trees yshadwed was his place.
>
> 606-7

Not only has he thoughtfully provided for himself from the manorial finances, but the shadow of the trees suggests both a degree of comfort and the secretiveness which is so much a part of his nature. The Monk's bridle, jingling like a chapel bell, reminds us of where the Monk *should* be.

We have, then, a blend of realistic reporting and literary convention, and all this is given by the Chaucer who joined the group of pilgrims at the Tabard and is quickly accepted as one of them. 'Chaucer the pilgrim', as he is now called since Professor Donaldson's brilliant essay,[9] provides the surface, reportorial 'realism'. He is enthusiastic, impressionable (fond of superlatives like *al*, *ryght* and *ful*), ready to gossip (both with his fellow-pilgrims and his audience), exhilarated by the spring season and excited at the prospect of good company on the journey. The links show him as

---

koude muchel of, knew a good deal about
Gat-tothed, with teeth set wide apart

wonyng, dwelling
yshadwed, shaded

plump, abstracted, not over bright (*Sir Thopas*, a *rym I lerned long agoon*, is the best poetry he is capable of), but anxious to please (obliging with the *Melibeus* when that same *Sir Thopas* is rudely interrupted). He is rather prolix about faithfulness to his source, as he is about using blunt language, lest anyone should be offended (*General Prologue*, 725–42 and *Miller's Prologue*, 3170–86). Although he can make a joke (I 443–4 and 691), and although he is sure the Summoner goes too far in pooh-poohing excommunication (I 659–62), he admires most of the pilgrims, the bad as well as the good, for those who are less than perfect are manly men, or companionable, or at least clever and efficient thieves: they are successful, what they do really comes off. It would have been easy to let this Chaucer be the link between the stories. But it would never have worked, for he is too loath to criticise, and the Host, a man who knows what he likes and will let no one persuade him otherwise, is far better at the job. For what Chaucer the pilgrim gives us is all surface impression. Even when he has evidently found out about some of the pilgrims' lives at home (the Wife of Bath's love of precedence in church, the Friar marrying off girls he had seduced, the social climbing of the Guildsmen's wives), he is doubtful rather than overtly critical; the Lawyer *seemed* busier than he was. The irony, the discrepancy between the worldly values described and the deeper values professed, is the contribution not of Chaucer the pilgrim but of Chaucer the poet – and his audience – who knows what monks and nuns and physicians and reeves and the rest of them *ought* to be, but who has allowed his fictional *alter ego* to describe them, blandly and without distraction, as they so evidently *are*.

If one considers together the descriptions of the pilgrims in the *General Prologue*, the links, and the prologue to the individual tales where these occur, it is clear that there is an opportunity for developing dramatic characterisation. The *gentils*, as a group, intervene twice: once to praise *The Knight's Tale* (I 3113) and once to prevent the Pardoner telling a tale of *ribaudye* (IV 324). Polite as he is, the Knight cannot stand any more of the Monk's tragedies. The Miller and the Reeve quarrel in the links and each tells a tale against the other. So do the Friar and the Summoner, and there is a hint, in *The Manciple's Prologue*, of an incipient third quarrel, between the Manciple and the Cook. Probably these enmities result from opposed business interests and are sparked into life by the presence of an audience and the good Southwark ale. *The Reeve's Prologue* shows that his thin body and cropped head conceal a warped mind. Yet, as Shakespeare demonstrates with Shallow and Silence, old age can be at once comic, loathsome and curiously pathetic:

> As many a yeer as it is passed henne
> Syn that my tappe of lif bigan to renne.
> For sikerly, whan I was bore, anon
> Deeth drough the tappe of lyf and leet it gon;
> And ever sithe hath so the tappe yronne
> Til that almoost al empty is the tonne.   I 3889–94

Conditions are bad in the Cook's London eating-house, and the Host, as a London innkeeper, knows this well enough. The *General Prologue* does not mention the Merchant's unhappy marriage, and it is true that some manuscripts omit the *Merchant's Prologue*, but the pent-up bitterness is in character with his earlier secretiveness. The Franklin only wishes that his son had a quarter of the Squire's *gentilesse*, which, with its attendant *fraunchise*, is the moral of *The Franklin's Tale*. The claim that he is ignorant of rhetoric, made in the *Franklin's Prologue*, is belied by his *Tale*, but his Prologue does help to establish him as a man of a certain standing yet limited literary appreciation; a lot of medieval literature was probably written for people like him. We would expect from the Parson the *Moralitee and vertuous mateere* he promises in his tale. He adds that, being a *Southren man*, he cannot compose alliterative poetry which he seems to regard as monotonous and old-fashioned (although the next line shows that he is not attracted to the more fashionable rhyming poetry either). The most obvious examples of

henne, away
Syn that, since
sikerly, truly
anon, straightaway
drough, turned on

tonne, cask
gentilesse, nobility
fraunchise, generosity
mateere, subject-matter

close integration between teller and tale are the prologues to *The Wife of Bath's Tale* and *The Pardoner's Tale*. The former describes in detail the Wife's life with five husbands and her aggressive sexuality. The latter is an example of the preaching at which the *General Prologue* tells us the Pardoner excelled. With these two pilgrims (and perhaps the Canon's Yeoman as a third, although naturally he is not described in the *General Prologue*) we may go further. Their tales are also suited to their characters. To find the Wife retailing a straightforward medieval romance at first comes as a surprise, but she twists the story to illustrate her favourite doctrine that the only happy marriages are those in which the wife is firmly in control. *The Pardoner's Tale* is an *exemplum* of his sermon's text, *Radix malorum est cupiditas*. *The Merchant's Tale*, implicitly but not directly, reflects its teller's marital predicament. Other tales, such as the Knight's, the Clerk's or the Franklin's, seem generally suitable to their tellers; one or two, the Monk's or the Physician's perhaps, do not seem so well adapted to the pilgrim who relates them.[10] There is, however, a general correspondence between the social class of pilgrim and the tale he tells. The *gentils*, on the whole, tell the more refined and sophisticated stories, while the fabliaux are reserved for the lower classes or for those like the Shipman and the Merchant who, while not *cherls* themselves, probably had more in common (at least in literary taste) with the Miller and the Reeve than with the Knight or the Prioress. Naturally we must not assume that the Miller, *a janglere and a goliardeys*, is himself capable of the artistry shown in his tale: it is simply that its tone and morality are suitable to him.

The most fascinating case of the growth of a pilgrim's character throughout *The Canterbury Tales* is perhaps that of the Host. The first impression, from the *General Prologue*, is of an imposing figure, a born leader, a man who would be likely to make his mark in society (as he had perhaps done).[11] He it is who suggests the scheme of four tales per pilgrim, and he is businessman enough to ensure that they will all return to his inn, the Tabard, for the final supper in honour of the winner. It comes as no surprise when the pilgrims beg him to be master of ceremonies and judge of the best story.[12] He sees to it that (*by aventure, or sort, or cas*) the Knight, socially the most important member of the company, gets the first cut and so tells the first tale. A successful innkeeper such as the Host must, if he is to avoid trouble, be able to make a quick judgment of people. He is polite to the Knight and agrees with his estimate of *The Monk's Tale*, adding that a collection of such tragedies is not only painful, what is worse it is wearisome, and he (the Host) is normally as good a listener as the next man (VII 3564 ff.). Why (and we remember the *General Prologue*) doesn't the Monk tell a hunting story now? The Monk had been the Host's choice for the second tale, following the Knight's, but the Miller, already the worst for drink, had insisted on telling the story. The Host first tries to persuade the Miller to *Abyd, and lat us werken thriftily* ('Wait a bit and let's act sensibly'), but when he fails is wise enough to give the Miller his head and let him continue (I 3128–35). A similar polite request to stop the later argument between the Friar and the Summoner also having failed, he this time raises his voice and subdues them both (III 1286–1300). A hint of blackmail by the Cook – condoned by the Host – is enough to quieten the Manciple. Harry Bailey – we learn his name from the Cook at I 4358 – is even more polite to the Prioress than to the Knight; perhaps, like Chaucer the pilgrim, he is very impressed by this nun with such exquisite manners:

> . . . and with that word he sayde,
> As curteisly as it had been a mayde,
> 'My lady Prioresse, by youre leve,
> So that I wiste I sholde yow nat greve,
> I wolde demen that ye tellen sholde
> A tale next, if so were that ye wolde.
> Now wol ye vouche sauf, my lady deere?'

VII 445–51

by . . . cas, by luck, or fate, or chance
as it, as if he
So . . . greve, provided I was sure I wouldn't offend you
wolde demen, would like to ask
if . . . wolde, if you're sure you wouldn't mind
vouche sauf, agree

With the lower-class pilgrims, though, or with those who seem unlikely to give trouble, he knows where he is. The contemptuous *thou* is good enough for the Miller, Reeve or Cook, and even for the Nun's Priest whom he addresses *with rude speche and boold* (VII 2808). He interrupts Chaucer's Tale of *Sir Thopas* crudely and decisively. He is more polite, but jocular, with both Clerk and Physician, and at first to Chaucer himself. He is oddly puzzled at how to take the interruption of the pilgrimage by the Canon and his Yeoman (a relationship like theirs is clearly outside his experience), and some of his lines echo the uncertainty by their lameness (VIII 595, 596, 634, 639, 663). But once he learns more details his interest is aroused, and no plea by any canon whatsoever is going to deprive the company of what promises to be an intriguing tale (VIII 697–8). He has a good taproom joke about ecclesiastics, especially monks, making better lovers than laymen:

> Religioun hath take up al the corn
> Of tredyng, and we borel men been shrympes.
>
> VII 1954–5

as *The Shipman's Tale* had already illustrated. The Monk, who has probably heard it all before, deliberately does not rise to the bait. The Host, unabashed, tries the joke over again on the Nun's Priest, of all people (Epilogue to *The Nun's Priest's Tale*).

If we are to believe him, however, the Host's own married life is far from serene. He twice, after *The Merchant's Tale* and after the *Melibeus*, speaks of his own shrewish Goodlief whose truculence is going to get him into trouble one of these days. But domineering wives, like lecherous clerics, are the very stuff of one sort of entertainment, so perhaps some of this talk should be attributed to his affability rather than to his true marital situation. He prefers to appear as a plain man who knows what he likes, educated enough to quote Seneca (but in conjunction with Malkin's maidenhead!),

takc . . . tredyng, got hold of the   *borel,* ordinary
best stallions

unable to *speke in terme* like the Physician (VI 311), *nat depe
vstert in* [astrological] *loore* (II 4) but knowing enough to
calculate the date and time of day. He occasionally blunders
over names or difficult phrases. He is impatient with the
Franklin's preoccupation with *gentilesse*, but very much
affected by the Physician's tragedy of Virginia. The Man of
Law's story of Constance he simply calls *thrifty* ('suitable',
'very good'). Despite his plea, twice over, for tales of *best
sentence and moost solaas* (I 798) and *som murthe or som doctryne*
(VII 935), he is determined that *sentence* and *doctryne* shall not
predominate. This, after all, is partly a holiday occasion: no
Parson or Clerk is going to treat the pilgrims to a *predicacioun*
(II 1176). The Pardoner's sermon is, presumably, a different
matter – at least until he tries to make a sinful Harry Bailey
pay for kissing his sham relics. So, for a very different
reason, is the final *Parson's Tale*:

> For, as it seemed, it was for to doone,
> To enden in som vertuous sentence.   X 62–3

We have seen that in only a very few cases is the tale
expressly tailored to the teller, although in rather more it is
generally appropriate. Is there any principle of organisation
which will enable us to apprehend the *Tales* as a whole?
Medieval religious allegory often visualised life as a spiritual
pilgrimage, and the final position of *The Parson's Tale* is no
accident:

> And Jhesu, for his grace, wit me sende
> To shewe yow the wey, in this viage,
> Of thilke parfit glorious pilgrymage
> That highte Jerusalem celestial.   X 48–51

A hint in *The Knight's Tale*, at the beginning of the series,
uses the same biblical metaphor, even though the lines are
spoken by the pagan Egeus:

speke in terme, use learned terms
depe ystert, expert
gentilesse, nobility
sentence, significance
moost solaas, greatest entertainment

predicacioun, (lengthy) sermon
for to doone, the right thing to do
wit, skill
viage, journey
thilke, that
highte, is called

This world nys but a thurghfare ful of wo,
And we been pilgrymes, passynge to and fro.[13]

I 2847–8

These references make a satisfactory framework for the *Tales*, but it is undeniable that for long stretches we lose sight of the pilgrimage motif. Attempts to see in the various pilgrims representations of the seven deadly sins described in *The Parson's Tale* have not attracted any support. There are, however, certain tales which may be especially concerned with the question of 'sovereignty' or 'mastery' in marriage, that is, whether the husband or the wife shall dominate. Professor Kittredge, who first formulated the idea of the 'Marriage Group',[14] believed that the debate was begun by the Wife of Bath and concluded by the Franklin. This would neatly span groups III, IV and V, although we should remember that, even if each group is coherent within itself, there is no demonstrable manuscript connection between groups. The Wife of Bath's belief is that the only really happy marriages are those in which the woman is in control, and this is not only the thesis of the whole of her Prologue but the final point of her Tale, when the knight who has yielded sovereignty is rewarded by seeing his hag of a wife turn into a beautiful princess. The Wife's story is followed by those of the Friar and the Summoner who, busy with their own private quarrel, have no time to spare for the philosophy of marriage. Griselda, the heroine of *The Clerk's Tale*, is wholly submissive to her husband and incredibly patient throughout all the tests he imposes on her. In the Envoy to this tale, however, the Clerk first states that there are no Griseldas nowadays, and then appears to reverse his moral by arguing that wives should take upon themselves the *governaille* and, if necessary, make their husbands' lives thoroughly miserable. He refers to the Wife of Bath by name, and the exaggerated style of the Envoy may be meant to match her own extreme position and to suggest that married life would be wrecked if she had her way. The Merchant first tells of the bitter disappointment of his own recent marriage, and the

nys but, is nothing but

tale which follows is a story of an old husband deceived by a young wife. The Wife of Bath would appear to have been refuted once more, although apportioning blame between the characters of *The Merchant's Tale* is none too easy. The Squire who follows does not say anything directly about marriage, but his story is (as might be expected from the *General Prologue*) concerned with *fine amour* in which the woman is unquestionably superior. *The Franklin's Tale* ends the discussion with the solution that mutual tolerance is the only recipe for a truly happy marriage.

Attempts have been made to extend the discussion to include *Melibeus* and *The Nun's Priest's Tale* in particular, but these tales are not concerned with sovereignty. *Melibeus* is about the qualities (especially prudence) required in a *governour*, and *The Nun's Priest's Tale* with what happens when a man takes his wife's advice. It is undeniable that the same words – *lordshipe, maistrie, soveraynetee, governaunce* – recur throughout the 'Marriage Group' and that the opening lines of *The Franklin's Tale* make the point of equal tolerance at some length, as if this were to be the final solution to the problem, but surely the three tales (Friar's, Summoner's and Squire's) which interrupt the discussion direct attention away from the subject of marriage rather than making the debate more dramatic, as Kittredge claimed. Kittredge viewed *The Canterbury Tales* as an English Human Comedy – *act, stage, dramatic* are words he uses regularly – and this approach is somewhat out of fashion at present, although it was revived in part by Lumiansky in his book *Of Sondry Folk*. A more serious objection is that the Host, either by his remarks in the links or in his choice of pilgrim to tell the next tale, never seems at all conscious that this group of stories is meant as a running debate on marriage. We must remember, of course, that in medieval catholic England marriage is assumed to be indissoluble, and therefore some degree of compatibility between the partners was highly desirable. There can be little harm in our allowing that Chaucer gave a few of his pilgrims conflicting opinions on a subject of perennial interest, so long as we do not turn this admission into a conscious device used to organise these three groups of tales. If we must have an organising principle, we may observe it in the fact that a serious tale is apt to be followed by a comic one (or if it is not, it is not for want of the Host trying) or else, as Professor Lawlor has suggested, in the tension between *auctoritee* and *pref*, what the books will tell you and what experience demonstrates to be the case.

In this book, *The Canterbury Tales* will be considered primarily as the stories they claim to be. Chaucer's remarks, at the close of *The Miller's Prologue*, to the effect that those whose sensibilities are too refined for fabliaux may easily find matters more to their taste elsewhere in *The Canterbury Tales*, and also the joking reference in the introduction to *The Man of Law's Tale* to the number and divergence of Chaucer's works, imply a deliberate attempt to achieve variety of narrative. The three main types of medieval narrative – romance, fabliau and legend – are all well represented. *The Knight's Tale*, *The Squire's Tale*, *The Wife of Bath's Tale* and *The Franklin's Tale* are all romances, basically stories of adventures or tests through which a knight or squire seeks to win the love of his lady or to vindicate his own position. The form is parodied in *Sir Thopas*. At the other extreme from the romances comes the anecdotal, often crude, fabliau whose plot usually involves one or more bourgeois attempting to cheat another. *The Miller's Tale*, *The Reeve's Tale*, *The Summoner's Tale* and *The Shipman's Tale* are fabliaux, and in its plot at least *The Merchant's Tale* also conforms to the type. Thirdly, there is the legend. The word (from Latin *legenda*, 'what is read') did not, in the Middle Ages, imply that the story was a fiction – rather the contrary. These legends will often be of saints or martyrs, as in *The Physician's Tale*, *The Second Nun's Tale* and *The Prioress's Tale*; *The Clerk's Tale* and *The Man of Law's Tale* can be included here, because although their heroines are not strictly saints, their behaviour is incredibly and consistently saintly. A further link between this third group is the fact that, with the exception of *The Physician's Tale*, these stories are in rhyme royal, the seven-line stanza which seems to be employed in *The Canterbury Tales* only for serious, dignified poetry. This classification, however, omits two of the best tales, those of the Pardoner and the Nun's Priest. I would propose, in order to include these, a fourth category, the sermon, and to consider as well *The Parson's Tale*, since we should remember that Chaucer wrote prose as well as verse. To call *The Nun's Priest's Tale* a sermon is perhaps to direct attention away from its primary qualities of beast-epic and mock-heroic, but its narrator is a priest, fond of his 'authorities', and he does advise us, at the end of his tale, to concentrate on the *moralite*, taking the *fruyt* and leaving the *chaf*. Two further points should be made. The work of a really great writer cannot be categor- ised as simply as this. Frequently our interest will be not so much in the traditional features of the genre as in what Chaucer added to these. Finally, it will, I think, be better to concentrate on one or two tales in each class and to invoke the others occasionally as corroborative evidence.

Romance
The Knight's Tale and *The Franklin's Tale*

Romances are like novels, and not only because they were the staple narrative diet of the Middle Ages. We all *feel* we know what a novel is, but when we try to define it we end with as many definitions as there are critics. Similarly, medieval English metrical romances have been defined by their relation to epic, by their probable audiences, by their characters, by length even, since with a work recited aloud there must be a limit to what an audience will put up with at one sitting. Yet the most recent historian of the Middle English romances has to admit that the word could mean something as vague as 'a good story',[15] and 'romance' appears to have passed in French from 'a composition in or transla- tion into the vernacular' to 'a courtly poem in the vernacu- lar', such as the Roman *de la Rose*. But not all English romances were courtly. Most of those based on French originals show signs of having been adapted to the taste of a far less courtly audience for whom action was much more important than the psychology of *fine amour*. Some, both metrically and by reason of their exaggeration, are almost unbelievably bad, and in *Sir Thopas* Chaucer seems to be satirising these. One can learn a lot from *Sir Thopas* about the range of Chaucer's reading and the worst features of medieval romance in general, but nothing very much (except by contrast) about Chaucer's own romances: he is hardly likely to parody himself. Chaucer's romances proper, *The Knight's Tale*, *The Franklin's Tale*, *The Squire's Tale* and *The Wife of Bath's Tale*, are sophisticated to a degree not often seen in other English romances. (Easily the best, and the best-known, non-Chaucerian romance, the North-West Midland *Sir Gawain and the Green Knight*, is here, as in so much else, an exception.)

One ends, therefore, not with a definition of romance, but with a few critical remarks which apply to many romances. Their characters, on the whole, are not very realistic, except sometimes some of the minor ones. We often do not know, at the crises of the story, what they are thinking, although this is more serious for us who have read later psychological novels, than it was for the Middle Ages. Quests are common, but in *The Wife of Bath's Tale* the Knight is in search not of love or adventure but of the answer to the question 'What do women most desire?' (Which, naturally, gives the Wife of Bath an opportunity to suggest her own characteristic reply.) Disguises are frequent, and recognition is often achieved by talismans such as rings previously exchanged between the lovers. Many romances invoke magic or the supernatural, and some have an eastern setting which the Crusades had perhaps helped to make popular: *The Squire's Tale* takes place *At Sarray, in the land of Tartarye*, and tells of a marvellous brass horse which will transport its rider anywhere, a magic mirror which reflects the future, a ring which enables its wearer to speak the language of birds and to know the virtues of herbs, and a sword which can both wound and heal. A few are romantic in a more recent sense of the word, and tell of far away and long ago, of shadowy forests and half-realised but

intriguing characters. Once or twice *The Wife of Bath's Tale*
approaches this:

> In th'olde dayes of the Kyng Arthour,
> Of which that Britons speken greet honour,
> Al was this land fulfild of fayerye.
> The elf-queene, with hir joly compaignye,
> Daunced ful ofte in many a grene mede.
> This was the olde opinion, as I rede;
> I speke of manye hundred yeres ago.   857–63

> And in his wey it happed hym to ryde,
> In al this care, under a forest syde,
> Wher as he saugh upon a daunce go
> Of ladyes foure and twenty, and yet mo;
> Toward the whiche daunce he drow ful yerne,
> In hope that som wysdom sholde he lerne.
> But certeinly, er he cam fully there,
> Vanysshed was this daunce, he nyste where.
> No creature saugh he that bar lyf,
> Save on the grene he saugh sittynge a wyf –
> A fouler wight ther may no man devyse.   989–99

although the pragmatism of its teller impels her to point out
that the elves which once peopled the countryside have
lately been replaced by begging friars. The end of a romance
usually shows poetic justice, even if, as in the non-Chaucerian
Sir Orfeo where Orfeo and Herodis (Eurydice) live happily
ever after, this involves changing the story. The hero and
those who have helped him are lavishly rewarded and the
villains horribly tortured or killed. Perhaps the most
important single feature of the medieval romance is that it
is never in a hurry, unlike epic which spotlights the main
events and moves rapidly over intervening material, or

which that, whom
Al . . . fayerye, This whole land
   was full of fairy folk
mede, meadow
it happed hym, he chanced
care, worry
under . . . syde, along the edge
   of a forest

yet mo, still more
yerne, eagerly
nyste, had no idea
wyf, woman
wight, creature
devyse, imagine

fabliau which is concerned above all with plot. The romance writer could linger wherever he liked and whenever he wished. He often finds himself describing the good things of the aristocratic life, like the sumptuous feast Chaucer hints at (under cover of *occupatio*) near the beginning of *The Squire's Tale* or the amphitheatre and the tournament which he describes fully in *The Knight's Tale*.

THE KNIGHT'S TALE

Two of Chaucer's earlier critics, Dryden and Joseph Warton, pick out *The Knight's Tale* from among *The Canterbury Tales* for special praise.[16] Although this may simply reflect an Augustan fondness for epic and the high style, the poem is undeniably impressive. It is set in Ancient Greece, but, with the usual medievalisation of the classics, Theseus becomes a duke and Palamon and Arcite young knights, rivals for the love of Emily, Theseus's sister-in-law, who has all the charm of a romance heroine. Chaucer's source for *The Knight's Tale* was, in fact, a romantic epic, Boccaccio's *Teseida*, *c.* 1340, comprising over nine thousand lines in twelve books. Chaucer does not say that his story is from Boccaccio, any more than he mentions *Il Filostrato* as the source of *Troilus and Criseyde*. There he had expanded Boccaccio; here his problem is the reverse, and the *Teseida* is reduced by almost two-thirds.[17] The cuts come principally at the beginning of the story where Boccaccio tells of Theseus's war against the Amazons which he has just concluded, in Arcite's wanderings as an exile from Athens, and in the replacement of the epic catalogue of the champions attending the tournament by two representative figures. *The Knight's Tale*, in fact, uses *occupatio* extensively. Its opening lines provide an admirable summary of Theseus's return from war, using the excuse of the Knight's concern over the length of his own story – the first of *The Canterbury Tales* – and the number of other tales to follow:

> But al that thyng I moot as now forbere.
> I have, God woot, a large feeld to ere,

forbere, leave   *ere*, plough
woot, knows

And wayke been the oxen in my plough.
The remenant of the tale is long ynough.
I wol nat letten eek noon of this route;
Lat every felawe telle his tale aboute.   885–90

Theseus's subsequent championing of the Theban ladies and
his defeat of Creon are recounted almost equally briefly:

But shortly for to speken of this thyng . . .
But it were al to longe for to devyse . . .
But shortly for to telle is myn entente . . .
985, 994, 1000

This episode is an illustration of Theseus, the *trewe knyght*,
avenging ladies in distress, and it demonstrates, early in the
story, his concern for justice tempered with mercy. But it
must not illustrate this at too great length.

For in this romance we are concerned with the two young
knights, Palamon and Arcite, sworn brothers-in-arms, left
for dead in the heap of bodies at Theseus's sack of Thebes
and imprisoned by the victor. From their dungeon, high up
in a castle tower, they catch sight of Emily in the garden
below, and instantly each falls in love with her. Our interest,
from now on, is in the conflict between military comrade-
ship and romantic love (in another romance, *Amis and
Amiloun*, sworn brotherhood is set against the love of children)
and in which knight will win the lady. In other words, it is
the situation rather than the characters which is stressed. The
situation demands that each knight shall be both brave, as
we see in the tournament and in the earlier fight in the grove
(where they are separated with the blood up to their ankles
and still rising!), and in addition the perfect lover suffering
the torments of *fine amour*. They have equal claim to Emily
who cannot decide between them; nor can Theseus without
the tournament. There is some indication that Arcite is the
more practical and Palamon the more reflective. Palamon
thinks that he has seen a goddess in the garden, Venus

I . . . route, · Besides, I don't
want to hold up anyone
among the company

aboute, in turn
were . . . devyse, would take
much too long to describe

transfigured. Arcite knows a woman when he sees one, and rebuts Palamon's prior claim to the lady's affections with the remark that in love it is a case of every man for himself. Arcite prays to Mars for victory in the tournament, Palamon to Venus that he shall win Emily. But these are details and should not be elevated into a complete contrast in character. Emily, the object of their affections, does practically nothing in *The Knight's Tale*, and therefore remains beautiful, perfect and infinitely desirable. She is as *fresshe* as the May to which she is so often compared. In consequence she acts passively: after praying to Diana that she may remain a virgin, she accepts the idea of marriage to the victorious Arcite and ends up apparently happily married to his rival Palamon. All this is in contrast to Boccaccio's Emilia who is distinctly coquettish. She knows the imprisoned knights are watching her from their tower and breaks into song whenever she thinks they are looking at her. When Arcite, in disguise, takes service with Teseo, Emilia recognises him but pretends not to know that he is in love with her. As she watches the tournament, she remarks that she just cannot choose between two such handsome men.

The only really interesting character in *The Knight's Tale* is Theseus, who is not only the guardian of Emily but the legal possessor (as his prisoners) of Palamon and Arcite. He is also, in his closing speech, the executant of destiny, a point to which I shall return. His concern for justice and mercy, too, already illustrated from the beginning of the tale, continues throughout. He is always impartial towards Palamon and Arcite. He interrupts their fight in the grove because it is a battle *Withouten juge or oother officere* (1712), and spares them both at the request of the women in the company and because he is *gentil* (1761) and reasonable (1766). He appreciates both the irony of the situation – two knights fighting over a woman who doesn't even know they are in love with her – and also its necessity as a part of a man's development, for he too has been a servant of love in his time. He entertains the visiting knights lavishly both before and after the tournament whose rules are framed to prevent unnecessary shedding of blood. He makes preparations for

Arcite's ceremonial funeral. Theseus presides efficiently and generously over everything. It is fitting that he should conclude by arranging the marriage of Palamon and Emily, 'political' since it unites Athens and Thebes, but also a love-match in the romance tradition.

It is arguable that Chaucer's interest in *The Knight's Tale* is not in the characters but in the opportunity to display the whole chivalric panorama.[18] In the Ellesmere manuscript (but not in many others) the story is divided into four parts, probably by an early scribe but the breaks seem clear enough to have been intentional. The whole of the third part is devoted to the description of the amphitheatre in which the tournament is to take place and the three temples which are its chief ornament. The pause in the action allows for the year which intervenes between the fight in the grove and the tournament, but perhaps Chaucer's professional interest was also engaged here, for in 1389 he was responsible, as Clerk of the King's Works, for the construction of seating for two tournaments at Smithfield. Tournaments, as Maurice Hussey says,[19] provided 'practical chivalric education' and a certain amount of combat training, as well as being fine set pieces. This is, after all, a tale told by a Knight who is renowned for his campaigns and whose son is the pattern of the gay young lover. Its idealised aristocratic universe naturally presupposes *fine amour*: a tournament to fight for a lady, *benedicitee* (2115) – Lord bless you, yes! But the story is also full of ritual, from the obsequies for the kings killed in the war against Creon at the beginning to Arcite's magnificent funeral at the end. Ceremony presupposes symmetry, and again this is most clearly seen in the third section, with the hundred knights (with one representative figure described) on each side and the three prayers in the respective temples. It has often been noticed how a speech by Arcite is apt to be answered by one of almost equal length from Palamon. This is the high rhetorical style (as in *Troilus*) which, by slowing down the pace of the story, provides appropriate dignity.

Into this glittering world intrude darker questions about the part played by Fortune and the gods. The Theban women have been changed from duchesses and queens into wretched petitioners by the turn of Fortune's wheel (925). Arcite blames the knights' imprisonment on Fortune acting through the planetary influences (1086). When he is released from prison but prevented from seeing Emily, Arcite regards Palamon as fortunate, since he can at least see her (1238), but for Palamon, in captivity still, the gods are cruel (1303), arbitrary (1314) and revengeful (1328 and cf. 1559–60). There is not much hope for mankind in a puzzling, hostile world:

> We seken faste after felicitee,
> But we goon wrong ful often, trewely.   1266–7

> And whan a beest is deed he hath no peyne;
> But man after his deeth moot wepe and pleyne,
> Though in this world he have care and wo.
>
>   1319–21

Yet Palamon eventually escapes from prison by *aventure or destynee* (1465), and is discovered fighting with Arcite in the grove by Theseus who has chosen that very day and place to go hunting through

> The destinee, ministre general,
> That executeth in the world over al
> The purveiaunce that God hath seyn biforn.
>
>   1663–5

Theseus's solution to the quarrel is the tournament where each will achieve his *destynee* (1842) and where Emily will be given as bride to whichever knight Fortune wills (1860). The three temples in the lists are dedicated to Mars, Venus and Diana whose votaries are respectively Arcite, Palamon and Emily. Since some of the classical gods had become identified with the medieval planets, they could properly be said to govern the destiny of humans. Yet however magnificent these temples may be, they are also frightening.

---

faste, eagerly   *purveiaunce*, providence
moot, may   *seyn biforn*, foreseen
over al, everywhere

Chaucer seems to have gone out of his way to stress the least attractive manifestations of these deities: the cruel and destructive aspects of war, the unhappy lovers, the vengeance on those who fall foul of Diana, goddess of chastity, and the suffering of women in childbirth (Diana as Lucina). As Professor Salter shows,[20] the gods do not come very well out of *The Knight's Tale*. Mars and Venus bicker over the claims of their disciples, and Saturn has to intervene to placate them. Saturn's stratagem is in character with his usual malevolence, since the solution depends not (as it might in a normal romance) on Palamon's or Arcite's prowess in battle but on a blatant *deus ex machina*. For just as Arcite is celebrating his victory with a lap of honour, a fury causes his horse to stumble, as a result of which he is thrown and mortally wounded. So Arcite achieves the victory for which he had prayed to Mars, but Palamon, after an appropriate interval, wins the lady.

A very few of the best medieval romances (and *Sir Gawain and the Green Knight* is another example) seem to use the romance form to raise wider issues of behaviour or morality. The philosophical material in *The Knight's Tale* is no part of the romance convention, and, as in *Troilus and Criseyde*, comes from Boethius's *Consolation of Philosophy*. Throughout the poem man has been shown to be subject to Fortune, a deity whose behaviour towards men may seem to them fickle and unjust but whose power (as Lady Philosophy tells Boethius) is in reality controlled by a divine foreknowledge. After Arcite's tragic and painful death, Theseus, no less than Palamon and Emily, cannot be comforted, and it falls to Egeus, Theseus's *olde fader*, to begin to fit this one death into a larger world-pattern:

> Joye after wo, and wo after gladnesse.   2841

Theseus gives Arcite a magnificent funeral, and it is fitting that he, who throughout has shown a stability perhaps characteristic of the Knight's ideal ruler, should give the final summing-up. In this, man takes his appointed place in the whole scheme of things ordered by the *Firste Moevere*, and he appears rather more than the mere pawn of gods that

The Knight's Tale sometimes seems to suggest. Even so, the best he can do is to realise that he has a fixed span of life which he cannot lengthen and so to *maken vertu of necessitee*.[21] He is lucky if, like Arcite, he dies in his prime and so departs

> Out of this foule prisoun of this lyf.   3061

Perhaps this is all Chaucer thought possible for a virtuous pagan, such as Theseus was, and the spiritual state of the virtuous pagan was a subject of dispute in the Middle Ages. Here there is no 'Epilogue', as in *Troilus and Criseyde*, to point to a Christian interpretation of the human condition. But Palamon has always been a true 'servant' and Emily is accommodating as ever, so *The Knight's Tale*, after all, can end, as romances often do, with a wedding.

THE FRANKLIN'S TALE

At first glance *The Franklin's Tale*[22] may seem to be about people in a way *The Knight's Tale* was not: certainly Dorigen is more alive than Emily. But we do not have to read very far into the tale to see that it is really concerned (as *The Knight's Tale* was) with a conflict of principles, that is, with plot. Will Aurelius manage to remove the black rocks, and if he does, will Dorigen keep her word? Once again, love is at the root of the dilemma, but this time, as often in the romances, a promise is of supreme importance, for Dorigen has agreed to grant her love to the squire Aurelius on what she clearly regards as impossible conditions – which he proceeds to fulfil. Folk tales based on a rash promise whose conditions are finally waived because of the integrity of the giver are not difficult to find. *The Franklin's Tale* is closest to an episode in Boccaccio's prose romance *Il Filocolo*. This also has a contest in generosity between the husband, the lover and a magician, and furthermore the husband tells his wife to keep the promise secretly (cf. *Franklin's Tale*, 1483). In Boccaccio, though, there are no threatening black rocks to be removed; instead the lover has to provide a garden which flowers in January (it is in January, however, that Aurelius and the magician travel back to Brittany). In his Prologue the Franklin says his story is an old Breton lay, and it does have a setting which can be identified even in present-day Brittany. The *lai* was a short narrative poem, originally to music (712), with a strong love interest, often of a pathetic kind. The form was particularly associated with the late twelfth-century writer, Marie de France, but only some half dozen lays are extant in Middle English; they may have gone out of fashion by the late fourteenth century when Chaucer revived interest in the genre. For that very reason the story may have seemed an appropriate one for the rather conservative Franklin. It has been suggested that Chaucer derived his knowledge of the Middle English lays from a manuscript collection seen in a London bookshop,[23] but perhaps there was indeed a lay, now lost, with resemblances both to *The Franklin's Tale* and to *Il Filocolo*. In the lays, characters – especially heroines – are often carried off by otherworldly creatures, but the magic in *The Franklin's Tale* is less mysterious and explained more 'scientifically' in accordance with Chaucer's own interests. For our purposes there would seem little point in distinguishing lays from romances, except perhaps on grounds of their comparative brevity.

Several romance conventions appear in *The Franklin's Tale*. Early in the story Arveragus sets out for England to seek fame in arms, and he stays there two years. (It is, of course, convenient to have him out of the way while the plot develops.) He is away again at the crisis of the story where Dorigen needs her husband to advise her – as Criseyde needed Troilus and later Diomede – and in his absence she can only consider suicide. It is thoroughly conventional for the squire to be in love with his master's wife (as with Damian and May in *The Merchant's Tale*). In fact, Aurelius has loved Dorigen secretly and despairingly for two years, and all he can do is compose songs bewailing his grief in general terms (like the Black Knight in *The Book of the Duchess*). We first see Aurelius at a dance in a garden in May – a typical setting and season for *fine amour* – where Dorigen and he get into conversation and he finally summons up enough courage to blurt out his love for her. He has all the typical virtues:

> Oon of the beste farynge man on lyve;
> Yong, strong, right vertuous, and riche, and wys,
> And wel biloved, and holden in greet prys.   932–4

and spends two more years with the arrow of loved fixed deep in his heart, wondering how he can make the rocks disappear. He has a single confidant, as the tradition allowed; this is his brother who, by recalling the interest in magic during his student days at Orleans, brings about the resolution of the dilemma. Aurelius, like Troilus and most courtly lovers, is volatile: he alternates between initial despair and an impulsive joy which immediately agrees to the magician's steep fee (1227). His speech to Dorigen reminding her of her promise now the rocks have disappeared is a mixture of conventional abasement before his lady and an assurance of his eventual success in obtaining her love. The means used to remove the rocks need not destroy our enjoyment of the tale, for we can appreciate it without knowing all about the language of astrology. There is, in fact, only one passage of technical detail, 1273–90. Aurelius originally prays to Phoebus Apollo, god of the sun, to persuade his sister, the moon, to join him in producing abnormally high tides. We know that the moon does control the tides, and the whole aim of the magician is to use his astrological skill to emphasise and prolong these natural forces. It is enough if the technical language sounds impressive and is not obviously wrong.

Arveragus and Dorigen, husband and wife, are characterised mostly in their reactions to the all-important promise. For Dorigen the black rocks around the coast of Brittany represent a possible barrier to the return of the husband on whom her whole life is centred. It is natural, as well as paradoxical, that she makes their removal the price for granting Aurelius her love. She speaks *in pley* (988) and probably out of a misjudged wish to soften her originally uncom-

---

Oon . . . lyve, one of the handsomest men alive

prys, esteem

in pley, in jest

promising rejection of his advances. This is good psychology, as is her numb reaction to the well-meaning friends who try to cheer her up during her husband's absence. But it does not turn Chaucer into Henry James. Nor does it offset the apparent total unreality of Arveragus's direction to Dorigen to keep her promise to Aurelius. The objection has been stated most cogently by Professor Robertson:

> When the time comes in the Franklin's story for Arveragus to assert his husbandly authority, all he can do is advise his wife to go ahead and commit adultery.[24]

And the Franklin, as he tells his tale, would seem to be struggling too, in the face of such unlikely guidance:

> Paraventure an heep of yow, ywis,
> Wol holden hym a lewed man in this
> That he wol putte his wyf in jupartie.
> Herkneth the tale er ye upon hire crie.
> She may have bettre fortune than yow semeth;
> And whan that ye han herd the tale, demeth.
>
> 1493–8

But this is no answer at all, for Dorigen could not *expect* such a stroke of luck. Yet there is more to it than this. The long introduction to *The Franklin's Tale* has been at pains to show that this is an ideal marriage, based not on the *maistrie* of either partner but on mutual trust and forbearance. This has usually been interpreted as Chaucer's compromise solution to the 'marriage debate' and his rejection of the extreme attitudes of *The Wife of Bath's Prologue* and *The Clerk's Tale*. And so perhaps it is. Yet its relevance to this particular story is that Arveragus has promised his wife *suffrance* (788). It is a great struggle for him, but he is being consistent as well as stoical when he tells her to keep her promise, for *trouthe* ('the highest thing that man may keep') is,

Paraventure, perhaps
heep, lot
ywis, indeed
lewed, stupid

upon hire crie, cry out against her
demeth, judge

like tolerance, a part of *gentilesse*. And the Franklin, from the beginning, had been greatly (even excessively) concerned with *gentilesse*.[25] It is what he admires in the Squire; it is a characteristic of the Bretons from whom he got his tale (709); and it becomes the pivot on which the whole story turns. He has first spent some time demonstrating that *maistrie* is a negative quality; it remains to show that *gentilesse* is equally positive. Aurelius finally respects Dorigen, and even more Arveragus, for their integrity, so much so that Dorigen is released of her promise in formal, legal language (1533–8), almost as if it had been written rather than verbal. It is a commonplace in Chaucer (and elsewhere in medieval literature) that true *gentilesse* is only incidentally and etymologically a question of rank. A long passage in *The Wife of Bath's Tale*, for instance, shows that it is really a question of character: there *gentilesse* is twice (1122, 1176) defined as 'living virtuously'. Towards the end of *The Franklin's Tale* the terms *gentilesse*, *franchise* (generosity) and *trouthe* are constantly brought into association:

> Aurelius gan wondren on this cas,
> And in his herte hadde greet compassioun
> Of hire and of hire lamentacioun,
> And of Arveragus, the worthy knyght,
> That bad hire holden al that she had hight,
> So looth hym was his wyf sholde breke her *trouthe*;
> And in his herte he caughte of this greet routhe,
> Considerynge the beste on every syde,
> That fro his lust yet were hym levere abyde
> Than doon so heigh a cherlyssh wrecchednesse
> Agayns *franchise* and alle *gentillesse*.   1514–24

The story ends with a typical *demande*, put to the pilgrims: which was the most *fre* (or *gentil*) – the husband in his advice to his wife, the squire in his decision to release her from her promise, or the magician in refusing his thousand pounds?

cas, matter	would rather forgo his own
hight, promised	happiness than carry out
routhe, pity	such a very mean act against
That . . . gentillesse, So that he	generosity and great nobility

It provides a neat end to the story, but what matters more is the demonstration of a moral excellence which commands universal respect. This supreme *gentilesse* in its turn gives rise to a compassion great enough to allow the willing renunciation of lordship, love and a fat fee.

V

The Canterbury Tales

[II]

Fabliau
The Miller's Tale and *The Merchant's Tale*

The modern counterpart to the fabliau is the bar-room story, although regrettably few of these are as well told as Chaucer's. Because they are such good stories, Chaucer's fabliaux usually have world-wide analogues, although attempts to find actual sources have not met with much success. With the possible exception of the Manciple's account of why crows became black, they would appear to represent some of Chaucer's later work, and *The Manciple's Tale* is held to be early chiefly on grounds of its slight story, its evident rhetorical padding and its lack of any obvious relation to its narrator or even to its own prologue. Quite apart from their other virtues, the Miller's and Reeve's tales on the one hand and the Friar's and Summoner's on the other stand out by reason of the mutual animosity of their tellers and by Chaucer's dramatic exploitation of this within the scheme of the Canterbury pilgrimage. *The Shipman's Tale* is about adultery and money, and contains rather less action than the others. Props like tubs, cradles or pear-trees therefore play no part in it, but its intrigue and final fooling of the stuffy husband by both wife and lover show that it conforms to the type. *The Merchant's Tale*, as we shall see, while having a fabliau plot, goes some way beyond the mere requirements of the genre.

Curiously enough, there are almost no Middle English fabliaux outside Chaucer, although there are plenty from

France, and the name itself is, of course, French. It used to be thought that they were designed for the amusement of the newly-rich bourgeois of thirteenth-century France, with leisure but not much sophistication, but since the fabliaux often seem to satirise this class – and, incidentally, the clergy with whom they came into contact – it is nowadays assumed that they were meant for more aristocractic entertainment, although the appeal of a risqué story well told does not limit itself to any one class. Two sorts of plot recur. The first is that of the old, jealous husband whose young wife deceives him, despite all his precautions, with a more attractive and sprightly lover. The second is that of the biter bit, as in *The Reeve's Tale*, where the miller, having stolen some of the clerks' meal to bake a cake, is not only humiliated by the *swyvyng* of both wife and daughter but also loses the cake and the expense of entertaining the clerks. Or, on another level, the rapacious summoner of *The Friar's Tale* is tricked in his turn and carried off to hell by the devil who has assumed the guise of a bailiff. The two motifs are combined in *The Miller's Tale*, where Alison first deceives her old husband John the carpenter with the young lodger Nicholas and then tricks her other suitor Absolon with the misdirected kiss, and where Nicholas, thinking to improve on the joke, is himself painfully outsmarted by Absolon. The outcome of the fabliau is thus predictable within general limits – old husbands marrying young wives must expect to be cuckolded, and young men (especially clerics) are apt to be too clever by half – but the interest is sustained by watching the method by which these obvious conclusions are to be achieved. The fabliaux therefore sometimes depend on huge practical jokes which, in their way, are as unrealistic as anything in the romances. They demand an extravagance of action and gesture which goes well with Chaucer's frequent extravagance of description in *The Canterbury Tales* whose pilgrims are often, according to the author, the best (or cleverest, or wickedest) at their job you ever saw.

The solutions are deliberately ingenious and hence keep up our interest to the end of the story. The summoner of

swyvyng, seduction

The Friar's Tale actually condemns himself to hell. The seemingly insoluble problem of *The Summoner's Tale* is in fact solved, and in a way which humiliates the friar most of all by rewarding him with the chief share in the disgusting ritual at the end. Nicholas's fantastic arrangements for the flood culminate in a way he never imagined. *The Shipman's Tale* tells how a smooth young monk borrows money from his merchant friend in order to pay a debt for the merchant's wife. In return she agrees to spend the night with the monk. The monk later tells the merchant that he has repaid his loan to the wife, but when challenged she – with the quick thinking characteristic of fabliaux wives – claims she thought the money was a gift from her husband. The merchant has lost his hundred francs and the monk has enjoyed his wife, but, as Craik points out,[1] we are left in some doubt whether the wife really desires the monk or is simply using him as a means to get the money. If the latter, there is a further irony in that *he* eventually uses *her* for his own convenience. However things go, the fabliaux often end with a demonstration that what has been achieved is, within the terms of the genre, something approaching poetic justice, although we may note that the wife usually comes off better than the others:

> Thus swyved was this carpenteris wyf,
> For al his kepyng and his jalousye;
> And Absolon hath kist hir nether ye;
> And Nicholas is scalded in the towte.
> This tale is doon, and God save al the rowte!
> > *Miller's Tale* I 3850–4

> Thus is the proude millere wel ybete,
> And hath ylost the gryndynge of the whete,
> And payed for the soper everideel
> Of Aleyn and of John, that bette hym weel.

swyved, seduced	*rowte*, company
For, despite	*ylost*, got no money for
nether ye, backside	*everideel*, every bit of
towte, bottom	

His wyf is swyved, and his doghter als.
Lo, swich it is a millere to be fals!

Reeve's Tale I 4313–18

The lord, the lady, and ech man, save the frere,
Seyde that Jankyn spak, in this matere,
As wel as Euclide dide or Ptholomee.
Touchynge the cherl, they seyde, subtiltee
And heigh wit made hym speken as he spak;
He nys no fool, ne no demonyak.
And Jankyn hath ywonne a newe gowne. –
My tale is doon; we been almoost at towne.

Summoner's Tale III 2287–94

Should the fabliaux seem to exhibit a somewhat cynical view of human nature, especially in marriage, it might be replied that, firstly, jokes of this kind *are* often knowing and cynical, and, secondly, that similar situations occur elsewhere in medieval literature with a very different tone, as in this lyric which shows how intolerable a loveless marriage could become to a young wife:

Alas hou shold Y singe? Yloren is my playnge.
Hou shold Y with that olde man
To leven, and let my leman,
    Swettist of all thinge?[2]

To illustrate Chaucer's development of the fabliau form,[3] one might choose either *The Miller's Tale* or *The Reeve's Tale*. But *The Miller's Tale* is the better. *The Reeve's Tale* is clever enough, but it lacks the variety of *The Miller's Tale*, the feeling that several things are going on at the same time. Roger the Cook calls it *a jape of malice in the derk* (I 4338), and it ends, in the true fashion of farce, with an almighty scrap.

---

swich it is, that's what comes of
subtiltee, intelligence
demonyak, madman

Yloren . . . playnge, All my happiness is gone
leven, live
let my leman, desert my beloved

THE MILLER'S TALE

The beginning of *The Miller's Tale* makes only passing reference to the carpenter who is to be characterised later by his reaction to events. For the present the description of him as a riche *gnof* and the mention of his age and possessiveness is enough to label him as the typical *senex amans*. Instead there are descriptions of Nicholas and Alison of a length and detail not often found for the stock characters of most fabliaux. Nicholas is *sleigh* (artful) and *privee* (secretive), as many students were evidently expected to be (cf. 3275). He has a local reputation as a fortune-teller and weather-prophet, so that his later revelation to the carpenter about the flood is accepted readily enough. The description of Alison is much more in the manner of the pilgrims in the *General Prologue* than of the formal rhetorical description of the Duchess Blanche. But then, she is not an aristocrat, for she is brunette not blonde, and line 3244 tells us she has a most uncourtly come-hither look under those carefully plucked eyebrows. The apparently disjointed observations which make up the description do, however, comprise two conflicting strands of imagery. On the one hand, the mention of morning milk, the white smock and cap, the early pear-tree, the soft wool of a sheep, the shining complexion like a newly-minted coin, the swallow singing on the barn roof, the honey drink, and apples stored in hay all suggest the wholesome country girl of eighteen she undoubtedly would like her husband and the world at large to believe her. On the other, the weasel (potentially deceitful as well as lively), the frolicsome kid and colt, together with the earlier mention of John the carpenter restraining her *narwe in cage* and her later reaction to Nicholas ('And she sproong as a colt dooth in the trave') suggest her restiveness and a willingness to find solace elsewhere, and perhaps also something of the 'shrill vulgarity' which, as

gnof, fellow (someone of no class)
senex amans, old man in love
narwe in cage, closely watched

trave, frame for holding horses being shod

Kaske notices,[4] she reserves almost wholly for Absolon. The concluding lines of the description suggest for Alison alternative, and socially different fates:

> She was a prymerole, a piggesnye,
> For any lord to leggen in his bedde,
> Or yet for any good yeman to wedde.
>
> 3268–70

Prymerole and *piggesnye*, while terms of affection, may also have been (we can hardly be sure now) knowingly colloquial: 'a nice little thing', perhaps.

Naturally Nicholas and Alison, under the same roof, soon come together. Alison's initial rebuff to this urgent and uncourtly lover is made in a suitably genteel idiom ('Do wey youre handes, for youre curteisye!', 'Be so good as to take your hands away!'), and is probably for form's sake anyway, since she gives in soon enough. It is only after the two of them have agreed to watch their chance to deceive the carpenter in his own bed that Chaucer introduces a further complication in the person of Absolon, the young parish-clerk besotted with an Alison who is already too busy with Nicholas to return his love. He is a sharp dresser and accomplished at several useful trades, but suffers in comparison with Nicholas. The latter is a lodger in Alison's house, whereas Absolon has to creep up outside the bedroom window. Nicholas is neat, but Absolon is positively affected, taking endless trouble over his appearance and chewing liquorice before visiting Alison in order to make his breath smell sweet. In Beichner's phrase he is 'more ladylike than Alison'[5] and is clearly intended to be a foppish version of the biblical Absalom who, as II *Samuel* xiv tells us, was more beautiful than any man in Israel with 'no blemish in him'. In contrast with Nicholas's directness of approach to Alison, Absolon is more uncertain, coy and serious, and although he shares some of the stock attributes of the courtly lover, he is too self-conscious about his emotions. Whereas Nicholas (and Alison) sing loud and clear, Absolon's voice is a thin,

leggen, lay

quavering falsetto.[6] Absolon, however, is not wholly effeminate. He is unfortunately limited to watching Alison from a distance, but in a manner most uncharacteristic of the true courtly lover's adoration:

> I dar wel seyn, if she hadde been a mous,
> And he a cat, he wolde hire hente anon.

3346-7

He has been called a 'curious mixture of the predatory and the romantic'.[7] In fact, all three men – Nicholas, Absolon, and even her husband, John the carpenter – have possessive designs on Alison, so that it is not perhaps too unreasonable that, however much she may lead them on, she eventually gets off scot free.

The success of *The Miller's Tale* comes not only from an elaboration of character unusual in the fabliaux but also from the careful dovetailing and pacing of the plot. Nicholas omits no detail to make John believe that something terrible is about to happen. When the door to his room has been broken down, he swears the carpenter to secrecy before the latter knows what the secret is, and flatters him up to the hilt with the impression that he is the only sensible man worth trusting. As a result John is 'left filled with apprehension and heroic responsibility'.[8]

The story quickens with a wealth of circumstantial detail which, ridiculous in itself, taken together is enough to convince the old man:

> And whan thou thus hast doon, as I have seyd,
> And hast oure vitaille faire in hem yleyd,
> And eek an ax, to smyte the corde atwo,
> Whan that the water comth, that we may go,
> And breke an hole an heigh, upon the gable,
> Unto the gardyn-ward, over the stable,

wolde . . . anon, would have pounced on her straightaway
vitaille, provisions
faire, properly

eek, also
Unto the gardyn-ward, facing the garden

That we may frely passen forth oure way,
Whan that the grete shour is goon away . . .

3567–74

One might be tempted to forgive him his credulity, especially as his first thought is for the danger to Alison and not to himself, were it not that he is so complacent about his own rightness. He is a more attractive character than the ruffian miller of *The Reeve's Tale*, but, like him, he believes that, in the last resort, a simple man can outwit a student, however clever the latter.[9] Furthermore, he is insufferably sententious:

And seyde, 'I am adrad, by Seint Thomas,
It stondeth nat aright with Nicholas.
God shilde that he deyde sodeynly!
This world is now ful tikel, sikerly.
I saugh to-day a cors yborn to chirche
That now, on Monday last, I saugh hym wirche.'

3425–30

and is convinced that he foresaw Nicholas's 'breakdown' from overmuch studying and meddling with matters that are *Goddes pryvetee*. Once convinced that Nicholas's prophecies will come to pass, he quickly goes off to obtain the tubs and provisions and to make the ladders.

Absolon's first visit to the house comes some time before his second (in the interval Nicholas and Alison have been making plans) and at first sight might seem to be unnecessary. But besides establishing Absolon's feelings towards Alison, it makes us familiar with the all-important geography, especially the *shot-wyndowe* which must be set low in the wall and able to open quietly. Later (3695–6) we only need a reminder in the colloquial tone which befits the anecdote the tale essentially is. At the second visit the plot proceeds to its hilarious climax (or rather two successive climaxes) but, like

shour, storm
It . . . aright, there's something wrong
shilde, forbid
tikel, unreliable
sikerly, certainly

cors, corpse
That . . . wirche, Of someone I saw working just last Monday
Goddes pryvetee, God's concern
shot-wyndowe, casement window

all the best raconteurs, Chaucer slows the pace for a moment immediately before the joke:

> This Absolon gan wype his mouth ful drie.
> *Derk was the nyght as pich, or as the cole,*
> And at the wyndow out she putte hir hole,
> And Absolon, *hym fil no bet ne wers,*
> But with his mouth he kiste hir naked ers
> Ful savourly, er he were war of this.   3730-5

The joke is crude and the words are blunt, but hardly unnecessarily coarse. Chaucer has apologised twice over (at the end of the *General Prologue* and in *The Miller's Prologue*) for the occasional plain language, but he is not guilty of elaborating the indecent aspects of the tale, and the smith's knowing wink to Absolon (3767-71, which is the funnier because his guess is true) is the only possibly salacious part of it. And there is still a final twist to come. Just as, in the earlier part of the story, Nicholas and Alison have been left in bed while we watch Absolon plotting how to see Alison while her husband is away, so at the end we have almost forgotten John hanging up there in the roof, until Nicholas's agonised cry of 'Water' brings him crashing down to earth to become an object of ridicule to all his neighbours.

It may be that there is meant to be a further level of amusement to *The Miller's Tale*. The Host had originally asked the Monk for a story to follow and *quite* (match) *The Knight's Tale*, and the Miller uses the same word when he insists on telling a tale first. Now *The Knight's Tale*, as we have seen, is a story where two young men are in love with the same girl. So is *The Miller's Tale*. Furthermore, *The Knight's Tale* is pervaded by the code of fine amour. In *The Miller's Tale* Absolon suffers from *love-longynge* and cannot sleep for thinking of Alison. The overwhelming difference is one of rank, for *fine amour* is above all aristocratic, *courtly* love, while this is a provincial version of the same, in which, as will always happen, people are trying to ape their betters. Absolon consequently is not quite the perfect lover who

hym . . . wers, and this is ex-   *savourly,* enjoyably
actly what happened to him

might well *swelte* for his lady but hardly *swete* as well.
Nicholas, too, is introduced as

> This clerk was cleped hende Nicholas.
> Of deerne love he koude and of solas.

3199-3200

Fine amour is *deerne* by definition and *solas* (consolation) is its
aim. The first mention of *hende* Nicholas may slip by un-
noticed, for *hende* (pleasant, courteous) is a colourless word,
overworked by being applied to heroes (and heroines) in too
many romances.[10] Oddly enough, it is not common in
Chaucer's later work. But when the term is associated with
Nicholas so often (3272, 3397, 3401, 3462, 3487, 3526,
3742, 3832) it may acquire by repetition something of the
irony of Antony's description of Caesar's assassins as 'all
honourable men', and, if *The Miller's Tale* were read aloud,
the narrator could, by appropriate stress and facial expression, see that the audience did not miss the point. For
although Nicholas is etymologically *hende*, in the sense of
'at hand, close by', he is anything but courteous and gentle –
except now and then for his own ends. If this was Chaucer's
intention, *The Miller's Tale* is something more than the *nyce
cas* (ludicrous affair) that most fabliaux were, and some of the
diverse folk who laughed at it may have appreciated both its
intricate plotting and its stylistic achievement.

THE MERCHANT'S TALE

The Merchant's Tale is considerably longer than *The Miller's
Tale* which is itself longer than most fabliaux. Yet its plot is
simple, and firmly in the fabliau tradition. January, the
jealous old man, marries May, the young girl, who deceives
him with Damian, a squire in his household. The episode in
the pear-tree at the end of the story, and May's preposterous
'explanation' of her actions provide the sort of ending we
expect, and the language of the narrator changes (with the

swelte, swoon, die   *derne*, secret
cleped, called

usual apology for plain speaking) to the appropriate blunt style:

> Ladyes, I prey yow that ye be nat wrooth;
> I kan nat glose, I am a rude man –
> And sodeynly anon this Damyan
> Gan pullen up the smok, and in he throng.
>
> 2350–3 (and cf. 2376)

This bluntness occurs even though *The Merchant's Tale*, and *The Shipman's Tale* too, deal with characters of a higher social class than the other fabliaux. The background of *The Shipman's Tale* is that of a solidly prosperous household. January is a 'knight' and maintains a considerable retinue. The action comes almost entirely in the second half of the story, but it is the talk and the descriptions that ultimately prove the more interesting. In particular we see much more of January than we do of the old men in similar situations. We know why he marries, the way his mind works (his *heigh fantasye*) and how hypocritical almost all his actions are. He is exposed to an unmerciful close-up scrutiny. By contrast we are left to imagine May's reactions:

> But God woot what that May thoughte in hir herte.
>
> 1851

> How that he wroghte, I dar nat to yow telle;
> Of wheither hire thoughte it paradys or helle.
>
> 1963–4

In other words, *The Merchant's Tale* conforms sufficiently to its type. As usual, it is Chaucer's development of the tradition and his additions that engage our attention.

From the beginning of the story January has made up his mind to marry. He is over sixty and has had his fun for long enough. He claims that he wants a settled life, one that has

---

glose, pretend
rude, plain
sodeynly anon, all at once
throng, thrust

woot, knows
How . . . wroghte, What he did
hire thoughte it, it seemed to her

the blessing of Holy Church, and an heir to his lands. The Merchant pretends to give him the benefit of the doubt:

> Were it for hoolynesse or for dotage,
> I kan nat seye . . .   1253–4

but it is clear that what January is after is simply ready and legalised sex. However, since he is thoroughly hypocritical, the arguments for and against marriage are stated at some length, and his very long opening speech lasts from line 1263 to line 1392. Although he raises the arguments against taking a wife, he does so only to reject them contemptuously:

> But take no kep of al swich vanytee;
> Deffie Theofraste, and herke me.
>   1309–10 (and cf. 1568–9)

His speech is remarkable for its lack of logic:

> O flessh they been, and o flessh, as I gesse,
> Hath but oon herte, in wele and in distresse.
>   1335–6

> Suffre thy wyves tonge, as Catoun bit;
> She shal comande, and thou shalt suffren it,
> And yet she wole obeye of curteisye.   1377–9

but he is resolved on this course of action. He summons his friends to tell them *th'effect of his entente* (the gist of what he had in mind) and this takes a further sixty-odd lines. He is prepared to listen only to the sycophant Placebo, and he is rude to Justinus who states the case against marriage. After January has rejected all the latter's arguments, he chooses his wife *of his owene auctoritee*, as he had no doubt always intended. When he has fixed on his choice and called back his friends, he wants no opposition:

take . . . vanytee, take no notice of silly things like that
Deffie, ignore
O, one
gesse, suppose

but, only
wele, happiness
bit, bids
of curteisye, out of courtesy

And alderfirst he bad hem alle a boone,
That noon of hem none argumentes make
Agayn the purpos which that he hath take.

1618–20

The only thing that worries him is how he can possibly enjoy the heaven of wedded bliss here on earth and also expect salvation afterwards: it would surely be asking too much. Seeing there is no hope for it, Justinus becomes splendidly ironic (the word *skippe* is beautifully chosen):

And therfore, sire – the beste reed I kan –
Dispeire yow noght, but have in youre memorie,
Paraunter she may be youre purgatorie!
She may be Goddes meene and Goddes whippe;
Thanne shal youre soule up to hevene skippe
Swifter than dooth an arwe out of a bowe.

1668–73 [11]

and refers January to the Wife of Bath on marriage.

The allusion is apt, for it is in *The Wife of Bath's Prologue* (which had come some little way before *The Merchant's Tale* on the road to Canterbury) that the traditional antifeminist arguments against marriage had been brought forward, only to be triumphantly overturned by the Wife's combination of opposing 'authorities', her considerable experience and her readiness to take the initiative herself until her poor husbands are willing to give in for the sake of a moment's peace. She puts the arguments against marriage into their mouths so often that her continual *Thou seist . . .* makes them appear intolerable complainers. Briefly, the arguments against taking a wife are (*a*) women waste their husband's money on finery for themselves, (*b*) they are only waiting for their husbands to die so that they can get their hands on the inheritance and (*c*) the more attractive they are, the more likely it is that they will cuckold the husband. A true servant

alderfirst, first of all
boone, request
purpos . . . take, resolve he had made

the . . . kan, the best advice I know
Paraunter, perhaps
meene, instrument

is much more reliable than a wife, and cheaper too. Such antifeminist views go back at least to St Paul's Epistles, to St Jerome's *Epistle Against Jovinian* in the fourth century and to *The Golden Book of Marriage* by Theophrastus (cf. line 1310), a disciple of Aristotle. In the Middle Ages they are to be found in parts of Jean de Meun's continuation of the *Roman de la Rose* and in *The Mirror of Marriage* by Deschamps, Chaucer's contemporary. (The Wife of Bath's jibe was that such books are written by superannuated clerics, celibates by reason of their office and seeking revenge on woman-kind.) January counters such arguments with a list of faithful biblical wives – Rebecca, Judith, Abigail, Esther – but these, although successful in advancing the Israelite cause, could almost equally well be cited as examples of women's dupli-city, an irony which naturally escapes him.[12] The same anti-feminist sentiments recur towards the end of *The Merchant's Tale* in the dispute between Pluto and Proserpine. In the analogues to this story it is usually God or St Peter who restores the blind man's sight. Chaucer substitutes Pluto, the king of the fairies (as often in medieval literature). Pluto, incensed by May's treachery which he regards as thoroughly typical of women, resolves to restore January's sight at the crucial moment. Yet, on his wife Proserpine's spirited reply, he caves in just like the Wife of Bath's fifth husband. We remember that in the classical legend Pluto carried off Proserpine who was allowed to leave him for six months of each year, so that it might be said that he had trouble with his wife too. Proserpine vows that she will grant May *suffisant answere*, and, as at the end of *The Knight's Tale*, we are left wondering how the gods can both get their way. But the wife's quick thinking when it matters most is thoroughly in the fabliau tradition. The quarrel between celestial husband and wife also repeats the theme of *maistrie* in marriage which runs through these central tales.

But this is to anticipate. Once January has fixed on May as his bride, he is shown as progressively more despicable. The decorative machinery of the wedding feast is as much Renais-sance as medieval, with its profusion of victuals, music and riotous deities: the setting is, after all, in Italy. But all the

while January cannot wait to hurry the guests away so that
his fantasies about sleeping with May can become reality.
When the visitors have finally left, he takes aphrodisiacs, and
we next see him in the bridal chamber:

> And Januarie hath faste in armes take
> His fresshe May, his paradys, his make.
> He lulleth hire, he kisseth hire ful ofte;
> With thikke brustles of his berd unsofte,
> Lyk to the skyn of houndfyssh, sharp as brere –
> For he was shave al newe in his manere –
> He rubbeth hire aboute hir tendre face.   1821–7

Not only is his behaviour vulgar, so are his expressions. From
the outset he had been determined to have a young wife:

> 'I wol noon oold wyf han in no manere.
> She shal nat passe twenty yeer, certayn;
> Oold fissh and yong flessh wolde I have ful fayn.
> Bet is', quod he, 'a pyk than a pykerel,
> And bet than old boef is the tendre veel.
> I wol no womman thritty yeer of age;
> It is but bene-straw and greet forage.'   1416–22

Marriage for him simply sanctifies lust:

> And blessed be the yok that we been inne,
> For in oure actes we mowe do no synne.
> A man may do no synne with his wyf,
> Ne hurte hymselven with his owene knyf;
> For we han leve to pleye us by the lawe.[13]
>   1837–41

As if this were not enough, he builds a garden walled with
stone and with one small wicket gate of which he keeps the
single key. (Lest we should miss the literary antecedent of
this garden, it is said to be beyond description, even by the

make, mate	*pykerel*, pickerel
unsofte, harsh	*greet forage*, coarse fodder
houndfyssh, dogfish	*mowe*, may
brere, briar	*leve*, licence
in no manere, on no account	*pleye us*, enjoy ourselves

author of the *Roman de la Rose*. The garden is intended for
further refinement of marital delights:

> In somer seson, thider wolde he go,
> And May his wyf, and no wight but they two;
> And thynges whiche that were nat doon abedde,
> He in the gardyn parfourned hem and spedde.
>
> 2049-52

Meanwhile, however, two things have happened to abate
our growing revulsion at January's behaviour. May has not
yet spoken: it is not until line 2188, over nine hundred lines
from the beginning of the story and little more than two
hundred lines from its end, that she first speaks. Hitherto we
have simply been invited to imagine her feelings:

> But God woot what that May thoughte in hir herte.
>
> 1851

Now one of January's squires, Damian, has fallen deeply and
hopelessly in love with May. It is the textbook situation of
fine amour – the squire in love with his master's wife – and it
is to reach its culmination in the textbook garden setting
which ironically January had designed for his own pleasure.
Chaucer makes rhetorical play with the situation:

> Som tyrant is, as ther be many oon,
> That hath an herte as hard as any stoon,
> Which wolde han lat hym sterven in the place
> Wel rather than han graunted hym hire grace;
> And hem rejoysen in hire crueel pryde,
> And rekke nat to been an homycide.   1989-94

But not May. She is more than ready for an affaire with
Damian. We have been foolish if we supposed that her
beauty and her silence implied some special virtue, and our
natural sympathy for her begins to diminish.[14] Our feelings
may even start to veer in the other direction when January

spedde, enjoyed	*Wel rather,* much sooner
woot, knows	*grace,* favour
many oon, many a one	*rekke nat to been,* not care about
sterven, die	being

is suddenly struck blind. The Damian–May liaison is expressed in the stock courtly language of *mercy, pitee, grace,* and his 'sickness' which she speedily cures, but all romance is deliberately drained from it by his desire for self-preservation and her action in tearing up his note and putting the pieces in the privy. This relationship, just as much as January's with May, is based on physical desire alone.

The point of the possibly overlong introduction to the tale now becomes apparent. January's idealistic view of marriage (*so esy and so clene*) had been based on the assumption that a *yong thyng* could be moulded

> Right as men may warm wex with handes plye.
>
> 1430

(which is exactly how May takes an impression of the key to the garden and gives it to Damian) to humble and willing obedience:

> Al that hire housbonde lust, hire liketh weel;
> She seith nat ones 'nay', whan he seith 'ye.'
> 'Do this,' seith he; 'Al redy, sire,' seith she.
>
> 1344–6

Whether this is naïveté or hypocrisy, it is, as Justinus had seen at once, simply asking for disillusionment. But should the truth be as cruel as this? Is physical blindness too heavy a punishment for January's moral and spiritual blindness?

> For love is blynd alday, and may nat see. 1598

The very first time May speaks she is protesting her wifely devotion at the moment that Damian is waiting (by prior arrangement) in the garden. If we are tempted to feel too sorry for January at this point, we should remember that he has not really changed. He may promise May that after his death she will be his sole beneficiary, and even at times appear to be genuinely fond of her, but he will not let her out

---

so esy and so clene, so pleasant and so pure
plye, mould

Al . . . lust, Everything that pleases her husband
alday, always

of hand's reach. She eggs him on, it is true, but he is still very willing for another walk in the garden:

> 'Rys up, my wyf, my love, my lady free!
> The turtles voys is herd, my dowve sweete;
> The wynter is goon with alle his reynes weete.
> Com forth now, with thyne eyen columbyn!
> How fairer been thy brestes than is wyn!
> The gardyn is enclosed al aboute;
> Com forth, my white spouse! oute of doute
> Thou hast me wounded in myn herte, O wyf!
> No spot of thee ne knew I al my lyf.
> Com forth, and lat us taken oure disport;
> I chees thee for my wyf and my confort.'
> Swiche olde lewed wordes used he.   2138–49

This – which the bitter Merchant narrator calls *lewed* (old and silly) *wordes* – is the language of *The Song of Solomon* which had from early times been interpreted as an allegory of Christ's love for his church. As with the vocabulary of *fine amour* used in *The Merchant's Tale*, it is only the language not the spirit, lust and egotism instead of spiritual refinement, carnality and not courtesy. May perhaps finally persuades January that he may not have seen what he knows, in his heart, he did see (cf. the doubt expressed in *me thoughte*, 2386, and *I wende* 2393). Or did he, like Shakespeare, come to believe it is better to be deceived?

> Therefore I lie with her, and she with me.
> And in our faults by lies we flattered be.
>   Sonnet 138

or – to move from later sonnet to contemporary fabliau prologue:

> An housbonde shal nat been inquisityf
> Of Goddes pryvetee, nor of his wyf.

free, noble
columbyn, dove-like
oute of doute, truly
spot, blemish

disport, pleasure
chees, chose
pryvetee, secret concerns

> So he may fynde Goddes foyson there,
> Of the remenant nedeth nat enquere.
>
> *Miller's Prologue* 3163–6

Finally, this is the *Merchant's* tale. The *General Prologue* says nothing about the Merchant's marriage, although it says a good deal about his acquisitiveness and his secretive nature. The *Merchant's Prologue* is found in under half the manuscripts of the *Tale*, and it is possible to read the story without the bitterness of the introduction. But it surely loses by being so read. The Merchant in his *Prologue* complains that his wife is a *shrewe* and of her *crueltee* and *cursednesse*, all general terms, although the unhappy narrator may have considered it a small step from wickedness to infidelity. The bitterness of the *Prologue* has its continuation in the irony and cynicism manifest in the way the *Tale* is told. Marriage is consistently pictured by January as an economic transaction. If he had previously *despended* his body, a wife can yet become the 'fruit' of her husband's *tresor*, although he must be careful that *housbondrye* (economy) does not suffer. Wedlock is a *boond* (which, in his case, will become bondage) between husband and wife; one of her main duties is to 'keep his goods'. The legal arrangements for the marriage are watertight:

> I trowe it were to longe yow to tarie,
> If I yow tolde of every scrit and bond
> By which that she was feffed in his lond.
>
> 1696–8

but the spiritual arrangements should surely not be treated in the same perfunctory manner?

> Forth comth the preest, with stole about his nekke,
> And bad hire be lyk Sarra and Rebekke
> In wysdom and in trouthe of mariage;
> And seyde his orisons, as is usage,

foyson, plenty
Of . . . enquere, There's no need to bother about the rest.
tarie, delay

scrit, deed
feffed in, put in legal possession of
usage, custom

And croucheth hem, and bad God sholde hem blesse,
And made al siker ynogh with hoolynesse.   1703–8

What January in his depravity is shown to want is simply
legalised and sanctified sex. Once only does the Merchant
intrude into his tale:

Yet was he blent, and, God woot, so been mo,
That wenen wisly that it be nat so.
Passe over is an ese, I sey namoore.   2113–15

For the most part his revenge is an irony far more bitter than
that of his character Justinus. All the protagonists in this, one
of Chaucer's most complex tales, show a self-interest and a
cynicism underlined by their narrator, a man who, not two
months since, made the biggest mistake of his life, and,
unable to restrain himself after hearing *The Clerk's Tale*,
volunteers his own view of marriage even before the Host
asks for it.

The Saints' Legends and *The Clerk's Tale*

To move from the fabliaux to the saints' legends is to go from
the ridiculous to the sublime. Here there is no laughter or
irony, but instead piety and devotion. The type had begun to
gain popularity in the fourth century and from the eighth
century lives of the saints were read at matins. They are well
represented in the surviving Old English literature and in
the Middle Ages their number grew with the conversion of
the barbarians. There is often little firm historical evidence
for these 'lives', but saints were venerated because of their

croucheth hem, made the sign of
the cross over them
And . . . hoolynesse, And made it
well and truly binding in a
proper religious manner.

blent, deceived (literally,
'blinded')
mo, others
wenen wisly, truly believe
Passe . . . ese, It's as well to
leave the rest.

position as intercessors between God and man.[15] One of the best-known medieval collections was *The Golden Legend* (*Legenda Aurea*) compiled by Jacobus de Voraigne in the mid-thirteenth century. Legends of martyrs and virgins were especially popular, and it is natural that Chaucer included his *legendes of seintes* as a separate class in the books of 'morality and devotion' mentioned in the 'Retraction' at the end of *The Canterbury Tales*. *The Physician's Tale* and *The Second Nun's Tale* are stories of virgin martyrs, *The Prioress's Tale* of the killing of a Christian boy by the Jews. *The Man of Law's Tale* and *The Clerk's Tale* are not technically saints' legends, but Constance and Griselda are so very saintly that they may well be included. With the exception of *The Physician's Tale*, which is written in the rhymed couplets used for the majority of *The Canterbury Tales*, these are all in the seven line stanza (rhyme royal) which Chaucer had used earlier for *The Parliament of Fowls* and *Troilus and Criseyde*. While this metre may in some cases suggest earlier work refurbished for *The Canterbury Tales*, it is equally possible that others are late compositions where Chaucer considered that the stanzaic form, by slowing the pace of the story, would achieve a dignity compatible with the subject. The biblical parallels, the large amount of rhetoric and the repetitions characteristic of this group of tales also give them an impressive quality going far beyond the simple piety which may well have been the audience's first response. At the close of *The Prioress's Tale* the pilgrims are unusually silent:

> Whan seyd was al this miracle, every man
> As sobre was that wonder was to se.   VII 691–2

The Physician's Tale conforms most closely to the type. Virginia is the beautiful only daughter of a knight, and even more virtuous than beautiful. A heathen judge determines to have her for himself. The villains in the saints' legends usually try persuasion first, then gifts, and often torture: here the judge recognises that Virginia is so virtuous he has no hope. He therefore suborns a servant to claim that the girl has been stolen away as a child and should now be returned. When the case comes before him, the judge rules that she should be his ward before her return to the servant. Virginia's father tells her she must choose death or shame. When she chooses death, he smites off her head and sends it to the judge as he sits in court. At which the people, who had suspected all was not well, rise up and imprison the wicked judge. In *The Second Nun's Tale* (which Chaucer says is taken from *The Golden Legend* although it is a longer version of the story than the one now extant) Cecilia is married but, through a miracle, persuades her husband Valerian to live chastely with her. He is baptised and converts his brother Tiburtius. The brothers are eventually commanded upon pain of death to worship the image of Jupiter, but they convert their executioners. When they refuse publicly, however, they are martyred, and Cecilia buries them. She too is summoned before the prefect, but refuses to sacrifice or to deny her faith. She tells him he has no power in comparison with Christ, thus inviting martyrdom in a manner characteristic of this type of legend. The prefect finally loses patience and condemns her to be burnt alive. But the flames do not touch her, and she even lives three days with her neck half cut in two. (The saints' legends sometimes contain gory details of torture or privation comparable with details of battles in the romances, but the former were recommended reading by the Church whereas the latter were frowned upon by the stricter clerics.) Cecilia eventually dies after the three days respite she had prayed for in order to confirm her Christian followers in the faith.

THE PRIORESS'S TALE

The Prioress's Tale is short, but it nevertheless finds room for a formal Prologue which is (as in *The Second Nun's Tale*) an Invocation to the Virgin whose power (*vertu*) the story illustrates. Mary is present throughout the tale: the child kneels and says an *Ave Maria* whenever he sees her image; it is the *Alma Redemptoris* which he is most anxious to learn:

> 'And is this song maked in reverence
> Of Cristes mooder?' seyde this innocent.
> 'Now, certes, I wol do my diligence

maked, composed   *diligence*, utmost

To konne it al er Cristemasse be went.
Though that I for my prymer shal be shent,
And shal be beten thries in an houre,
I wol it konne Oure Lady for to honoure!'

537–43

and it is his singing this song as he passes through the Jewish
quarter on his way to and from school which leads the Jews,
who believe this is an insult to their race, to hire an assassin
to kill the boy. Miraculously, he continues to sing the *Alma*,
even after his throat has been cut. Mention of St Nicholas,
St Hugh of Lincoln and the Holy Innocents simply serves to
fix the legend more firmly into the tradition.

What shocks us, especially today in an age of greatly
increased ecumenical understanding, is the evident hatred
of Jews which would appear to be logically incompatible
with Christian piety. But medieval Catholics were usually
not tolerant in this matter (although a few, like Langland,
saw that the Jews shared part of our belief) and, forgetting
that Christ was himself a Jew, condemned them as murderers
of the Saviour. So the anti-semitism is in character for a
prioress, even for one who could show such kindness to lap-
dogs and weep over suffering animals. (*The Prioress's Tale*
contains nothing of the fashionable pretensions evident in
her description in the *General Prologue*.) In fact, the Prioress
could hardly have known about Jews at first hand, since they
had been expelled from England in 1290. In the early Middle
Ages the Jews had been prominent as great capitalists; the
lending of money for interest was forbidden to Christians,
but it frequently suited English kings to raise money from the
Jews when the Commons had limited the royal finances.
Their place as bankers was eventually taken by the Lombards
(hence Lombard Street in the City of London), although
some Jews may later have returned. Chaucer sets his tale in
Asia, but even so the Jews are usurers:

There was in Asye, in a greet citee,
Amonges Cristene folk, a Jewerye,

konne, learn
went, past

shent, punished
Jewerye, Jewish quarter

Sustened by a lord of that contree
For foule usure and lucre of vileynye,
Hateful to Crist and to his compaignye.

488–92

Even in countries from which they had not been expelled, the Jews lived in strictly supervised ghettoes, a name first applied to the Jewish quarter in Rome where they were under the special protection of the Pope to guard them against Christian fanaticism. The little boy in Chaucer's tale is killed when passing through just such a Jewish quarter. At the end, the Jews are not finally converted, as in some of the analogues. Instead, the Provost, called in to investigate the murder, condemns them to an unmerciful death:

He nolde no swich cursednesse observe.
'Yvele shal have that yvele wol deserve';
Therfore with wilde hors he dide hem drawe,
And after that he heng hem by the lawe.   631–4

This is another feature the saints' legends share with the romances: justice has to be seen to be done.

Chaucer's aim seems to be to increase the pathos of the story and also its realism, so far as such stories can ever be realistic. Consequently the child is a widow's son, seven years old (the usual age for starting school); his extreme youth is often mentioned:

This litel child, his litel book lernynge,
As he sat in the scole at his prymer.[16]   516–17

He is pathetically anxious to learn, even out of school hours, and begs an older boy to teach him the meaning of the anthem he overhears; this second boy would appear to be Chaucer's addition to the story. The mother searches distractedly for her lost son, even asking the Jews if they have

Sustened, supported
lucre of vileynye, filthy lucre
nolde . . . observe, would not countenance such wickedness

with . . . drawe, had them torn apart by wild horses
heng . . . lawe, hanged them according to the law

seen him. As he dies the Virgin speaks to him as gently as a mother to her child (667–9). The story finally impresses us as a strange mixture of delicacy and horror.

THE MAN OF LAW'S TALE

The Man of Law's Tale is closer to the saint's legend than is *The Clerk's Tale* and so may be considered briefly first. Constance is, I think, less realistic than Griselda; on the other hand, Walter's motivation in testing his wife is less obvious than that of the heathens or seducers of *The Man of Law's Tale*. The two tales have several points in common with romances which, indeed, they have sometimes been called.[17] Constance is twice cast adrift in a boat and miraculously preserved from death. The plot of *The Man of Law's Tale* depends on counterfeit letters, and in both stories there is a final recognition scene at a ceremonial banquet. Yet *The Man of Law's Tale*, at least, might conceivably have ended up as a true saint's legend. Constance is an emperor's daughter and so perhaps less likely to become a virgin martyr; instead the Sultan is so much in love that he chooses to become baptised and marry her. The heathens, led by the wicked mother-in-law, take their revenge by murdering the Sultan and his fellow converts at the marriage feast. A later wrongful accuser of Constance is miraculously struck down as he swears to her guilt, and a still later would-be seducer falls overboard and is drowned after he and Constance had been struggling in the boat. Her second husband, Alla, is converted too, and since the plot requires Constance to produce a child, the narrator feels he must offer some explanation:

> They goon to bedde, as it was skile and right;
> For thogh that wyves be ful hooly thynges,
> They moste take in pacience at nyght
> Swiche manere necessaries as been plesynges
> To folk than han ywedded hem with rynges,

skile, reasonable   *Swiche . . . plesynges,* Such things as are necessary to please

> And leye a lite hir hoolynesse aside,
> As for the tyme, – it may no bet bitide.   708–14

The story is much more explicitly Christian than *The Clerk's Tale*. No opportunity is lost to point the moral:

> O foule lust of luxurie, lo, thyn ende!
> Nat oonly that thou feyntest mannes mynde,
> But verraily thou wolt his body shende.
> Th'ende of thy werk, or of thy lustes blynde,
> Is compleynyng. Hou many oon may men fynde
> That noght for werk somtyme, but for th'entente
> To doon this synne, been outher slayn or shente!
>
>   925–31

Christ and the Virgin continually preserve Constance from death:

> And thus hath Crist unwemmed kept Custance.
>   924

> Thus kan Oure Lady bryngen out of wo
> Woful Custance, and many another mo.[18]   977–8

The pathos of the story is similarly stressed, e.g. at 267–71, 617–18, 834–40, 1051–71, and in the best-known passage of the tale:

> Have ye nat seyn somtyme a pale face,
> Among a prees, of hym that hath be lad
> Toward his deeth, wher as hym gat no grace,
> And swich a colour in his face hath had,
> Men myghte knowe his face that was bistad,

---

lite, little	*entente*, intention
As . . . bitide, For the time being – that's all there is to it.	*outher*, either
	shente, ruined
luxurie, lechery	*unwemmed*, unspotted
feyntest, weaken	*mo*, more
shende, destroy	*prees*, crowd
compleynyng, lamentation	*gat no grace*, got no pardon
werk, deed	*bistad*, desperate

Amonges alle the faces in that route?
So stant Custance, and looketh hire aboute.

645–51

It is surprising how little of *The Man of Law's Tale* (roughly
one-fifth) is a translation from the source, the early
fourteenth-century Anglo-Norman prose *Chronicle* of Nicholas
Trivet. Although the plot is much as in Trivet, Chaucer has
added a great deal of rhetoric, especially apostrophe, not
only to differentiate poetry from prose but also to achieve
the dignity required of a near saint's life. Where *The Man of
Law's Tale* fails is in its heavy use of coincidence, especially in
part three, where the boat returning to Rome from the
punitive expedition sent against the Syrians by Constance's
father (because of their earlier treatment of her) encounters
the boat in which she and her child are drifting, and in its
repetition of incident: there are two wicked mothers-in-law,
twice Constance is cast adrift, and two would-be seducers. A
story which is none too easy to follow in any detail would
also have been improved by division into more than the
three sections it has compared with the six in the shorter
Clerk's Tale.

THE CLERK'S TALE

The Clerk's Tale is not nowadays admired so much as it
evidently was in the Middle Ages. It is the last story in
Boccaccio's *Decameron*, probably the position of greatest
honour. Petrarch was so pleased by the story that he translated it from its original Italian into Latin so as to give it a
wider European currency. The Clerk acknowledges the
debt to Petrarch, although Chaucer also used *Le Livre
Griseldis*, a translation of Petrarch into French prose: rather
more of *The Clerk's Tale* comes directly from the French than
from the Latin.[19] The sequence of events in all four versions –
Boccaccio, Petrarch, the French and Chaucer – is nevertheless the same, although both Petrarch and Chaucer in turn

route, throng   *hire aboute,* around her
stant, stands

develop the characterisation. Many readers today, however, are offended by Griselda's passivity. Not only does she submit to the loss first of her daughter and then of her son, but she finally agrees to withdraw in favour of Walter's new 'wife' and even to supervise the preparations for her welcome. Worse than this: she would like to *anticipate* her husband's every wish so that she could immediately obey it, however unpleasant it might be:

> And certes, if I hadde prescience
> Youre wyl to knowe, er ye youre lust me tolde,
> I wolde it doon withouten necligence;
> But now I woot youre lust, and what ye wolde,
> Al youre plesance ferme and stable I holde;
> For wiste I that my deeth wolde do yow ese,
> Right gladly wolde I dyen, yow to plese.
>
> Deth may noght make comparisoun
> Unto youre love.   659–67

Even as she consents to return to her father's house to make way for her successor, she thanks the marquis for all his past kindness:

> That ye so longe of youre benignitee
> Han holden me in honour and nobleye,
> Where as I was noght worthy for to bee,
> That thonke I God and yow, to whom I preye
> Foryelde it yow; ther is namoore to seye.   827–31

She is continually protesting her unworthiness to be wife to such a lord. Her one direct reproach to him is immediately followed by an assurance of her continued cooperation:

> But sooth is seyd – algate I fynde it trewe,
> For in effect it preeved is on me –

certes, truly	*benignitee*, goodness
prescience, foreknowledge	*nobleye*, noble rank
lust, pleasure	*Foryelde*, Reward
woot, know	*algate*, at least
wiste I, if I knew	*in effect*, in the event

Love is noght oold as whan that it is newe.
But, certes, lord, for noon adversitee,
To dyen in the cas, it shal nat bee
That evere in word or werk I shal repente
That I yow yaf myn herte in hool entente.

855–61

The most she can bring herself to do is to give Walter some
advice on how to treat his new wife, but even then she does
not use anything so direct as the first person:

O thyng biseke I yow, and warne also,
That ye ne prikke with no tormentynge
This tendre mayden, *as ye han doon mo*;
For she is fostred in hire norissynge
Moore tendrely, and, to my supposynge,
She koude nat adversitee endure
As koude *a povre fostred creature*.

1037–43

Can Chaucer really be asking us to admire someone as
spineless as this?

In fact, both Petrarch and Chaucer admit that Griselda
has few, if any, successors (1142, 1164, 1180), so that the
story did not correspond to fourteenth-century reality any
more than to twentieth. Although Chaucer repeats Petrarch's
moral – that the story advises us to be equally patient in the
face of adversity that God may send us – he does not make
very much of it. Again, medieval audiences, remembering a
procession of fictional or semi-historical saintly women, and,
in theory at least, believing that a husband was his wife's
superior, might not have been so outraged as we may be.
Griselda is introduced in language that could apply equally
to Virginia or Cecilia or Constance:

Love . . . newe, Love grown old
is not the same as when it is
new
certes, truly
for . . . cas, no matter what
happens, even if I have to
die for it
werk, deed

in hool entente, unreservedly
biseke, beseech
prikke, goad
mo, others
is fostred . . . norissynge, has been
brought up
povre fostred, brought up in
poverty

> But thogh this mayde tendre were of age,
> Yet in the brest of hire virginitee
> Ther was enclosed rype and sad corage.
>
> 218–20

But Griselda's path is not to be theirs, although, like Constance, she is finally to be reunited with her husband and
children and everyone is to live happily ever after. Despite
the unpromising nature of the plot, *The Clerk's Tale* is set in
a world much more real than that of the typical saint's
legend. Griselda has an old father to look after; she *koude al
the feet of wyfly hoomlinesse*; she becomes adept at reconciling
quarrelling factions in the kingdom; the feelings of Walter's
subjects about the succession have to be considered; Griselda
is apparently the only person capable of supervising the
preparation of the palace for the new marchioness; she is
(twice over) stripped of her ragged clothes to be clad in
garments befitting her true rank. It would seem that Chaucer
frankly admits the intractability of the material, but does
his best to soften our utter disbelief. The result is that, without
ever believing that such events are at all likely, we are
brought to admit that they conceivably *could* happen, given
the premises of the story.

The clue to Chaucer's approach lies in the figure of the
marquis Walter. Viewed baldly, his function consists simply
of twisting Griselda's arm and seeing how long she will stand
it. His own justification of his actions is inadequate:

> For no malice, ne for no crueltee,
> But for t'assaye in thee thy wommanheede.
>
> 1074–5

for *wommanheede*, although one of Chaucer's highest compli-
ments (he uses the word about Criseyde), is too vague here.
Chaucer never *excuses* Walter: he makes it clear from the
beginning that his testing of his wife is both pointless and

brest . . . virginitee, virgin breast   *koude . . . hoomlinesse*, knew all
rype . . . corage, a mature and   the domestic duties of a wife
    steadfast spirit   *for . . . wommanheede*, in order
    to test your womanly virtues

ill-advised (the last three lines are Chaucer's addition to his source):

> He hadde assayed hire ynogh bifore,
> And foond hire evere good; what neded it
> Hire for to tempte, and alwey moore and moore,
> Though som men preise it for a subtil wit?
> But as for me, I seye that yvele it sit
> To assaye a wyf whan that it is no nede,
> And putten hire in angwyssh and in drede.
>
> 456–62

What he does is to give Walter just enough characterisation to make his behaviour barely credible. As Professor Sledd has pointed out,[20] the division of *The Clerk's Tale* into six parts is very carefully made. The poem begins, not with Griselda but with Walter. He is at once *biloved* and *drad* by his people. While he is young and noble, his ruthless determination is stressed early on:

> But on his lust present was al his thoght.   80

This trait can be taken up much later where it is specifically applied to his testing of Griselda:

> But ther been folk of swich condicion
> That whan they have a certein purpos take,
> They kan nat stynte of hire entencion,
> But, right as they were bounden to a stake,
> They wol nat of that firste purpos slake.
> Right so this markys fulliche hath purposed
> To tempte his wyf as he was first disposed.
>
> 701–7

Closely allied to his single-mindedness is his capriciousness, and Chaucer suggests, by carefully placed parentheses,

assayed, tried
tempte, test
subtil wit, clever trick
yvele it sit, it isn't right
condicion, nature
purpos, resolve

stynte of, give up
right as, just as if
of . . . slake, desist from that original idea
tempte, test

that this kind of behaviour is always possible with noblemen, especially married ones:

> Ther fil, *as it bifalleth tymes mo* . . .   449

> But natheless his purpos heeld he stille,
> *As lordes doon, whan they wol han hir wille.*
>
>   580–1

> But wedded men ne knowe no mesure,
> Whan that they fynde a pacient creature.
>
>   622–3

Janicula, Griselda's old father, had always known what might happen in a marriage like this, and is not really surprised when Griselda comes back to him (like Henryson's Cresseid returning to Calchas after Diomede). *The Clerk's Tale* probably began life, long before Boccaccio, as a folk-story in which a mortal woman is given to an otherworld lover. It has been held that this explains the unreality of Walter's motivation, but by the Middle Ages this situation had given place to an aristocratic world where lords' commands may be lamented but not evaded:

> Ye been so wys that ful wel knowe ye
> That lordes heestes mowe nat been yfeyned;
> They mowe wel been biwailled or compleyned,
> But men moote nede unto hire lust obeye.   528–31

Although Walter's subjects may later begin to grumble (722–32), they do nothing about it, and the common people, in Chaucer as in Shakespeare, are notoriously fickle: they are ready enough to welcome a second wife *right for the noveltee*. Walter makes Griselda swear unquestioning obedience to him before marriage, and it is this oath that she will on no account break:

Ther . . . *mo*, It turned out, as it sometimes does happen	*mesure*, moderation
	heestes, commands
wol . . . *wille*, intend to have their way	*yfeyned*, evaded
	lust, will

She shewed wel, for no worldly unreste
A wyf, as of hirself, nothing ne sholde
Wille in effect, but as hir housbonde wolde.

                                                        719–21

(a sentiment that January would have welcomed). His love
of secrecy shows itself in his determination to choose his own
wife and to conceal her identity until the very wedding-day;
Griselda is actually planning to get her work done early in
order to watch the marchioness on her way to the castle.
The childish love of surprise is seen again in his dramatic
revelation of his choice to his subjects (366–71) and in the
elaborate arrangements – including forged papal bulls – for
the second 'marriage'. Walter is not quite the callous monster
he is sometimes painted: he does, in fact, take special care
that no harm comes to the children, and at times he is almost
overcome by Griselda's total lack of resentment so that he
can scarcely continue the experiment (667, 892). His is a
complex personality, if never an admirable one.

In the face of all her trials Griselda maintains the *rype
and sad corage* of her introduction to the story. We must be
careful to translate *sad*, not by its modern equivalent, which
would seem natural enough in the circumstances, but by
some such word as 'constant' or 'sober'; what Chaucer
means is that she shows a maturity far beyond her years. It
was just this quality in her that led Walter to choose her in
the first place. We cannot question her constancy any more
than we can question the avarice or jealousy or uxoriousness
of one of Ben Jonson's 'humour' characters: nothing less
than the absolute will do. Griselda's admirable *pacience* is
also deepened, as has often been noticed, by biblical phras-
ing.[21] Nevertheless, Chaucer does pass over quickly the
twelve-year separation from her daughter and the eight-year
loss of her son, so quickly that we are not conscious of such a
long period. He also takes us into his confidence, so that we
are sure everything will eventually come out right. There is
no surprise in *The Clerk's Tale*.

wel, clearly
unreste, misery
A wyf . . . wolde, A wife, for her
part, should not desire anything except what her husband desires.

As Sledd suggests, what finally offends us in *The Clerk's Tale* is less Griselda's unnatural forbearance than the sentiment which Chaucer wrings from the situation. She begs the fearsome *sergeant* for a final kiss for her daughter before he carries her away, and implores him to bury the body so that neither beasts nor birds shall tear it to pieces; this last request is repeated as he seizes her small son. She returns Walter not only the clothing and jewels he had given her, but also her wedding ring. Her father throws an old coat around her as he leads her back to his cottage. The reconciliation scene is played for all it is worth:

'O tendre, o deere, o yonge children myne!
Youre woful mooder wende stedfastly
That crueel houndes or som foul vermyne
Hadde eten yow; but God, of his mercy,
And youre benyngne fader tendrely
Hath doon yow kept,' – and in that same stounde
Al sodeynly she swapte adoun to grounde.   1093–9

She clutches her children so tightly in this swoon (her second) that the onlookers can scarcely tear them away from her grasp. All this is to medieval taste, and, more to the point, very much in the vein of the saints' legends. Yet the moral to *The Clerk's Tale* is not stressed regularly, as it is there. There is also far less obvious rhetoric than in (say) *The Man of Law's Tale*. If the Clerk is throughout following the tradition of the sermon or legend in exalting a single virtue, and if he cannot quite reproduce here the reticence and the brevity for which he is praised in the *General Prologue*, he does seem to follow the Host's advice:

Youre termes, youre colours, and youre figures,
Keepe hem in stoor til so be that ye endite
Heigh style, as whan that men to kynges write.

wende stedfastly, thought for certain
benyngne, kind
Hath . . . kept, Has had you looked after
stounde, instant

swapte, fell
Youre . . . figures, Your technical terms, your rhetorical language and your figures of speech
endite, practise
Heigh, elevated

Speketh so pleyn at this tyme, we yow preye,
That we may understonde what ye seye.   16–20

The Clerk had not been one to push himself forward: like Chaucer the pilgrim, he has to be reminded by the Host that it is his duty to tell a tale. But in the end he proves more than a match for some of his more vocal companions. He first of all emphasises the unlikelihood of meeting many Griseldas. Then he promises a song (headed *Lenvoy de Chaucer* in several manuscripts) in honour of the Wife of Bath and her *heigh maistrie*. The word is deliberately chosen, for the Wife's Prologue and Tale had been one long advocacy of feminine *maistrie* in the struggle for power which is her view of marriage. The story of Griselda, told by a *clerk*, is the direct antithesis of this:

> If the Wife is a compendium of all the nightmares a celibate clergy might have about women, Griselda is a collection of all the elements of their fondest dreams. ... The Wife jeers that no clerk ever speaks well of women: Griselda proves her wrong.[22]

For Griselda is loyal, long-suffering, even (apparently) inexpensive to maintain. The 'Envoy' comes as something of a shock, for the Clerk appears to stand his whole story on its head, to argue that wives should firmly take the initiative and, if necessary, make their husbands' lives unbearable. But this does not put him in the Wife's camp: quite the contrary. For the evident exaggeration of his language suggests that he regards both positions – Alice of Bath's as well as Griselda's – as too extreme:

Ye archewyves, stondeth at defense,
Syn ye be strong as is a greet camaille;
Ne suffreth nat that men yow doon offense.
And sklendre wyves, fieble as in bataille,

pleyn, plainly	*camaille*, camel
archewyves, arch-wives	*offense*, harm
at defense, on the defensive	*sklendre*, slender
Syn, since	

Beth egre as is a tygre yond in Ynde;
Ay clappeth as a mille, I yow consaille.

Ne dreed hem nat, doth hem no reverence,
For though thyn housbonde armed be in maille,
The arwes of thy crabbed eloquence
Shal perce his brest, and eek his aventaille.
In jalousie I rede eek thou hym bynde,
And thou shalt make hym couche as doth a quaille.

1195-1206

The battle is ridiculous and the armour several sizes too big (except perhaps for the *archewyves*). Any kind of *maistrie*, if taken to extremes, is unreasonable. Petrarch tells how, when two of his friends first read the story, one twice broke down weeping while the other declared the tale far too unreal. It was left to Chaucer's Clerk to demonstrate that unreality rests in the eye of the beholder.

'Homilies and Morality and Devotion' *The Pardoner's Tale* and *The Nun's Priest's Tale*

At the very end of several manuscripts of *The Canterbury Tales* occurs a paragraph headed, in five of them, *Heere taketh the makere of this book his leve*. In it Chaucer asks forgiveness for works of *worldly vanitees* and gives thanks for his translation of Boethius 'and othere bookes of legendes of seintes, and omelies, and moralitee, and devocioun'. I have already spoken of Boethius and of Chaucer's saints' legends. 'Devotion' is a comprehensive term and presumably would include the saint's legend as well as other works inculcating Christian living. So, we might think, is 'morality', but it is used surprisingly often in *The Canterbury Tales*. At the end of

egre, fierce
clappeth, clatter
crabbed, perverse

aventaille, (movable) front of a helmet
rede, advise
couche, cower

The Miller's Prologue, moralitee and hoolynesse are together distinguished from a *cherles tale* and from *storial* (historical?) *thyng that toucheth gentilesse.* When the Host interrupts Chaucer's own *Tale of Sir Thopas* he asks instead for something containing *som murthe or som doctryne* (the same antithesis between 'entertainment' and 'instruction' occurs near the end of the *General Prologue* where the Host again asks for *Tales of best sentence and moost solaas*). Chaucer replies with *The Tale of Melibeus* which he calls *a moral tale vertuous.* The Parson, when his turn comes, offers *Moralitee and vertuous mateere.* Earlier the Pardoner's appearance, and the fact that he calls for a drink, lead the alarmed gentlefolk among the pilgrims to fear some *ribaudye*, a coarser fabliau than any so far perhaps. (The author of the fourteenth-century romance *King Alisaunder* says there are those

> þat hadden leuer a ribaudye
> þan here of God oiþer Seint Marie.
> Oiþer to drynk a copful ale
> þan to heren any gode tale.)

They ask for *som moral thyng* and the Pardoner agrees to think of *som honest* ('suitable', 'decent') *thyng* while he drinks; afterwards he tells what he himself terms *a moral tale.* At the close of his story of Chanticleer, Pertelote and the Fox, the Nun's Priest concludes:

> But ye that holden this tale a folye,
> As of a fox, or of a cok and hen,
> *Taketh the moralite*, goode men.
> For seint Paul seith that al that writen is,
> To oure doctrine it is ywrite, ywis;
> Taketh the fruyt, and lat the chaf be stille.

3438–43

Some recent critics, following the lead of Professor D. W. Robertson,[23] have argued that much of Chaucer, and indeed of medieval literature generally, is concerned with demonstrating the Augustinian antithesis between *caritas*,

hadden leuer, would rather have *ywis*, truly
doctrine, instruction *lat . . . stille*, let the chaff alone

love of God, and *cupiditas*, love of any earthly good for its own
sake, between Jerusalem and Babylon. Gluttony, gambling
and swearing in *The Pardoner's Tale*, for example, are all
manifestations of *cupiditas*. These critics suggest that the
most profitable approach to medieval texts, secular as well as
religious, is through exegesis, by which the literal exterior,
the bark or *cortex*, may be made to yield up the interior
kernel, *fructus* or *nucleus* of its religious message. In the Nun's
Priest's image, we are to ignore the *chaf* and eat the *fruyt*.[24]
In the case of scripture, the traditional codefied interpreta-
tions (or glosses) did often provide one or more additional
and more pointed allegorical meanings for an apparently
literal event, and, of course, the painter or architect,
medieval as well as modern, does often suggest interpreta-
tions going beyond the obvious surface representation. However, even with scripture, the exegetical method was possibly
losing ground in the late Middle Ages, and I am not persuaded that we should apply it consistently to secular
literature. This is not to deny that (more often in a poet like
Langland than in one like Chaucer) there may occasionally
be one (or even more) secondary meanings behind the literal
story or character. But, to my mind, there is usually a direct
invitation in such cases to make the allegorical interpretation, a plain hint, as with the Nun's Priest, that it is the
sentence that matters. We are not normally intended, of our
own accord, to associate the context with another scriptural
context that mentions the same figure or situation and then
apply the scriptural gloss to the secular story. Even where
we are invited to do so, the lesson is often a simple one ('be
on your guard, avoid flattery', in *The Nun's Priest's Tale*) or
the parallel is very general – Absolon in *The Miller's Tale* is
simply handsome and vain like the Absalom of II *Samuel*.

Naturally, most sermons have a *sentence* of this general
kind; the preacher has a message or a text which the sermon
illustrates. Chaucer's two sermons or *omelies*, *Melibeus* and
The Parson's Tale, are in prose. They are both translations:
Melibeus closely follows a French prose text which was itself
a paraphrase of a Latin original, and *The Parson's Tale*
depends on two thirteenth-century Latin works on penitence.

Melibeus is a lengthy argument for patience and tolerance in the face of extreme provocation, the moral of *The Clerk's Tale* in a different setting. Melibeus's house is attacked in his absence by enemies who break in and wound his daughter. He summons several counsellors to decide what action to take. His wife Prudence examines their views in detail and, following her advice, Melibeus becomes less headstrong, forgives his enemies and is reconciled with them. *Melibeus* may have been first assigned to the Man of Law who says he will speak in prose. Its emphasis on legal processes instead of violent revenge would, of course, have been suitable to him. Yet, in its rectification of an initial misguided conception of worldly honour, it is equally (or more) suited to Chaucer the diplomat and the philosopher who had translated Boethius. *The Parson's Tale* is a consideration of the three stages of confession – contrition, confession and satisfaction. The second stage includes a long section on the seven deadly sins in which a description of each sin (and its 'branches' or subdivisions) is followed by the *remedium* against that sin. It is possibly less of a sermon to be preached than the 'treatise' which Chaucer twice calls it: manuals of confession for the guidance of parish priests were beginning to appear in the vernacular by the fourteenth century. Neither tale appeals greatly to a modern audience,[25] paradoxically because of what would have been regarded as a virtue in the Middle Ages, the extremely methodical progression of the argument. Here are two examples:

> And certes, sire, as I have seyd biforn, ye han greetly erred to han cleped swich manere folk to youre conseil, which conseillours been ynogh repreved by the resouns aforeseyd. But nathelees, lat us now descende to the special. Ye shuln first procede after the doctrine of Tullius. Certes, the trouthe of this matiere, or of this conseil, nedeth nat diligently enquere; for it is wel wist whiche they been that han doon to yow this

certes, truly
cleped, called
manere folk, sort of people
to youre conseil, to advise you

ynogh, sufficiently
wel . . . been, well known what sort of people they are

trespas and vileynye, and how manye trespassours, and in what manere they han to yow doon al this wrong and al this vileynye. And after this, thanne shul ye examyne the seconde condicion which that the same Tullius addeth in this matiere. For Tullius put a thyng which that he clepeth 'consentynge'; this is to seyn, who been they, and whiche been they and how manye, that consenten to thy conseil in thy wilfulnesse to doon hastif vengeance.   *Melibeus*, 1352–60

Now been ther three maneres of humylitee; as humylitee in herte; another humylitee is in his mouth; the thridde in his werkes. The humilitee in herte is in foure maneres . . .   *Parson's Tale* 477–8

Ire, in *The Parson's Tale*, includes homicide, swearing, lying, flattery, chiding and other branches as well, and each is considered. The frequent use of proverbs and the over-illustration of a point we have easily grasped are not to our taste either. Illustration is often by *exempla*, the citation of analogous characters or incidents from scripture or the classics. *Melibeus* and *The Parson's Tale* fail, for us, because these demonstrations are not clothed in flesh and blood. Nor are the sins of *The Parson's Tale* seen in action, as they are in the early thirteenth-century *Ancrene Wisse* or, to come closer to Chaucer's day, in *Piers Plowman*. There are a few attractive details, for example of outrageous dress under Pride or of divination under Ire, and one or two intriguing allegorical phrases ('Flaterers been the develes norices') that cry out for development but do not get it. If the treatment of the subject, while retaining its orderly progression, could be made less rigorously schematic, and if the *exempla*, while retaining their relevance, could become entertaining in their own right – if, in fact, more consideration might be given to keeping the attention of the audience by whatever rhetorical devices – the sermon might engage our interest.

This is what happens in *The Pardoner's Tale* and *The*

trespas and vileynye, wrong and   *wilfulnesse*, stubborn resolve
   shameful deed   *hastif*, rash
put, sets out   *norices*, nursemaids

Nun's Priest's Tale. The Pardoner's Tale is in the form of a
sermon with its own text, *Radix malorum est cupiditas*, and the
tale of the three 'rioters' to illustrate its theme. The beast-
fable of *The Nun's Priest's Tale* teaches how men as well as
cockerels must beware of flattery and how silence is better
than *janglynge*. Yet neither is *simply* a sermon. *The Pardoner's
Tale* uses the form of the sermon, but keeps up a running
commentary by its preacher on his proficiency. *The Nun's
Priest's Tale* employs the technique of mock-heroic, first to
inflate and then suddenly to topple its hero, because, as any
preacher would tell you

> . . . evere the latter ende of joye is wo.
> God woot that worldly joye is soone ago.
>
> 3205–6

Of course, neither rhetorical devices like *apostrophe* (frequent
in sermons) nor *exempla*, nor the citing of 'authorities', nor
the drawing of morals is confined to the sermon form.
Chaucer's early work is among his most obviously rhetorical.
It is perfectly possible to interpret *The Clerk's Tale* (with
Petrarch) as an *exemplum* illustrating *pacience* in the face of
trials which God may send us or *The Man of Law's Tale* as a
demonstration of the devout soul's constancy in persecution,
and *The Wife of Bath's Tale* is clearly intended to be an *exemplum* pointing out the advantages of a wife having the
maistrie. *The Monk's Tale* which precedes *The Nun's Priest's
Tale* is a collection of *exempla* showing the operation of Fortune in the scheme of medieval tragedy. The four biblical
good women – Rebecca, Judith, Abigail and Esther – are
cited together both in *Melibeus* and, in a very different context, by January in *The Merchant's Tale*. Authorities crop up
on almost every page of Chaucer. The Host draws a possible,
but somewhat odd, moral from *The Physician's Tale*:

> Wherfore I seye al day that men may see
> That yiftes of Fortune and of Nature

janglynge, chattering   *Wherfore*, Therefore
woot, knows   *al day*, always
ago, past

Been cause of deeth to many a creature.
Hire beautee was hire deth, I dar wel sayn.

VI 294–7

But all these features are found together most often in
sermons. It is, too, perfectly characteristic of Chaucer, in his
later work, to take the sermon form and to develop it into
something far more exciting.

THE PARDONER'S TALE

The Pardoner is Chaucer's most consummate hypocrite. He
claims that his indulgences (which are bogus) have the power
to absolve sinners both *a poena* and *a culpa*, that is, both from
the punishment due to the sin and from the guilt itself,
whereas indulgences, by drawing on the Treasury of Merit,
could excuse only the former. He accepts cash for satisfaction
without bothering to see if there has first been contrition.
The text of his sermon is – is always – *Radix malorum est
cupiditas*, yet he himself is the very personification of the
avarice he preaches against. His relics are a sham and
he despises his audience, *lewed peple* who will fall for a *gaude*
and whom he can easily trick by any of a *hundred false
japes*:

Of avarice and of swich cursednesse
Is al my prechyng, for to make hem free
To yeven hir pens, and namely unto me.
For myn entente is nat but for to wynne,
And nothyng for correccioun of synne.
I rekke nevere, whan that they been beryed,
Though that hir soules goon a-blakeberyed!

400–6

I . . . sayn, I'm sure of that
lewed peple, stupid folk
gaude, trick
cursednesse, wickedness
free . . . pens, ready to give their
   money
namely, especially

nat . . . wynne, only to get
   money
nothyng, not in the least
rekke nevere, don't care
beryed, buried
Though . . . a-blakeberyed, If their
   souls go blackberrying

He is, as the *General Prologue* suggests, a eunuch, or at least highly effeminate. His thin, high voice, lack of beard, long hair, long neck, even his exhibitionism, all point in that direction, and his physical shortcoming is surely meant to imply spiritual sterility too. Yet this impotent fellow presents himself as a very devil with the women:

> Nay, I wol drynke licour of the vyne,
> And have a joly wenche in every toun.

452-3

He had earlier interrupted the Wife of Bath (III, 163) calling her a *noble prechour* – half in impudence and half in admiration, no doubt – and saying that he was about to wed. Unabashed by the Wife's warning of *tribulacion in mariage*, he begs her to continue

> And teche us yonge men of youre praktike.

III 187

He is on a pilgrimage designed to obtain forgiveness for sins, yet he believes the whole affair a fairy-tale and a fraud.

Nevertheless we accept him and his tale because, although it takes the form of a sermon, it is above all a performance. He is fascinated by the sins he condemns and he lets the pilgrims into the tricks of his trade. He is 'Half-Confessor, half Witch-doctor'[26] and, one might add, *all* actor. We do not need to go to Browning to find the origin of the dramatic monologue in which the speaker confesses his own hopes and shortcomings as well as describing his profession. Chaucer's own *Wife of Bath's Prologue*, the confessions of the Sins in Langland's *Piers Plowman*, parts of Gower's *Confessio Amantis* and, even earlier, several characters in the *Roman de la Rose* like False-Seeming, the hypocritical churchman from whom Chaucer took several hints for the Pardoner, all show that the form was (as one would expect) known to medieval Catholic England. The Pardoner begins by demonstrating to the pilgrims how he first fools his audience with his false bulls

praktike, practice

and relics and then preaches them a sermon on avarice. Since his living depends on the reception of the sermon, it must be both convincing and entertaining:

> Thanne telle I hem ensamples many oon
> Of olde stories longe tyme agoon.
> For lewed peple loven tales olde;
> Swiche thynges kan they wel reporte and holde.
>
> 435–8

It may be that, by his constant reference to the stupidity of the peasants from whom he usually exacts money, he is deliberately inviting the pilgrims to regard themselves as sophisticated men of the world, sharing with the Pardoner himself the knowledge of the true state of affairs, how things really work.[27] But he remembers that he had promised the pilgrims a *tale*, and, fortified by his drink, proceeds to give them one. Whether or not the tale is meant to take place at the ale-house does not really matter; since the Pardoner inveighs against the sins of the tavern, perhaps such a setting would provide an additional irony. Having begun his tale, he is, within a few lines, preaching once more. Preaching is what he knows, and the tale of the rioters, when it comes, is itself an *exemplum* illustrating avarice, *cupiditas*, the subject of the sermon and its text.

The *riotoures* ('wasters', 'debauchees') are, however, guilty of gluttony (especially drunkenness, one of its chief branches), swearing and dicing, as well as of avarice in their search for the gold, so the tale of the treasure is not the only *exemplum*. Lot, Herod and Attila are examples of the evils of drink; it was gluttony (for the apple) that drove Adam from Paradise; the Spartan ambassador, 'Stilboun', will not see his country allied to a collection of gamblers. 'Authorities' abound, as they do in many medieval sermons: Seneca and Paul on gluttony, Matthew and Jeremiah on swearing. The sermon proceeds, as sermons should, methodically from one sin to the next, but it also demonstrates, like *The Parson's Tale*, that sins are interdependent:

lewed, ignorant

wel . . . holde, easily repeat and keep in mind

Now comth hasardrie with his apurtenaunces, as tables
and rafles, of which comth deceite, false othes, chid-
ynges, and alle ravynes, blasphemynge and reneiynge of
God, and hate of his neighebores, wast of goodes,
mysspendynge of tyme, and somtyme manslaughtre.

X 792

The connection between the sins extends from the Pardoner's
sermon into his tale. The rioters are three of a company of
yonge folk, and the predominately middle-aged pilgrims
might be ready enough to hear ill of the younger
generation.[28] They punctuate their dicing by violent
oaths, their friend is slain by Death as he is *fordronke* and
they want the gold in order to continue their dissolute
life:

> This tresor hath Fortune unto us yiven,
> In myrthe and joliftee oure lyf to lyven,
> And lightly as it comth, so wol we spende.

779–81

> And thanne shal al this gold departed be,
> My deere freend, bitwixen me and thee.
> Thanne may we bothe oure lustes all fulfille,
> And pleye at dees right at oure owene wille.

831–4

The Pardoner can, therefore, finally and triumphantly
demonstrate the relationship between gluttony, swearing
and dicing, and between these three and murder and
lechery:

> Thus ended been thise homycides two,
> And eek the false empoysonere also.
> O cursed synne of alle cursednesse!

hasardrie, gambling	*yiven*, granted
tables, backgammon	*lightly*, easily
rafles, raffles	*departed*, shared out
chidynges, reproaches	*lustes*, desires
ravynes, thefts	*right . . . wille*, to our heart's
reneiynge, denying	content
fordronke, dead drunk	

> O traytours homycide, O wikkednesse!
> O glotonye, luxurie, and hasardrye!
> Thou blasphemour of Crist with vileynye
> And othes grete, of usage and of pride!   893-9

This last quotation also serves to illustrate the *apostrophe* or *exclamatio* that occurs throughout the sermon and tale. Not only this, however; the Pardoner, like any good performer, appeals to what his audience will already know for themselves. Hence the shared jests about the cooks who dress up food to *turnen substaunce into accident* (a philosophical 'in' joke) and the vintners who adulterate strong wine by mixing in cheaper, and the imitation of the drunk (*Sampsoun, Sampsoun!*) or the dicers with their great oaths (once again showing the relationship between the sins):

> 'By Goddes precious herte' and 'By his nayles,'
> And 'By the blood of Crist that is in Hayles,
> Sevene is my chaunce, and thyn is cynk and treye!'
>   651-3

Less needs to be said about the Tale proper, since everyone can understand its message. The three revellers are equally guilty, yet each has his own personality. The 'first' rudely accosts the old man, and it is his idea to kill the third; the 'second', rather slower-witted, takes his cue from the first but is justifiably suspicious of his friend's true intentions; the 'third', whom we wrongly expect to be more innocent because he is the youngest, shows his own brand of devilish cunning in plotting to kill his companions and in tricking the apothecary. They are all three out to seek and slay Death, who is to them, as to the innkeeper and his boy, a kind of brigand who goes about terrorising the countryside. But

traytours, treacherous
luxurie, lechery
hasardrye, gambling
vileynye, sinful language
of usage, from habit
substaunce, essence
accident, external form

Hayles, Abbey of Hailes (Gloucestershire) where there was a phial supposedly containing some of Christ's blood
chaunce, throw
cynk and treye, five and three (from hazard)

Death is more insidious than they imagine, for it is the gold, *cupiditas*, one of Death's manifestations, which kills *them*. They had not taken the boy's advice:

> Beth redy for to meete hym everemoore. 683

nor that of the old man who is also seeking Death, but who knows far more about his nature than the rioters do and who could have been a valuable *memento mori* to them if they had been less insulting and more considerate.[29] Like Everyman, they had been too ready to be distracted:

> O Deth, thou comest whan I had the leest in mynde!

The Pardoner knows that the grisly end to his tale can be quickly told. He does not – of course – forget to remind his congregation to make their offering to him to protect themselves against avarice, or indeed against any sin. The pilgrims, and we ourselves, are suddenly reminded that this has been not only a Canterbury tale but a specimen sermon:

> And lo, sires, thus I preche.
> And Jhesu Crist, that is oure soules leche,
> So graunte yow his pardoun to receyve,
> For that is best, I wol yow nat deceyve.
>
> 915–18

And lo, sires, thus I preche. This is how it is done, this is how the rabbit is pulled out of the hat. Can the Pardoner really be serious when he immediately afterwards offers absolution to the pilgrims if they will come up and kiss his relics, or indeed whenever or wherever they wish, *So that ye offren*? Professor Elliott argues that he is not, since his offer is so ridiculous and his tone so exaggerated that no pilgrim can possibly be fooled. Father Beichner, too, believes that his offer to the pilgrims is a continuation of his self-exposure in his Prologue, a piece of horseplay which comes disastrously unstuck. His relics were fakes and he knows that everyone of any

leche, physician   *So . . . offren*, provided you make an offering

intelligence (the pilgrims, not the *lewed* country people)
would realise this.[30] Yet the Host, the Pardoner's intended
first victim, is not sarcastic – as he might have been if
everyone had seen the joke – but furiously angry. Perhaps,
on the other hand, we are wrong to stress the *his* of line
917. Lumiansky reminds us that the Pardoner, like all
pardoners, always claimed to be selling Christ's pardons as
His agent.[31]

I think that we should remember that the Pardoner's
real confession had ended two hundred and fifty lines back,
at line 642. The intervening sermon, with the tale embedded
in it, is unexceptionable:

> For though myself be a ful vicious man,
> A moral tale yet I yow telle kan. 459–60

It might have been preached by the Parson, had he been
capable of the necessary verve. The Pardoner is, furthermore, perfectly serious about the *theory* of Christ's pardon. It
is best, but he has the next best, which is, happily, much
more readily available: instant pardon. And so the patter –
which has been so successful that we have almost forgotten
it is patter – continues, and the pilgrims (were it not for the
Host) might have taken the place of the Pardoner's imaginary
congregation. No trick is too outrageous for this hypocrite to
try. He is guilty not only of *cupiditas* but also of *superbia*, Pride,
a turning away from God to self. Pride was usually placed
first in the list of the deadly sins and was often regarded as
the origin of all seven. For to know that you are sinning
against what is right, but nevertheless wilfully to go on
sinning – that is the deadliest sin of all.

THE NUN'S PRIEST'S TALE

The Nun's Priest is, like the Pardoner, a performer in complete command of his material. But here there is no desire for
gain, simply a delight in manipulating his subject-matter to
inflate a ridiculously commonplace incident: a cock flies
down from his perch and is carried off by a fox who later

unintentionally opens his mouth and lets the cock escape. Like *The Pardoner's Tale*, *The Nun's Priest's Tale* is sought as relief from the preceding serious story. For all his politeness, the Knight cannot face any more of the hundred tragedies the Monk claims as his repertoire: he has already suffered seventeen. Like the Pardoner too, the Nun's Priest uses sermon techniques, for he is, we should remember, a *priest*. The dispute between Chanticleer the cock and Pertelote, his favourite wife, is over the power of dreams to foretell the future. Pertelote is sure that Chanticleer's dream has a simple, physical explanation and prescribes laxatives. In any case:

> Lo Catoun, which that was so wys a man,
> Seyde he nat thus, 'Ne do no fors of dremes?'
>
> 2940–1

This will never do, however. How could Chanticleer ever hold up his head again if he were to submit so meekly to a woman? So he outbids Pertelote's single 'authority' with no less than seven of his own, three of which are expanded into illustrative stories, *exempla*: the man who dreamt that his companion was murdered and hidden in a dung-cart, the man who ignored his friend's dream of shipwreck and was drowned, and the murder of the child-martyr, St Kenelm. Yet Chanticleer, for all his pretended learning, is not only concerned about the interpretation of dreams; really he doesn't like laxatives because they taste nasty:

> Shortly I seye, as for conclusioun,
> That I shal han of this avisioun
> Adversitee; and I seye forthermoor,
> That I ne telle of laxatyves no stoor,
> For they been venymous, I woot it weel;
> I hem diffye, I love hem never a deel!   3151–6

Ne . . . dremes, Don't pay any attention to dreams
han of, have from
ne . . . stoor, set no store by laxatives

For . . . weel, For I'm absolutely sure they're horrible
diffye, spurn
I . . . deel, I don't like them one bit!

The little woman is sure she knows best, and the husband is not the brave fellow he would like to appear.

The moral of the first *exemplum* is, of course, that dreams come true, but *The Nun's Priest's Tale* draws a further one, that *Mordre wol out*. This often happens in sermons, for everything is grist to the preacher's mill, and no opportunity is lost to emphasise a point that arises, as it were, in passing. Occasionally, the Nun's Priest seems to be addressing not the pilgrims but a different congregation:

> Allas! ye lordes, many a fals flatour
> Is in youre courtes, and many a losengeour,
> That plesen yow wel moore, by my feith,
> Than he that soothfastnesse unto yow seith.
> Redeth Ecclesiaste of flaterye;
> Beth war, ye lordes, of his trecherye.   3325-30

His story turns out to have not one moral but two:

> Lo, swich it is for to be recchelees
> And necligent, and truste on flaterye.
>
>   3436-7

Chanticleer shut his eyes when they should have remained open, and the fox opened his mouth when he should have kept it shut. The double moral is like the double explanation of Chanticleer's action in leaving the safety of his perch for the danger of the farmyard. Is the cock's fall from happiness due to Fortune (like all those princes in *The Monk's Tale* immediately preceding):

> O destinee, that mayst nat been eschewed!
>
>   3338

or is it simply the result of female charm?

flatour, flatterer	*recchelees*, careless
losengeour, deceiver	*eschewed*, avoided
soothfastnesse, truth	

'For whan I se the beautee of youre face,
Ye been so scarlet reed aboute youre yen,
It maketh al my drede for to dyen.

. . . . .

I am so ful of joye and of solas,
That I diffye bothe sweven and dreem.'
And with that word he fley doun fro the beem.

3160–2, 3170–2

Things are clearly rather more than they seem. But not so
much more that, as one interpretation suggests, we are
directed to leave the cabbage-patch for the world of *Paradise
Lost*. Chanticleer is Adam, the first man (3188), deceived
by a woman (3256), guilty of the lust of the eyes, the lust of
the flesh, and the pride of life. The fox, black-tipped, is the
devil, or at least Judas (3227), and the farmyard chase at
the end is 'the moral confusion following the Fall of Man'
(3389, 3401).[32] Not only is there no direct hint to interpret
the fable in this way – as there almost always is with medieval
allegories – but, as Muscatine points out, Man, however
shaken by his experience, here remains still in possession of
his farmyard Paradise.[33]

It is surely not necessary to be as solemn as this. We begin
from a beast-fable, a well-known medieval form:

For thilke tyme, as I have understonde,
Beestes and briddes koude speke and synge.

2880–1

The Nun's Priest's Tale opens with the widow's cottage and
yard and, with the chase at the end, returns to the countryside in which it had been anchored. But, within the tale, the
viewpoint switches from animal to human and back again,
as it had not done in the earlier *Parliament of Fowls* in which
the birds appear only in the final section of the poem. A
commonplace incident is given a commonplace setting, but

yen, eyes   *sweven*, vision
drede, fear   *fley*, flew
solas, happiness   *thilke*, that
diffye, scorn

it is, by a number of devices found in epic and not often in fable, built up into something much more impressive-sounding. This is the technique of mock-heroic, as in Pope's *Rape of the Lock* where the whole poem springs from the snipping off of a lock of Belinda's hair. Mock-heroic is not meant to be taken too seriously, for its aim is to show how pretentious and self-important we are in our little world. *The Rape of the Lock* is therefore more gentle and less specific in its satire than the *Dunciad*, and *The Nun's Priest's Tale* is similarly not *The Parson's Tale*.

The debate on dreams thus takes its place as the first major device for inflating the plot. In the *Roman de Renart*, which Chaucer may have used as a source, Chanticleer has a wife and he has a dream, but his wife accepts her husband's view that the dream is prophetic. If we wish, we can also view the difference of opinion between husband and wife as a continuation of the running debate on 'mastery' else-where in *The Canterbury Tales*. At one moment Pertelote behaves as any medieval wife might, concerned at her husband's groans in his sleep and sure that everything has a medical explanation; at another she is the disdainful courtly lady, desiring a husband who is *secree* and *noon avauntour*. Furthermore, did Chanticleer fly down to the ground of his own accord or because it was predestined? Did the Almighty's foreknowledge *compel* him to leave his perch, or was it his own decision? This debate on predestination versus free-will we have met before in *Troilus and Criseyde*, where Chaucer borrowed from Boethius but appeared not to fol-low his compromise solution of allowing man a measure of free choice. Boethius is mentioned in *The Nun's Priest's Tale*, as are Augustine and Bradwardine, another authority on this subject who had died only a few years after Chaucer was born. But the whole matter, although of the greatest inter-est in its own right, is here treated as a joke and as another means of humorously augmenting the story: cocks, after all, are carried off by foxes every day.

There is much more in *The Nun's Priest's Tale* which fits into the mock-heroic technique. Several of the rhetorical

secree, discreet   *noon avauntour*, not a boaster

figures which Chaucer uses seriously elsewhere are here employed solely for fun. The early *descriptio* of Chanticleer, with his red comb, azure legs and body of burnished gold, makes the cock into an epic figure, and he later struts like a *grym leoun* and *roial, as a prince is in his halle*. He is, as Miss Corsa puts it, '*Homo Sapiens* and *Rara Avis* at one and the same time'.[34] The astrological *circumlocutio* from 3187 to 3197 is simply a roundabout way of saying nine o'clock on 3 May. An *exclamatio* rhetorically compares the lurking fox to other deceivers, Judas, Ganelon and Sinon; the figure is common in medieval sermons and hence doubly suitable here. The fall of Chanticleer is ironically likened to another tragedy, which also took place on a Friday, the death of Richard I (the Lion Heart), described in one of the set pieces in that thirteenth-century treatise on the art of poetry, Geoffrey de Vinsauf's *Poetria Nova*. The riotous chase after the fox with the cock in his mouth, where all within earshot, humans and animals alike, join in, is compared in turn to the fall of Troy, the sack of Carthage, Nero's burning of Rome and the massacre of the Flemings in the Peasants' Revolt. All this is padding with a purpose in one of the most learned of *The Canterbury Tales*.

Three times at least (3214, 3251, 3374) the Nun's Priest says he must get back to the story. But this protestation of helplessness in the face of his material is all part of the fun. He is enjoying himself enormously, switching from the proud but secretly frightened Chanticleer to the honey tones of the flattering colfox. The *doctrine*, if somewhat obvious, is perfectly serious, the method of presenting it considerably less so. Some stricter ecclesiastics, like Chaucer's own Parson,[35] evidently regarded secular fables (as opposed to holy writ) as a questionable method of moral exhortation. All right then, the story *is* true – or at least as true as some of the Arthurian legend, the bits that appeal to the ladies:

> Now every wys man, lat him herkne me:
> This storie is also trewe, I undertake,

roial, regal
also, just as

undertake, guarantee

> As is the book of Launcelot de Lake,
> That wommen holde in ful greet reverence.
>
>   3210–13

At which, perhaps, the Prioress took notice; but I doubt if she really saw the joke.

VI

Chaucer and his Contemporaries

In this concluding chapter I want to look at Chaucer in relation to the best known of his contemporaries. This is obviously to falsify, to some extent, those contemporaries, for I shall concentrate on their treatment of topics I have already discussed in Chaucer's work and shall often ignore other of their more important concerns. My excuse is that the chapter may help to fill out the picture of late medieval English literature and to prevent any idea that such themes are peculiar to Chaucer. Comparison with other authors may also provide jumping-off places for a deeper exploration of their work. Clearly some limitation in scope will also be necessary. Imitation of Chaucer began even before his death; he is the first poet we know of to have several disciples. However, the Chaucerian tradition in fifteenth-century England consisted far too often of an exaggeration of his metre and diction, especially in the love-allegories. A lot of this literature is pretentious and it contains far too little of the Chaucerian spirit. Things were better in Scotland where we encounter not only mellifluous aureate diction but often (as in Henryson, Dunbar and Gavin Douglas) genuine poetic fervour; yet this very independence makes its practitioners less obviously 'Chaucerian'.[1]

Even if one excludes fifteenth-century literature, one is still faced with a considerable body of late fourteenth-century English literature, most of it anonymous, especially in the fields of romance, lyric and drama. A little has already been said about the romances in the first chapter on *The Canterbury Tales*. Chaucer himself wrote several lyrics, some of which are occasional poems and are included in the

section 'Short Poems' in Robinson's edition, others of which
are embedded in longer works, like the 'complaint' of the
Black Knight in *The Book of the Duchess* (475–86) or the
rondel which ends *The Parliament of Fowls*. He probably wrote
several more which are lost; the chances of survival for a lyric
of a few stanzas were even slimmer than those for medieval
poems in general. Chaucer borrowed his metrical and
stanzaic forms, like the *ballade* and the *rondel*, and his genres,
like the 'complaint', from France. Machaut, Deschamps,
Froissart and Graunson are his exemplars here, as in the early
poems generally. Even his apparently autobiographical
lyrics are usually conventional, and the remainder are often
concerned with the ritualised behaviour of *fine amour*. If all
this seems unimaginative on Chaucer's part, one should
remember that the Middle English secular lyric is less varied
than the religious lyric (although many more of the latter
have survived) and that Chaucer was something of a pioneer
in England. As R. H. Robbins puts it: 'From Chaucer the
English court poets learned what the international French
set were saying and how they were saying it.'[2] The development of English religious drama was proceeding apace in the
late fourteenth and in the fifteenth century, but the majority
of our surviving texts are from the North. The Wife of Bath
says she loved going to *pleyes of myracles*, the Miller cries out
in Pilates voys and Absolon was adept at playing Herod (both
were presented as rumbustious, ranting characters), but if
Chaucer had any particular plays in mind we cannot now
know which they were. But miracle plays and also minstrels
must have been competitors with the sermon for the public's
interest (the Wife of Bath mentions *prechyng* as another
attraction) and consequently sermons were driven to become
more entertaining.

Gower, to whom together with the philosopher Ralph
Strode Chaucer dedicated his *Troilus and Criseyde*, wrote in
French and Latin as well as in English. His long poem
Confessio Amantis, in English despite its Latin title, was
probably finished by 1390 and survives in nearly fifty manuscripts. It is a valuable comparison, not only because Gower
was almost certainly addressing the same audience as

Chaucer, but because it takes the form of a framework and a collection of tales; in fact some of Gower's stories were also told by Chaucer in *The Canterbury Tales* and *The Legend of Good Women*. Finally, there is a large body of alliterative poetry in late Middle English, perhaps tracing its ancestry back to Old English poetry, almost all of it from the West and the North and therefore in a dialect more difficult for us than Chaucer's which was to become standard English.[3] Most of this poetry is anonymous, and its patrons were probably often aristocrats who were national as well as local figures. It was evidently a strong and flourishing tradition. The poet of *Sir Gawain and the Green Knight* says his story was recited (*with tonge*):

> If ȝe wyl lysten þis laye bot on littel quile,
> I schal telle hit as-tit, as I in toun herde,
>   with tonge,
>   As hit is stad and stoken
>   In stori stif and stronge,
>   With lel letteres loken,
>   In londe so hatz ben longe.   30–5

With lel letteres loken could mean simply 'embodied in truthful words', but it is more likely to mean 'linked with the correct letters' and to refer to the technique of alliterative verse. Set beside Chaucer's Parson's statement:

> But trusteth wel, I am a Southren man,
> I kan nat geeste 'rum, ram, ruf,' by lettre.
>   X 42–3

this would seem to imply one metrical tradition in the North and West and another in the South and East, yet the alliterative poetry is by no means completely apart from Chaucer's work. *Sir Gawain and the Green Knight* and the three

---

laye, story
quile, time
as-tit, straightaway
in toun, among men
stad and stoken, set down and fixed

stif, good
hatz ben longe, has long been the custom
trusteth wel, believe me
geeste, recite alliterative poetry

other poems in the same unique manuscript and in the same North-West Midland dialect, *Pearl, Patience* and *Purity* (or *Cleanness*), may be provincial in some of their words and grammatical forms, but *Gawain* and *Pearl* especially are sophisticated in their use of courtly diction and ideas. These and other contemporary alliterative poems use fashionable devices such as allegory, dreams and spring mornings. Some alliterative poems even have London affinities. William Langland, the probable author of *Piers Plowman*, seems to have lived in London for part of his life, and *St Erkenwald* (once thought to have been the work of the *Gawain* poet) celebrates an ancient bishop of London. *Piers Plowman* exists not in one version but in three, conventionally called A, B and C and perhaps to be dated in the late 1360s, 1377–9 and *c.* 1387 respectively.[4] All three versions are in alliterative verse, and the poem employs not one dream but several, including two dreams within dreams. Its style, and most probably its audience too, was less aristocratic than that of most other alliterative poems. Nor does it seem to aim at any regional interests in the manner of some works in the same metre. It would therefore be wrong to speak of an alliterative tradition and a Chaucerian tradition as if these were quite distinct. There are considerable areas of overlap between Chaucer, Gower, the *Gawain* poet and Langland, and I shall concentrate on three: the author as a character in his own poem, the conception of *fine amour*, and the extent to which the four can be called 'realistic'.

The fact that there is usually some degree of correspond-ence between the narrator of a medieval poem (the 'I' of the text) and its author may be simply one more manifesta-tion of the medieval desire for authority, the reluctance to cut the audience off completely from the known world. Or it may be a natural result of oral delivery, and I have already argued that Chaucer frequently exploited this situation. Just as the Dreamer in *The House of Fame* is called 'Geoffrey' by the Eagle who is carrying him through the heavens, so the Dreamer in *Piers Plowman* is called 'Will', Langland's own

name. The Lover of *Confessio Amantis* tells Venus, near the
end of the poem, that his name is 'John Gower' and refers
to himself as old and sick, as Gower may well have been at
the time of writing. Since we do not know who the *Gawain*
poet was, we cannot be sure if his poems reflect the circumstances of his life, but the likeliest explanation of *Pearl* is that
it is a personal poem: the pearl which at the beginning slips
through the Dreamer's fingers to be lost in the long grass of
a garden represents the Dreamer's daughter who died before
she was two years old. If this is indeed so, the poem is an
elegy, like *The Book of the Duchess*, meant to provide consolation to the bereaved rather than to mourn the deceased. The
Dreamer sees his dead child on the far bank of a stream
which separates earth and heaven, and the discussion
between them is intended to lead to the Father-Dreamer's
spiritual consolation and benefit. The Narrator of *The Book
of the Duchess* provides no such religious solace for the Black
Knight: instead he brings him to accept the fact of death by
the recall of happiness during life.

Only Chaucer seems to need bedside reading to put him
to sleep. The Dreamer of *Piers Plowman* drops off quickly,
at the sound of a stream burbling or in the middle of the
church service. For him the springtime setting is merely
functional, and the interludes in the 'real' world between
visions are usually short. Knowledge comes through dreams:
awake the Narrator is a poor creature, misunderstood and
despised by society. There is no setting within most of his
dreams either; this may be why much of the earlier part of
the *Vita* is apt to seem so abstract. Gower, too, has little
background scenery, although the stories themselves provide
the movement which would otherwise have been almost
completely absent. The wood of *The Book of the Duchess*, the
park of *The Parliament of Fowls*, and the Gothic variety of
Fame's temple achieve just enough by way of landscape to
prevent the poems becoming mere discussions. Most visual of
all, however, is *Pearl*. From the garden in August at its
beginning the poem moves to the brilliance of the open
spaces on the earthly side of the river and finally to the
colour and light of the New Jerusalem.

At the simplest level these dreamers observe events and ask questions of a kind the dullest member of the audience might raise. It would appear to have been part of Chaucer's technique to let his dreamer remain primarily an observer and to exploit his assumed naïveté. When he becomes a narrator, as in *Troilus and Criseyde*, or a pilgrim, as in *The Canterbury Tales*, more pointed comments become possible. The dreamers in *Pearl* and in *Piers Plowman* are much more argumentative. In *Pearl* the Dreamer is almost impossibly literal-minded. He will believe nothing unless he sees it (he has to be shown a vision of the New Jerusalem to assure him that it is not simply a city in Palestine) or else he has to be defeated in argument by a collection of texts or *exempla* more impressive than his own. It is perhaps because of his limitations that the early multifold symbol of the pearl gives way for a time to literal argument in the middle of the poem. We know virtually nothing of who William Langland was or what he did. The situation is the direct opposite of Chaucer's case (where we know a good deal about his public life), and in any 'autobiographical' interpretation of *Piers Plowman* we are consequently forced to rely to a very considerable extent on internal evidence from the poem itself and the supposition that Dreamer and poet are one and the same. This Dreamer becomes more of an individual as the poem progresses. In the A text and in the B and C text *Visio* (roughly the first – and easiest – third of the poem) he is almost wholly an observer. Only towards the close of A does he show signs of the argumentative nature which manifests itself in the *Vita* (the last two-thirds) of B and C where he becomes a participant in the action – it is *his* search for salvation, and he betrays not only a healthy intellectual curiosity but a pronounced disposition to query the statements of those whose advice he had sought. It was, in all probability, the assurance that he knew what was best, and his consequent involvement in a series of difficult and related arguments, which brought about the premature conclusion to the A text. Yet, from another point of view, this fallible guide is one of the successes of *Piers Plowman* because, as he grows in understanding, the argument of the poem grows with him. Such involvement of the audience is especially necessary in a long poem like this. When we read *Piers Plowman*, however misty sections of the poem may seem, we have the feeling of what one critic has called 'the mind struggling with the fundamental issues of life'.[5] When the dream poem reaches its end (as *The House of Fame* does not) the Dreamer is often by that time a sadder and wiser man. The Dreamer of *Pearl* sees he cannot yet join his daughter in heaven, but he is reconciled to her loss. The hero of *Sir Gawain and the Green Knight* (although not a dreamer) has fallen a little short of his own tremendously high standards and will be less proud in future. Not only the Black Knight but also the Dreamer of *The Book of the Duchess* realises that 'To lytel while our blysse lasteth' and that prolonged mourning is a profitless exercise. Most of all – because in this case there is an 'epilogue' as well as a 'prologue' – the Dreamer of *Confessio Amantis* is brought to understand that *fine amour* is not for an old man like him. The endings are not, however, always so diminuendo or so aesthetically satisfactory as this. At the oddly inconclusive end of *The Parliament of Fowls* the Dreamer goes back to his books. In the closing lines of *Piers Plowman* he sets out on yet another search, for Piers who he is convinced will put everything right.

Love in Chaucer ranges from the ascetic's love of God, as in *The Second Nun's Tale* or *The Man of Law's Tale*, to the frank sensuality of Alison and Nicholas in *The Miller's Tale* or the Miller's wife and daughter in *The Reeve's Tale* who happily accept whatever lover fortune may send them. In between come Troilus and Criseyde who pursue the evanescent and fragile pleasure of a *fine amour* which is finally seen to be *false worldes brotelnesse*, an *estat* in which there is *litel hertes reste*. If this is Chaucer's most considered view of *fine amour*, we must remember that it is not his only one. Elsewhere it can be a proper feature of leisured aristocratic society (*The Book of the Duchess*), or a formal, somewhat arid, potentially dangerous pastime (*The Parliament of Fowls*), or again, the language of *fine amour* may be present but its spirit

conspicuously absent (*The Merchant's Tale*). Of the other
three writers considered here – Gower, Langland and the
Gawain poet – it is Langland who has least to say about *fine
amour*. His concern is with other things: man's spiritual state,
the right use of the goods of this world, the harmonious
functioning of society. On one occasion, near the beginning
of his long poem, a smooth-talking friar (just such another
as the Friar of *The Summoner's Tale*) is seeking money from
Lady Meed, an allegorical figure who represents the power
of the purse (for good or evil, but mostly for evil). The
conversation turns to the behaviour of the aristocracy, whose
lax morals the friar is anxious to excuse since they are his
likeliest benefactors:

> It is frelete of flesh, ʒe fynde it in bokes,
> And a course of kynde wherof we komen alle;
> Who may scape the sklaundre, the skathe is sone amended;
> It is synne of the seuene sonnest relessed.　　B iii 55–8

The reference to the 'bookish' view of *fine amour* is interesting,
perhaps analogous to the opinion of the husband in *The
Manciple's Tale*[6] that, whatever gloss is put upon it, lechery
remains lechery.

Whereas in *The Book of the Duchess fine amour* is clearly
approved of as a polite accomplishment for courtiers and its
ennobling role stressed, in *Sir Gawain and the Green Knight* its
pre-suppositions become the means of repulsing sexual
temptation. Gawain is pledged to keep his half of a bargain
(one of those bargains ridiculous in real life but made
credible in the world of romance) that he shall seek out the
Green Knight and endure one stroke from the latter's axe in
return for having dealt him a similar stroke in Arthur's
court the preceding Christmas. He spends the second
Christmas at the castle of Bertilak, the Green Knight's *alter
ego*, although Gawain does not know this. While Bertilak is
out hunting on three successive mornings, Gawain is visited

ʒe, you
course . . . alle, fact of nature
　　through which we all get
　　born

sklaundre, slander
skathe, harm
relessed, absolved

in his room by Bertilak's attractive wife who is bent on seduction. Gawain's reaction to her advances, as both he and we discover later on, is to determine his future treatment by the Green Knight, so the test becomes also one of loyalty (*trawþe*) – both to his plighted word and to his host – versus the considerable charms of the host's young wife. *Trouthe* was the most important tenet of Arveragus's somewhat inflexible code in *The Franklin's Tale*, the 'highest thing that man may keep'. Here it is again put to the test and emerges almost, but not quite, triumphant. (*Trawþe* is linked with 'cleanness' – spiritual purity, freedom from defilement – in *Purity*, probably the work of the same poet.) Elsewhere, and especially in French literature, Gawain is one of Arthur's noblest knights but too ready for casual *amours*, in the matter of love not to be trusted. This side of his nature emerges in Malory (most of whose sources were French) and, through Malory, in Tennyson. In *Sir Gawain and the Green Knight*, however, his reputation is for *luf-talkyng*, for skill in courtly language, the *lel layk of luf*. The situation between Gawain and the Lady is the age-old motif of Potiphar's wife, and its resolution need not depend on *fine amour*. But Gawain decides to talk himself out of the dilemma he is in, to refuse the Lady's advances but without offending her, and he does this by a combination of self-deprecation and extravagant praise of the Lady, both attitudes encouraged by the code of *gentil* behaviour. The poet is deliberately exploiting the ambiguities of the language of *fine amour*, for often the Lady is clearly saying one thing and Gawain is pretending to understand another.[7]

Other alliterative poems, in fact, adopt a similar moral tone. Particularly interesting in relation to *Sir Gawain and the Green Knight* is *The Awntyrs of Arthur*, a late fourteenth-century alliterative poem in thirteen-line stanzas (each ending with a four-line 'wheel', as in *Sir Gawain*).[8] In this romance Gawain and Guinevere, who have together left Arthur's hunting party, are visited by the ghost of Guinevere's mother. The couple, and particularly the Queen, are warned against

luf paramour, listes, and delites.   213

luf . . . delites, passionate love, pleasures and delights for which Guinevere's remedies are to be meekness, mercy, pity on the poor and chastity. In the second half of the poem, a straightforward knightly combat, Gawain could almost be said to uphold the honour of the Round Table, as he does in *Sir Gawain and the Green Knight*. The ghost had earlier accused Arthur and his knights of covetousness for lands, but at the end Arthur redeems himself by his generosity towards the knight Gawain had defeated.

The most sensitive and delicate treatment of *fine amour* is, however, that of Gower. The scheme of *Confessio Amantis* requires the Lover (Amans) to confess to Genius, the priest of Venus. Genius takes him through the deadly sins one by one, with their 'branches' and sub-divisions, and illustrates each by stories of lovers. Religious imagery is characteristic of the language of *fine amour*, but this is the most extensive use of it in Middle English:

> So thenke I to don bothe tuo,
> Ferst that myn ordre longeth to,
> The vices forto telle arewe,
> Bot next above alle othre schewe
> Of love I wol the propretes,
> How that thei stonde be degrees
> After the disposicioun
> Of Venus, whos condicioun
> I moste folwe, as I am holde.   i 253–61

In each case Amans discusses this sin with the priest and receives advice from him. As elsewhere, love of this kind is for *gentils*. The Lady has all the usual virtues, such as *bounte* and *good governaunce*. Amans is infatuated (*assoted*), tongue-tied before her (as was Chaucer's Black Knight at the beginning of his courtship), wholly attentive to her slightest wish. At church his book is in his hand, but his thoughts are on her. He spends sleepless nights through love. She has several other suitors and can well look after herself, but in

thenke, intend	*telle arewe*, enumerate
bothe tuo, both	*propretes*, special qualities
that . . . to, what is the job of my order	*condicioun*, regime
	holde, bound

any case is always protected by Daunger. Several times we
are told that poor Amans gets absolutely no encouragement;
seemingly she has no *pite*, or at least not for him. The sins of
Amans are perforce those of intent:

> And in this wise I mot forsake
> To ben a thief ayein mi wille
> Of thing which I mai noght fulfille.   v 6604–6

He confesses to being guilty of 'love delicacy', of eyes, ears
and thought, but his feasting is *al of woldes and of wisshes*. He
is not keen on going on expeditions abroad to win his Lady's
favour (Blanche was less heartless; she did not prescribe
them, *Book of the Duchess*, 1024–33), for what if while he was
away he should ruin his chances at home?

Gower does not stress the spiritually ennobling aspects of
fine amour nearly so often as Chaucer, perhaps because his
plan demands confession of sins. Occasionally the characters
of moralist and high priest of Venus sit somewhat uneasily
on the shoulders of Genius. In the *Roman de la Rose* Genius
had been Nature's priest and spokesman, the advocate of
plenitude and reproduction. In the *Confessio Amantis* he is the
priest of Venus, and is occasionally embarrassed over her
evident promiscuity. Gower's ideal emerges as *honeste* love,
which is a part of *gentilesse*:

> For evere yit it hath be so,
> That love honeste in sondri weie
> Profiteth, for it doth aweie
> The vice, and as the bokes sein,
> It makth curteis of the vilein.   iv 2296–300

It is also opposed to adultery (we never learn whether or
not the Lady of *Confessio Amantis* is married). In fact, its end
is marriage:

> Mi ladi Venus, whom I serve,
> What womman wole hire thonk deserve,

forsake, deny   *doth*, puts
yit, yet   *vilein*, low-born
sondri weie, different ways

Sche mai noght thilke love eschuie
Of paramours, bot sche mot suie
Cupides lawe; and natheles
Men sen such love sielde in pes,
That it nys evere upon aspie
Of janglinge and of fals Envie,
Fulofte medlid with disese:
Bot thilke love is wel at ese,
Which set is upon mariage;
For that dar schewen the visage
In alle places openly.
A gret mervaile it is forthi,
How that a Maiden wolde lette,
That sche hir time ne besette
To haste unto that ilke feste,
Wherof the love is al honeste.   iv 1467–84

and marriage is based on *trouthe*:

Forthi scholde every good man knowe
And thenke, hou that in mariage
His trouthe plight lith in morgage,
Which if he breke, it is falshode.   vii 4226–9

Gower, one feels, would wholeheartedly have approved of *The Franklin's Tale*.

Genius has been able to give little comfort to Amans, for there is no real cure for *tristesse* in love (iv 3507). Amans must keep hoping that his fortune may change. His final advice, in Book viii, is that love is blind and, in Amans's case, unprofitable. Amans objects that advice is easy to give:

Mi wo to you is bot a game,
That fielen noght of that I fiele.
          viii 2152–3

thilke, that
eschuie, avoid
paramours, sexual
suie, follow
sielde, seldom
nys . . . aspie, is always having to
    watch for
disese, harm

the visage, its face
forthi, and so
lette, delay
besette, bestow
feste, celebration
trouthe plight, solemn pledge
That . . . fiele, You who feel
    nothing of what I feel

Genius agrees to carry his letter of intercession to Venus who appears personally to answer. She tells Amans that her medicine is not for such *olde sieke* as he and shows him two companies of lovers, one young and led by Cupid, the other, led by Elde, of those older, wise men who have nevertheless been overcome by love and who tread with *softe pas* and have *sobre chier*. Cupid pulls out his dart from the Lover's breast and Venus anoints the wound with healing ointment. In her mirror Amans sees himself as an old man. She excuses him from further service to love, and he receives absolution from Genius. So poor Amans leaves, also with *softe pas*, an unheroic figure as he has been throughout the poem, but now sadder and wiser and almost reconciled to his future. Although there is some indication, at the close of the *Confessio Amantis*, that *caritas* is better than *amor*, this cannot be the wider perspective of the end of *Troilus and Criseyde*, addressed to *yonge, fresshe folkes*. For Troilus and Criseyde were themselves young, while Amans is old. And love – or at least *fine amour* – is a young man's game.[9]

Realism is a large subject, and for us who set high store by realism (or at least verisimilitude) in literature a potentially dangerous one when we read the literature of the distant past.[10] In my attempt to show how much of interest Chaucer still has for us, I may have been guilty occasionally of exaggerating the realistic qualities in his writing. If so, perhaps a view of him in relation to his contemporaries will help to redress the balance.

Chaucer has little and the *Gawain*-poet nothing to say about the political events of the age. These, remember, included the social and economic discontent culminating in the Peasants' Revolt of 1381, the turbulent reign and eventual deposition of Richard II, the decline of English influence in France, the changing relationship between the city merchants and the central government, the papal schism, and the challenging doctrinal teaching of Wyclif. The

softe pas, gentle step   *sobre chier*, serious expression

Gawain poet is concerned, above all, with the way in which a spiritual or ethical crisis in the life of an individual forces him to re-examine his hitherto strongly-held principles of behaviour. Chaucer's reticence about public affairs may be the result either of his position as a court poet or of a feeling that such contemporary happenings were not the proper subject of poetry. Langland, on the other hand, is far more committed. Behind the *Visio* (especially) is the impact of fourteenth-century labour problems – the result of high wages demanded by workmen after the Black Death – and the problem of how the poor and the genuinely disabled are to be fed. The disarray of the Church, with rival popes in Rome and Avignon, is evident from a reading of the *Vita de Dobest*, the last part of his poem. His hero is a ploughman, a type (like Chaucer's ploughman) of the honest and willing workman. Elsewhere in the poem, especially in the C text, Langland gives a view of the plight of the miserable poor, a class which none of the other three writers we are discussing seems to consider. But two caveats are necessary: although Langland sympathises with the poor, he does not idealise them, much less use them as a political rallying-cry, and he always sees contemporary problems from the viewpoint of Christian teaching. His advice is that rich men and professional men (like lawyers and the clergy) should voluntarily do more to help poor men, that a radical change of heart would cure most of society's ills. There must also be a willingness on the part of the individual to submit humbly to the will of God. His conception of 'patient poverty', developed in the *Vita*, is paralleled in *Patience* and by Chaucer's 'glad poverty' in *The Wife of Bath's Tale*, although Langland devotes far more time to it than do either of these other works.

Gower reacted very differently to the political events of his time. His horror at the Peasants' Revolt emerges more clearly from his Latin and French works than from the *Confessio Amantis*. Even so, the Prologue to the latter gives us a picture of a nation troubled by discord, by the selfishness of each of the three Estates (knighthood, clergy and commons), a situation not to be compared with the stability of the former age. Love is therefore only part – although the main part – of the subject-matter of the *Confessio Amantis*. 'Digressions' on inventions in Book iv, on religions in Book v and on learning for the whole of Book vii, may not be digressions at all but an attempt to give a wider perspective to the poem. There is little contemporary detail since the stories are from the past, but more about political principles:

> And ech of hem himself amendeth
> Of worldes good, bot non entendeth
> To that which comun profit were.
>
> *Prologue* 375–7

Devotion to the 'common profit' had also been advocated by Scipio in *The Parliament of Fowls*. At the end of Gower's poem, Amans is advised by Venus:

> That thou nomore of love sieche.
> Bot my will is that thou besieche
> And preie hierafter for the pes.
>
> viii 2911–13

Gower's ideal is national peace and unity, promoted by love and dependent on personal virtue, legal restraint and the authority of the king. It is significant that whereas the first version of *Confessio Amantis* is said to be *A bok for king Richardes sake*, in the revised text this becomes *Engelondes sake* and the work is dedicated to Henry of Lancaster, the future Henry IV. Later, Gower addressed his poem entitled *In Praise of Peace* to the same monarch.

One minor but interesting aspect of the fourteenth-century background is the wide interest in astrology and magic. Langland has a few very puzzling astrological (perhaps alchemical) prophecies, mostly of a pessimistic nature. The plot of *Sir Gawain and the Green Knight* depends upon the enchantment of Bertilak into the Green Knight by Morgan le Fay in an attempt to discredit the *sourquydrye*

amendeth *Of,* profits by   *sieche,* seek
entendeth *To,* bothers about   *besieche,* entreat

(excessive pride) of Arthur's court and frighten Guinevere to death. Some critics have seen this explanation as perfunctory and not properly integrated into the poem. However this may be, the poet shows no interest in how the magic is achieved, in what way Bertilak is transformed; he simply accepts it as a necessary part of his story. In *The Franklin's Tale*, on the other hand, we are told of the mathematical calculations the magician used to remove the black rocks, and in *The Squire's Tale* everyone is very intrigued by the mechanism that drives the magic steed. Gower, too, is interested in the magic episodes he borrows from Ovid: Medea's recovery of Aeson's youth is perhaps the best example.

Chaucer, however, was well acquainted with the science of astrology.[11] He wrote *A Treatise on the Astrolabe* and most probably *An Equatorie of the Planetis*, both in the 1390s. (An astrolabe was an instrument for taking latitudes and calculating the position of the sun and stars, while an *equatorie* – evidently more complicated – ascertained the position of the planets.) He frequently uses a method of astrological dating in his other works. The opening of the *General Prologue* comes first to mind, but both the Host and Chanticleer (no common cock) tell the time by studying the progress of the sun. Mostly this is morning; the sun is getting higher in the sky and it is time to be up and doing. But not always; Criseyde goes to bed in the alien Greek camp to ponder the attractions of Diomede in the absence of Troilus:

> The brighte Venus folwede and ay taughte
> The wey ther brode Phebus down alighte;
> And Cynthea hire char-hors overraughte
> To whirle out of the Leoun, if she myghte;
> And Signifer his candels sheweth brighte,

Venus, the evening star	*Cynthea*, the moon
taughte, showed	*overraughte*, urged on
ther, where	*the Leoun*, the sign of Leo
Phebus down alighte, the sun had set	*Signifer*, the zodiac
	candels, signs

> Whan that Criseyde unto hire bedde wente
> Inwith hire fadres faire brighte tente.
>
> v 1016–22

Astrology, however, is not merely for dating; it is also predictive. It is the basis of the Physician's diagnoses. It is partly by astrological calculations (*calkulynge*) that Calchas foresees the fall of Troy and so deserts to the Greeks. Pandarus *caste* (took a horoscope) before setting out to acquaint Criseyde with Troilus' love for her (ii 74). He had *forncast* an auspicious time for the meeting of the lovers in his house, and it is a storm, caused by the rare conjunction of the Moon, Saturn and Jupiter in the sign of Cancer, that causes Criseyde to stay overnight. The Wife of Bath explains her boldness and amorousness by the conjunction of Mars and Venus at the time of her birth. The influence of the planets on men's destiny and the exploits of the gods with the same names (Mars, Venus, Jupiter) are sometimes woven together. This is so in some of the astrological imagery in *The Knight's Tale*, and it occurs again when Troilus prays for the gods' blessing on his visit to Criseyde's room.

The pseudo-science of alchemy is the subject of *The Canon's Yeoman's Tale*. The search for the means to turn base metals into gold and silver has caused the Canon's Yeoman to lose his own money and to get into debt. *The Canon's Yeoman's Prologue* is a confession in the manner of *The Wife of Bath's Prologue* and *The Pardoner's Prologue*, but, I think, not nearly so successful, since the *Tale* which follows does not illustrate and deepen the lessons of its *Prologue* to anything like the same extent, nor does the Canon's Yeoman really become a personality. There are too many names and not enough explanation for our taste. However, the mingled scorn and fascination for the science which has ruined him is well brought out:

> And yet, for al my smert and al my grief,
> For al my sorwe, labour, and meschief,
> I koude nevere leve it in no wise.   712–14

Inwith, within
smert, pain

meschief, misfortune
in no wise, on any account

A man may lightly lerne, if he have aught,
To multiplie, and brynge his good to naught!

1400–1

After the inevitable explosion, the canon of the *Tale* is ready
to sweep up the mess and begin all over again:

As usage is, lat swepe the floor as swithe,
Plukke up youre hertes, and beeth glad and blithe.

936–7

If the medieval story is about the past (and several were)
we must not expect any sense of period. History for them
was about *people* and how they behaved, not a careful re-
creation of the past, much less a demonstration of cause and
effect. They lived a long time before the theory of evolution.
In *Troilus and Criseyde* Chaucer remarks that things in classical
Troy differed from things in fourteenth-century England,
but he does not tell us *how* they differed, and the question
does not appear to have bothered him greatly. We might
expect, though, that the background, even if anachronistic
in some respects, should be realistic. This is most true of *Sir
Gawain and the Green Knight*. The several descriptions there of
armour, dress and architecture are functional in that they
are intended to convey the civilised life of the two courts,
Arthur's and Bertilak's, but the extensive vocabulary of the
alliterative tradition and the evident desire to impress by
fine writing would anyway encourage this elaboration. The
description of Bertilak's castle has been compared in its
technical detail with Chaucer's portrayal of Fame's palace,
and to Chaucer's detriment, but this is unfair, for Chaucer
seems to have been deliberately aiming for a grotesque effect.
Belshazzar's feast in *Purity* is medieval in its abundance and
formality. The three hunts of *Sir Gawain* are realistic in a

---

lightly, quickly
aught, any money
multiplie, technical term for
  changing base metals into
  gold or silver

usage, custom
lat . . . swithe, get the floor
  swept straightaway

more technical sense: the audience is expected to appreciate the proper method of hunting – and, in the case of the deer, dismembering – the animal.

It is Chaucer who seems to illustrate in his description of places most of the principles of medieval art and architecture. The best painting of the second half of the fourteenth century is in manuscript illumination, with the crowded scenes and lively faces of John Siferwas and the serious expressions and quiet, eloquent gestures of Herman Scheerre.[12] The Wilton Diptych (now in the National Gallery), painted on oak panels, with Richard II and his patron saints reaching out from the left-hand panel to the right-hand Madonna and child who seem to incline towards him, is one exception, and the portrait of Richard in Westminster Abbey another. But in many paintings of the period, despite the delicacy of shading and of colour, the figures are flat, the poses unnatural, the hands and the focusing of the eyes poor. There is almost no attempt at perspective, and not much in the way of spatial illusion is suggested by the backgrounds. Sometimes the birds which decorate the margins are far more real than the figures at the centre. The portrait of Chaucer in Hoccleve's *De Regimine Principium*, MS Harley 4866, painted after his death, manages to convey both age and intelligence; the art of portraiture became better understood in fifteenth-century England. The illustrations to the poems in the *Gawain* manuscript, on the other hand, are indistinct and undistinguished. There is much stylisation generally, for example in the habit of surrounding miniatures with late Gothic architectural settings. In architecture the process was often one of accretion, so that we are unable to take in the whole at a glance, although we may subsequently come to realise the interrelationship of the parts. The depiction of the temple of Venus in *The Parliament of Fowls* or of the three temples in *The Knight's Tale* similarly accumulates details rather than selecting salient ones. So does the description of Bertilak's castle (*Gawain* 763–802), although there Gawain's look is cleverly made to travel upwards from the moat to the towers, chimneys and battlements. The walls of the

Dreamer's room in *The Book of the Duchess* are painted; murals of the period exist from Italy and France, but the ones in the Chapter House of Westminster Abbey are now considerably damaged.

Descriptions of natural scenery are likewise apt to be generalised and all foreground. In the art of the time objects are seldom drawn to scale: their size is related to the emphasis to be put upon them. Chaucer does not seem to have felt the need to describe man's natural environment. The garden of *The Parliament of Fowls* is simply a conventional *locus amoenus*; the trees in the wood of *The Book of the Duchess* are equidistant from each other, and beneath them run small animals that are appropriate, not individual; the flower in the Prologue to *The Legend of Good Women* is a very literary daisy. Country objects are used for characterising human beings – like Alison (I, 3233–70) or Troilus (iv 225–31) or the comparison of the nightingale's song to Criseyde's first surrender (iv 1233–9) – or to describe the Squire's clothes.[13] Or again, the natural description may be rhetorical in function, as in the opening of *The Canterbury Tales*. The *Gawain* poet has similar passages, at the beginning of parts II and IV of his poem, to describe the passing of the seasons, but these go beyond the merely rhetorical. There is description which, while sometimes conventional in its diction, is nevertheless referable to actuality:

> Þe snawe snitered ful snart, þat snayped þe wylde;
> Þe werbelande wynde wapped fro þe hyȝe,
> And drof vche dale ful of dryftes ful grete.   2003–5

More important, the passing year, where the ripeness of autumn turns into the bleakness of winter, is meant to remind Gawain of his approaching doom:

> *þe snawe . . . grete*, the snow which cruelly nipped the wild creatures came shivering down bitterly. The wind rushed whistling from the high ground and drove each valley full of huge drifts.

Þenne al rypez and rotez þat ros vpon fyrst,
And þus ȝirnes þe ȝere in ȝisterdayez mony,
And wynter wyndez aȝayn, as þe worlde askez.

528–30

The plants and flowers in the 'arbour' at the beginning of
Pearl are colourful, but the time is August when the harvest
is gathered in, and the whole setting is meant to symbolise
decay at first to be followed by resurrection later. The
landscape of the river bank and still more the description of
the New Jerusalem are consciously literary in origin. The
hunts in *Sir Gawain and the Green Knight*, however, are once
again an exception: the scenery (especially in the boar hunt)
is that of North-West England.

We have seen often enough that, in the Middle Ages,
stories may be *exempla* and that characters may be types
rather than individuals. Dorigen produces a long list of
virtuous women. Each of Gower's tales in his *Confessio
Amantis* is intended to illustrate a particular sin against love.
The *Gawain* poet appears to have developed a technique of
exempla representing the *opposite* of his theme. Hence in
Patience Jonah acts impatiently, in order to prove that God's
mercy – through which man is enabled to survive – depends
on His patience. The three stories of *Purity* (the Flood,
Sodom and Gomorrah, Belshazzar's feast) all illustrate
uncleanness. Even the parable of the workers in the vineyard
in *Pearl* shows that strict justice is not what matters most to
God. Langland, too, has his *exempla* – this, for instance, on
the value of learning:

Take two strong men and in Themese caste hem,
And both naked as a nedle, her non sykerer than other.
That one hath connynge, and can swymmen and dyuen,

þenne . . . askez, Then everything that sprang up early
on ripens and decays. And so
the year slips away in a
series of yesterdays, and winter comes round again, as is
the way of the world.

nedle, needle
her . . . other, neither safer than
the other
connynge, skill

That other is lewed of that laboure, lerned neuere swymme;
Which trowestow of tho two in Themese is in moste drede?

　　　　　　　　　　　　　　　　　B xii 161–5

Langland's folk on the field are more types than Chaucer's pilgrims. Later on in his poem, in passus (section) v of the B text, Langland personifies the Seven Deadly Sins. Some of the details are memorable: Glutton's hangover, Wrath's snivelling manner, the worn tunic of Avarice on which there is scarcely room for a louse to leap about, but all these are symbolic of a particular sin. Furthermore, the personalities of the Sins can change: Sloth is sometimes a priest, sometimes a layman, and Wrath moves from being the convent gardener to the nuns' cook; later still he is seen getting short shrift in a monastery. Piers Plowman, who gives the poem its name, changes from the ploughman of the *Visio* to the human nature of Christ in the middle of the *Vita*, and again to the ideal pope towards the end of the poem.

What would appear to make Chaucer's work more realistic, or at least more plausible, than the writing of most of his contemporaries is that more often than they he will select a dramatic detail, one which, while appropriate and occasionally even conventional, will relate description or gesture to a state of mind. This is a question of frequency in Chaucer, for one could equally well cite the Green Knight nonchalantly using the handle of his battle-axe to vault over the stream, or Langland's gluttonous Doctor who lifts his cup to his mouth even as he extols abstinence, or Amans pretending to have forgotten something so that he may return and bid his Lady goodnight once more.[14] My earlier discussion of the Canterbury pilgrims will have demonstrated this feature in Chaucer, and it is far more common in *The Canterbury Tales* than in his earlier poetry. Other instances are the Friar of *The Summoner's Tale* settling himself comfortably beside the sick man's couch:

lewed . . . laboure, ignorant of
　　that art

trowestow, do you imagine
drede, fear

And fro the bench he droof awey the cat,
And leyde adoun his potente and his hat,
And eek his scrippe, and sette hym softe adoun.

1775-7

January sitting up in bed:

He was al coltissh, ful of ragerye,
And ful of jargon as a flekked pye.
The slakke skyn aboute his nekke shaketh,
Whil that he sang, so chaunteth he and craketh.

1847-50

or even a detail (probably original with Chaucer) from the
many in the description of the Temple of Mars:

The smylere with the knyf under the cloke.

Knight's Tale, 1999

These are typical of a begging friar, the *senex amans* and the
god of War. They also bring alive Thomas's confessor,
January, and the medieval assassin. By seizing on a dramatic
moment, they show character through action.

The realism, then, is most often a realism in detail. Now
and again there are sufficient details in the portrayal of one
character to make him seem psychologically 'real'. This is
true of Gawain. In many ways he is the archetypal romance
knight, yet his journey to the Green Chapel is tedious and
cold as well as adventurous. It lasts eight weeks. He cannot
sleep on the night before the second encounter with the
Green Knight and he flinches as the axe comes down for the
first time. It is also true, I think, of Dorigen. Despite the
blatant unreality of the plot of *The Franklin's Tale* (and also
of several other Chaucerian plots), its heroine comes to life
through her very neurosis. She broods over the black rocks
until she makes them the symbol of her separation from her

potente, staff
eek, too
scrippe, bag (for alms)
sette . . . adoun, settled himself
    comfortably down

ragerye, lust
jargon, chatter
flekked pye, spotted magpie
slakke, slack
craketh, croaks

husband and the barrier to his safe return; she cannot bring
herself to join in her friends' well-meaning attempts to 'take
her out of herself'; she gives her promise to Aurelius *in pley*,
scarcely realising what she is doing; she spends a day or two
considering whether suicide would not be preferable to
dishonour, but is saved from having to decide by Arveragus's
fortunate return; she later meets Aurelius, half-demented
and knowing only the terrible necessity of keeping her
word:[15]

> And he saleweth hire with glad entente,
> And asked of hire whiderward she wente;
> And she answerde, half as she were mad,
> 'Unto the garden, as myn housbonde bad,
> My trouthe for to holde, allas! allas!'   1509–13

Much of the Wife of Bath's *experience* is psychologically
credible, although her examples usually come from *auctoritee*.
Gower's forte is his almost invariable clarity of action and
his achievement of the correct mood for his story, rather than
very much dramatic detail. He is, in the main, a very
'literary' writer. But where a comparison with Chaucer is
possible, it is not always one-sided. In his tale of Florent
(Book ii), which is the same story as *The Wife of Bath's Tale*,
Florent is so embarrassed that when he takes the Hag back
to his castle they travel by night, and the wedding takes
place at night as well. But the sudden disclosure in open
court of her terms for having supplied the correct answer to
the all-important question is a dramatic detail of Chaucer's.
Gower's Medea (*Confessio Amantis* v, a story longer and
frequently better than its counterpart in *The Legend of Good
Women*) sees from the shore the sun shining on the golden
fleece in Jason's boat and knows her lover has returned
successfully. Chaucer misses the irony of Lucrece welcoming
Tarquin and entertaining him in her house (*Confessio Amantis*
vii), for in *The Legend of Good Women* Tarquin arrives in the
middle of the night. In Gower Lucrece breaks down when

saleweth, greets   *bad*, ordered
with glad entente, cheerfully   *trouthe*, word

she begins to inform her husband and her father of the rape; in Chaucer she tells all her friends. Yet Chaucer achieves some actuality by a greater use of direct speech, and Gower is not as imaginative as this:

> And as the se, with tempest al toshake,
> That after, whan the storm is al ago,
> Yit wol the water quappe a day or two,
> Ryght so, thogh that hire forme were absent,
> The plesaunce of hire forme was present.
>
> *Legend of Good Women* 1765-9

In the story of Virginia as told by Gower (Book vii), the father kills his daughter in the king's presence and then fights his way out of the room. This is more dramatic than *The Physician's Tale* where she herself begs him to kill her, but only after he has granted her time for meditation.

In medieval stories characters are apt to break off from dialogue to deliver a long speech addressed not particularly to the other speakers but to the world at large. This is so most often, as we might imagine, in formal poems like *The Knight's Tale* or *Troilus and Criseyde*. With the lower-class characters of the fabliaux the language is correspondingly more realistic and attuned to the particular situation. Professor Margaret Schlauch has demonstrated how Chaucer sometimes adapts his syntax to suggest a colloquial style for characters like the Wife of Bath or Pandarus.[16] In his book on *Sir Gawain and the Green Knight*, L. D. Benson shows that the syntax of alliterative poetry is typically coordinate, with the regular use of simple conjunctions and the frequent omission of connectives altogether. Juxtaposition of clauses is characteristic, whereas Chaucer's stylistic bent is for subordination, so that his sentences are longer and seem to run more fluently.[17] Gower's style is efficient and unobtrusive; it satisfies but seldom inspires. In alliterative poetry the most

---

toshake, tossed
al ago, quite over
Yit, still

quappe, heave
plesaunce, delight

elaborate diction, and also the most pronounced alliteration, is apt to occur in descriptive passages. This is the case in *Pearl*, where the argument between the Dreamer and the Maiden, although it can scarcely be realistic since a bereaved father is addressing a blessed soul on the borders of Heaven, is much less obviously impressive in its style than both the earlier and the later description: content has, for a time, become more important than language.

Langland, too, has lengthy speeches, sometimes so lengthy that by the end we have almost forgotten who the speaker is. Yet his style is less strained and more prosaic than that of much alliterative poetry. The digressions (of which there are several) are, in his case, not the product of rhetorical art but of nature. For he is a continual arguer, ready with a *contra* or an *ergo*, constantly making distinctions, getting distracted from the point at issue to ride away on a hobby-horse of his own. Arguments in life are seldom very tidy affairs; it is only when we write them up that clarity creeps in. He knows the ideal course for mankind, but the actual often pulls him up short, as it does in the episode of the half-acre (B vi) and in the *Vita de Dobest* (B xix and xx). There are two kinds of meed: unjust reward and the proper payment for work done, given and received by good men. There are two kinds of monk, those inside the cloister:

For in cloistre cometh no man to chide ne to fiȝte,
But alle is buxumnesse there and bokes, to rede and to lerne.
In scole there is scorne but if a clerke wil lerne,
And grete loue and lykynge, for eche of hem loueth other.

and those who cannot wait to get outside:

Ac now is Religioun a ryder, a rowmer bi stretes,
A leder of louedayes and a londe-bugger,

chide, quarrel	*A leder . . . londe-bugger*, good at
buxumnesse, obedience	settling disputes, and a buyer
lykynge, friendship	of land
a ryder . . . stretes, a horseman,	
a roamer along the highways	

A priker on a palfray fro manere to manere,
An heep of houndes at his ers, as he a lorde were.
And but if his knaue knele that shal his cuppe brynge,
He loureth on hym and axeth hym who tauȝte hym curteisye?

                                         B x 302–11

It is the old Gregorian joke of the monk out of the cloister
being like a fish out of water, which Chaucer had used in
his *General Prologue*, but here it comes with a bluntness and a
ferocity Chaucer does not dream of. The last thing Langland
would say, however ironically, would be that *his opinion was
good*. Langland's imagery is often unremarkable enough: the
covetous man is lured by 'something under the thumb', as a
hawk is; poverty and penance may be bitter like the shell
of a walnut, but they lead to Christ, the sweet kernel inside;
imperfect priests will not produce a good flock any more
than rotten boughs green leaves. Sometimes the comparison
of two objects, simple in themselves, is as startling as anything in metaphysical poetry. Love is the treacle of heaven;
rich men should become *Godes foules* to provide for the clergy,
since the old desert hermits were fed by birds; lords and ladies
should entertain the poor who are 'God's minstrels'. This is
a way in which Chaucer is seldom creative.

Should we conclude, then, that Chaucer was less realistic
in his own day than he appears to us, that his verisimilitude
resides mainly in his language or physical description and
only occasionally and intuitively in characterisation? Not
altogether. The picture of the urbane, ironic, detached
Chaucer, who left philosophical speculation to *clerkes* and
who could (like his own Pandarus) laugh ruefully at himself,
contains some truth but has perhaps been overstressed. It
fails to do justice to the man who was, much more than his
contemporaries, aware that no class has a monopoly of
what is right. If he chose, at the end of *The Parliament of Fowls*,
to go back to his books, it was, as he tells us, because he

A . . . palfray, galloping on a steed
manere, manor
And . . . curteisye, And unless the servant who brings his cup kneels, he glowers at him and asks him who taught him manners.

delighted in reading them, because they contained so much that was perennially valuable. He saw their lessons bodied forth in the everyday behaviour of men around him. When he adapts what he reads, it does not always come off and he grows bored with *The Squire's Tale* or with *The Legend of Good Women*. More often he enters wholeheartedly into the re-creation, so that he is captivated by Criseyde or revolted by the Pardoner. But most of all, six hundred years later, he is still able to communicate his enthusiasm to us.

Abbreviations used in the Notes

BD	Book of the Duchess
HF	House of Fame
PF	Parliament of Fowls
TC	Troilus and Criseyde
CT	Canterbury Tales
GP	General Prologue to The Canterbury Tales
KT	Knight's Tale
RT	Reeve's Tale
MLT	Man of Law's Tale
WBProl	Wife of Bath's Prologue
ClT	Clerk's Tale
MerT	Merchant's Tale
FT	Franklin's Tale
ParProl	Parson's Prologue
ParT	Parson's Tale

BURROW,   J. A. Burrow, *Geoffrey Chaucer* (Penguin Critical Anthologies, Harmondsworth, 1969)

MED   *Middle English Dictionary*, ed. H. Kurath, S. M. Kuhn and J. Reidy (Ann Arbor, 1952–)

DONALDSON, Poetry   E. T. Donaldson, *Chaucer's Poetry* (New York, 1958)

DONALDSON, Speaking   E. T. Donaldson, *Speaking of Chaucer* (London, 1970)

MUSCATINE   C. Muscatine, *Chaucer and the French Tradition* (Berkeley, 1957)

ROBINSON   F. N. Robinson (ed.), *The Works of Geoffrey Chaucer* (2nd ed., Boston, 1957)

ROWLAND   B. Rowland, *Companion to Chaucer Studies* (Toronto, 1968)

SCHOECK AND
TAYLOR, I   R. J. Schoeck and J. Taylor, *Chaucer Criticism*: I, *The Canterbury Tales* (Notre Dame, 1960)

SCHOECK AND
TAYLOR, II   R. J. Schoeck and J. Taylor, *Chaucer Criticism*: II, *Troilus and Criseyde and The Minor Poems* (Notre Dame, 1961)

Sphere History, I   *Sphere History of Literature in the English Language*, vol I: The Middle Ages, ed. W. F. Bolton (London, 1970)

WAGEN-
KNECHT,   E. Wagenknecht, *Chaucer: Modern Essays in Criticism* (New York, 1959)

JEGP   *Journal of English and Germanic Philology*
MÆ   *Medium Ævum*
MLR   *Modern Language Review*
MPh   *Modern Philology*
PMLA   *Publications of the Modern Language Association of America*
SPh   *Studies in Philology*

Notes to Chapter I (pp. 1-15)

1 *TC* v 1786–92. All references are to *The Works of Geoffrey Chaucer*, ed. F. N. Robinson (2nd ed., Boston, 1957). The point is made by Rosemary Woolf, 'Chaucer as a Satirist in the General Prologue to the *Canterbury Tales*', *Critical Quarterly* 1 (1959) 157.

2 Recently made conveniently accessible in Burrow, pp. 41–7.

3 T. S. Eliot, 'Philip Massinger', *Elizabethan Essays* (London, 1934) p. 155.

4 M. M. Crow and C. C. Olsen, *Chaucer Life-Records* (Oxford, 1966).

5 D. W. Robertson, *Chaucer's London* (London, 1968).

6 G. Mathew, *The Court of Richard II* (London, 1968) p. 62.

7 E. T. Donaldson, 'Chaucer the Pilgrim', *PMLA* 69 (1954) 928–36 (reprinted Schoeck and Taylor, I, pp. 1–13 and *Speaking*, pp. 1–12). For a different view, see J. M. Major, 'The Personality of Chaucer the Pilgrim', *PMLA* 75 (1960) 160–2.

8 Frequently reproduced, e.g. Burrow, opposite p. 164; in colour accompanying M. Galway, 'The "Troilus" Frontispiece', *MLR* 44 (1949) 162–77. (Many of Miss Galway's identifications should be treated with caution.)

9 Cf. *MerT* 2122–4, but Chaucer is not usually so obvious as this. A more subtle example is *FT* 1493–8, a valid objection by the pilgrims and a promise of its resolution later. The end of the story is a competition (for pilgrims and court audience) to decide which character was most *gentil*.

10 Mathew, pp. 108–10, Beryl Smalley, *English Friars and Antiquity in the Early Fourteenth Century* (Oxford, 1960) p. 26, suggests a 'half-lettered' audience, below this social level, of people who either could not read or who preferred to listen.

11 *The Words We Use* (London, 1954) pp. 235–9. For an excellent brief introduction to Chaucer's English, see

Appendix II of *The General Prologue to The Canterbury Tales*, ed. P. Hodgson (London, 1969).

12 B. M. H. Strang, *A History of English* (London, 1970) pp. 214–15.

13 For some important examples of semantic change, see M. Bowden, *A Reader's Guide to Geoffrey Chaucer* (London, 1965) pp. 196–206 and M. Hussey, A. C. Spearing and J. Winny, *An Introduction to Chaucer* (Cambridge, 1960) pp. 185–90.

Notes to Chapter II (pp. 16–55)

1 Text and translation, Burrow, pp. 26–8.
2 I quote from the Middle English translation in Robinson.
3 Muscatine, p. 76.
4 *The Art of Courtly Love*, by Andreas Capellanus, translated by J. J. Parry (New York, 1941). The Latin title is *De Arte Honeste Amandi* (or simply *De Amore*). *Honeste* means 'suitable', 'what is fitting' rather than Parry's 'courtly'.
5 C. S. Lewis, *The Allegory of Love* (London, 1936). Some of Lewis's ideas – on the 'newness' of twelfth-century love poetry, its limitation to courtly society and its rivalry with Christianity – have been rejected by Peter Dronke, *Medieval Latin and the Rise of the European Love Lyric* (Oxford, 1965). Most critics now agree that Lewis was wrong to regard adultery as a necessary concomitant of *fine amour*.
6 Cf. *TC* ii 607–9:

> For man may love, of possibilite,
> A womman so, his herte may tobreste,
> And she naught love ayein, but if hire leste.

7 Lewis, p. 23.
8 *TC* iii 1772–8.
9 *TC* iv 1672. *Trouthe* is 'the one human value the poem leaves entirely unquestioned', Donaldson, *Poetry*, p. 974. Aeneas, who deceives Dido, has *never a del of trouthe*, *HF* 331.

10 J. M. Steadman, ' "Courtly Love" as a Problem of Style', *Chaucer und Seine Zeit. Symposion fur Walter F. Schirmer* (Tubingen, 1968) pp. 1–33. See also E. T. Donaldson, 'The Myth of Courtly Love', *Ventures* (Magazine of the Yale Graduate School) 5 (1965) 16–23, reprinted *Speaking*, pp. 154–63.

11 Well illustrated by W. Clemen, *Chaucer's Early Poetry* (London, 1963) pp. 53–4, 62–3.

12 R. Jordan, *Chaucer and the Shape of Creation* (Harvard, 1967). I am not convinced that this is more than an interesting analogy. Cf. Clemen, p. 21 and A. K. Moore, 'Medieval English Literature and the Question of Unity', *MPh* 65 (1968) 285–300.

13 A good short introduction to Chaucer's rhetoric is R. O. Payne's chapter in Rowland, pp. 38–57.

14 Quoted by Robertson, *Chaucer's London*, p. 181.

15 Originally in 'The Pattern of Consolation in *The Book of the Duchess*', *Speculum* 31 (1956) 626–48, reprinted Schoeck and Taylor, II, pp. 232–60. More recently in *Chaucer* (London, 1968) pp. 25–6. For a contrary view, see I. Bishop, *Pearl in its Setting* (Oxford, 1968) pp. 23–4.

16 Clemen, p. 13.

17 Muscatine, p. 108.

18 R. W. Frank, 'Structure and Meaning in the *Parlement of Foules*', *PMLA* 71 (1956) 530–9.

19 D. S. Brewer, *The Parlement of Foulys* (London, 1960) p. 39.

20 Brewer, p. 3.

21 Brewer, pp. 37–8.

22 'The courtly without the vulgar makes of love a "sentiment" merely; the vulgar without the courtly makes of love sexuality and lust', H. S. Corsa, *Chaucer: Poet of Mirth and Morality* (Notre Dame, 1964) p. 27.

23 Muscatine, p. 141.

24 See the opening chapter of D. W. Robertson, *A Preface to Chaucer* (London, 1963).

25 Lawlor, *Chaucer*, p. 91. The lines are v 1772–85 (note the mention of Alcestis at 1778).

26 *CT* II 60.

27 For the laboured moral, cf. 799–801, 908–9, 1954–8.

Notes to Chapter III (pp. 56–98)

1 *Destruction of Troy*, Prologue, 33–45.
2 R. A. Pratt, 'Chaucer and *Le Roman de Troyle et de Criseida*', *SPh* 53 (1956) 509–39. I quote Boccaccio and Benoit in the translations of R. K. Gordon, *The Story of Troilus* (Dutton paperback, 1964). Two recent and well-annotated editions of Chaucer's poem are those of D. Cook (Doubleday Anchor paperback, 1966) and selections by D. S. and L. E. Brewer (London, 1969).
3 Cf. ii 1114–16, and further H. M. Smyser, 'The Domestic Background of *Troilus and Criseyde*', *Speculum* 31 (1956) 297–315.
4 *The Allegory of Love*, pp. 176–97; more explicitly in 'What Chaucer Really Did to *Il Folostrato*', *Essays and Studies* 17 (1932) 56–75 (reprinted Schoeck and Taylor, II, pp. 16–33). See also R. Sharrock, 'Second Thoughts: C. S. Lewis on Chaucer's *Troilus*', *Essays in Criticism* (1958) 123–37, and, for a detailed comparison, S. B. Meech, *Design in Chaucer's Troilus* (Syracuse, 1959).
5 A. Gaylord, 'Friendship in Chaucer's *Troilus*', *Chaucer Review* 3 (1969) 239–64. cf. I. L. Gordon, *The Double Sorrow of Troilus* (Oxford, 1970) pp. 110–13.
6 C. A. Owen, Jnr., 'Mimetic Form in the Central Love Scene of *Troilus and Criseyde*', *MPh* 67 (1969) 125–32.
7 D. R. Howard, *The Three Temptations* (Princeton, 1966) p. 154.
8 A. David, 'The Hero of the *Troilus*', *Speculum* 37 (1962) 566–81. For a different view of character, cf. R. O. Payne, *The Key of Remembrance* (New Haven, 1963) p. 180: 'an almost completely static concept of characterization in more or less set pieces'.
9 D. W. Robertson, *A Preface to Chaucer* (London, 1963) p. 497.
10 D. S. Brewer, 'The Ideal of Feminine Beauty in Medieval Literature', *MLR* 50 (1955) 257–69.
11 Donaldson, *Poetry*, pp. 965–80 (reprinted Burrow, pp.

190–206). This is easily the best short criticism of the poem.

12 For *unkynde* ('disloyal', 'inconstant') see Gordon, Appendix.

13 A fourteenth-century Italian manuscript of Benoit shows Diomede leaning over to talk to Criseyde even as Troilus and the Trojans are handing her over to the Greeks. (Margaret R. Scherer, *Legends of Troy in Art and Literature* (London, 1963) plate 82, p. 103.)

14 *Consolation of Philosophy*, I, metre 5. I owe this reference to Mr J. D. Burnley.

15 Quotations from Robert Henryson, *Testament of Cresseid*, ed. D. Fox (London, 1968).

16 'The lengthy wooing and the three years "bliss" of Chaucer's lovers are condensed by Shakespeare into a single meeting and one night's enjoyment.', M. C. Bradbrook, 'What Shakespeare Did to Chaucer's *Troilus and Criseyde*', *Shakespeare Quarterly* 9 (1958) 316.

17 G. Bullough, *Narrative and Dramatic Sources of Shakespeare* VI (London, 1966) p. 109.

18 Bullough, p. 86.

19 *Double Sorrow*, pp. 114–17. Her discussion is based on Gaylord, *SPh* 61 (1964).

20 *Double Sorrow*, p. 140.

21 D. R. Howard, 'Chaucer the Man', *PMLA* 80 (1965) 337–43. For a different view, see D. S. Brewer, 'Class Distinction in Chaucer', *Speculum* 43 (1968) 290–305.

22 D. Bethurum, 'Chaucer's Point of View as Narrator in the Love Poems', *PMLA* 74 (1959) 511–20 (reprinted Schoeck and Taylor, II, pp. 211–31).

23 'The Ending of Chaucer's *Troilus*', *Early English and Norse Studies presented to Hugh Smith* (ed. A. Brown and P. Foote, London, 1963) pp. 26–45 (reprinted *Speaking*, pp. 84–101). I think that Professor Donaldson somewhat overstresses the intractability of the material, just as Mrs Gordon's chapter on the Narrator (*Double Sorrow*, pp. 61–92) finds too much deliberate ambiguity.

24 The point is well made in T. P. Dunning, 'God and Man in *Troilus and Criseyde*', *English and Medieval Studies Presented to J. R. R. Tolkien* (Oxford, 1962) pp. 164–82,

and in Mrs Gordon's chapter on Boethius, *Double Sorrow*, pp. 24–60.
25 Muscatine, p. 123.
26 Perhaps expanding Boethius: 'For in alle adversites of fortune the moost unseely kynde of contrarious fortune is to han been weleful.' Book ii, prosa iv.

Notes to Chapter IV: Canterbury Tales I
(pp. 99–140)

1 This seems to me a better practice than wholesale modernisation. The Everyman edition, ed. A. C. Cawley, is both convenient and accurate.
2 J. R. Hulbert, '*The Canterbury Tales* and their Narrators', *SPh* 45 (1948) 565–77. For a comprehensive discussion of the organisation of the *Tales*, see W. H. Clawson, 'The Framework of *The Canterbury Tales*', *University of Toronto Quarterly* 20 (1951) 137–154 (reprinted Wagenknecht, pp. 3–22).
3 M. Bloomfield, 'Authenticating Realism and the Realism of Chaucer', *Thought* 39 (1964) 335–58.
4 For details about the pilgrims, I have drawn especially from P. Hodgson, *The General Prologue* (London, 1969), Donaldson, *Poetry* and M. Hussey, *Chaucer's World* (Cambridge, 1967).
5 The Prioress is accompanied by a second nun (nuns do not travel alone) and, the *GP* says, by three attendant priests. If, however, line 164 reads *the preest is thre* (rather than Ellesmere's *preestes thre*) there may have been only one, and we hear of only one Nun's Priest later. Neither the Second Nun nor the Nun's Priest is described in *GP*, although both later tell tales.
6 P. E. Beichner, 'Daun Piers, Monk and Business Administrator', *Speculum* 34 (1959) 611–19 (reprinted Schoeck and Taylor, I, pp. 52–62). A recent detailed examination of the Monk's probable duties (H. E. Ussery, 'The Status of Chaucer's Monk: Clerical, Official, Social, and Moral', *Tulane Studies in English* 17 (1969) 1–30) suggests that

outridere is unlikely to have been a monastic office in its own right. The monk in *The Shipman's Tale* rides out *because of* his office which was probably that of cellarer (VII, 65–6, 272–3). *Outridere* in *GP* may be pejorative: the Monk greatly abused his privilege of sometimes being allowed outside the monastery. Yet, since Langland and Gower make similar complaints, he was probably a realistic enough figure to the pilgrims.

7 Any good edition of *GP* will point out the parallels. For greater detail see M. Bowden, *A Commentary on the General Prologue to the Canterbury Tales* (2nd ed., New York, 1967), and for a comparison with Langland, J. A. W. Bennett, 'Chaucer's Contemporary' in *Piers Plowman: Critical Approaches*, ed. S. S. Hussey (London, 1969) pp. 310–24.

8 The passage from Jean de Meun is quoted by both Bowden and Hodgson, that from Bromyard by G. Owst, *Literature and Pulpit in Medieval England* (Cambridge, 1933) p. 327.

9 E. T. Donaldson, 'Chaucer the Pilgrim', *PMLA* 69 (1954) 928–36 (reprinted *Speaking*, pp. 1–12 and Schoeck and Taylor, I, pp. 1–13).

10 On this point see Lawlor, *Chaucer*, ch. v, 'Tales and Tellers'.

11 A Henri Bayliff appears as an innkeeper in Southwark records for 1380–1 and a Henry Bailey (probably the same man) held offices of M.P., tax collector and coroner at various times between 1376 and 1394.

12 'The Host is something of a guide, something of a referee, something of a master of revels, worse than the best of the pilgrims and better than the worst.' P. Ruggiers, *The Art of the Canterbury Tales* (Madison, 1965) p. 21.

13 Cf. *PF*, 53–4:

> And that oure present worldes lyves space
> Nis but a maner deth, what wey we trace.

14 G. L. Kittredge, 'Chaucer's Discussion of Marriage', *MPh* 9 (1911–12) 435–67 (reprinted Schoeck and Taylor, I, pp. 130–59 and Wagenknecht, pp. 188–215); also in his *Chaucer and his Poetry* (Cambridge, Mass., 1915).

15 D. Mehl, *The Middle English Romances of the Thirteenth and Fourteenth Centuries* (London, 1969) p. 17. See also J. B. Severs, *A Manual of the Writings in Middle English 1050–1500: The Romances* (New Haven, 1967), especially pp. 11–12, 38–40, 133–4, and A. C. Baugh, 'The Middle English Romance: Some Questions of Creation, Presentation and Preservation', *Speculum* 42 (1967) 1–31.

16 Burrow, pp. 72, 77.

17 A summary of the *Teseida*, pointing out the differences from *KT*, appears in the introduction to J. A. W. Bennett's edition, *The Knight's Tale* (London, 1954).

18 G. Kane, *Middle English Literature* (London, 1951) pp. 87–9.

19 *Chaucer's World*, p. 40.

20 E. Salter, *Chaucer: The Knight's Tale and The Clerk's Tale* (London, 1962).

21 Criseyde uses the same phrase, *TC* iv 1586.

22 Two good editions have appeared within the last few years, by P. Hodgson (London, 1960) and by A. C. Spearing (Cambridge, 1966).

23 L. H. Loomis, 'Chaucer and the Breton Lays of the Auchinleck Manuscript', *SPh* 38 (1941) 18–29.

24 *Preface to Chaucer*, p. 472.

25 L. A. Mann, '*Gentilesse* and *The Franklin's Tale*', *SPh* 63 (1966) 10–29. R. M. Lumiansky, however, views the tale as a not altogether successful attempt to combine the two systems of courtly love and marriage: the characters vacillate between the two attitudes, and this reflects the Franklin's own social uncertainty. (*Of Sondry Folk* (Austin, 1955) pp. 182–93.)

Notes to Chapter V: Canterbury Tales II
(pp. 141–94)

1 T. W. Craik, *The Comic Tales of Chaucer* (London, 1964) pp. 58–9.

2 Quoted by Rosemary Woolf, *Sphere History* I, p. 282.

3 For a representative selection, translated from French,

see R. Hellman and R. O'Gorman, *Fabliaux* (London, 1965). There is a good brief discussion by D. S. Brewer in Rowland, pp. 247–67.

4 R. E. Kaske, 'Patristic Exegesis: The Defence', *Critical Approaches to Medieval Literature*, ed. D. Bethurum (New York, 1960) pp. 27–60, reprinted Burrow, pp. 233–9.

5 P. E. Beichner, 'Characterization in *The Miller's Tale*', Schoeck and Taylor, I, p. 119.

6 3213–18, 3257–8, 3332, 3360, 3377. See E. Birney, 'The Inhibited and the Uninhibited: Ironic Structure in *The Miller's Tale*', *Neophilologus* 44 (1960) 333–8.

7 T. Whittock, *A Reading of the Canterbury Tales* (Cambridge, 1968) p. 84.

8 Craik, p. 21.

9 3448–64 (and notice the tone of self-satisfaction achieved by the heavy pause in 3461); cf. *RT* 4049–54, 4096, 4122–6.

10 E. T. Donaldson, 'The Idiom of Popular Poetry in the *Miller's Tale*', *English Institute Essays* (1950) 116–40 (reprinted *Speaking*, pp. 13–29).

11 Cf. *WBProl*, 489–90.

12 M. Hussey, *The Merchant's Prologue and Tale* (Cambridge, 1969) p. 13.

13 Cf. *ParT*, 859.

14 Donaldson, *Speaking*, p. 38.

15 *The Oxford Dictionary of the Christian Church*, ed. F. L. Cross, see 'Saints, Devotion to the'.

16 *litel* is also used at 495, 503, 509, 552, 587, 596, 667. Elsewhere in the tale *smale*, *sely* (innocent), *yong* and *innocent* are used. That the poem also achieves considerable dignity has been demonstrated by G. H. Russell, 'Chaucer: *The Prioress's Tale*', *Medieval Literature and Civilization, Studies in Memory of G. N. Garmonsway*, ed. D. A. Pearsall and R. A. Waldron (London, 1969) pp. 211–27.

17 e.g. by G. Kane, *Middle English Literature*, pp. 62–5.

18 Cf. 631–7, 907–10, 1041–3.

19 For a comparison of an extended passage of *ClT* with *Le Livre Griseldis*, see the appendix to the edition by J. Winny (Cambridge, 1966).

20 J. Sledd, '*The Clerk's Tale*: The Monsters and the Critics', *MPh* 51 (1953-4) 73-82 (reprinted Schoeck and Taylor, I, pp. 160-74 and Wagenknecht, pp. 226-39).

21 206-7, 394-9, 871-2, 932-8. Cf. 'This vertu [Pacience] maketh a man lyk to God, and maketh hym Goddes owene deere child.', *ParT*, 660.

22 R. A. Lanham, 'Game, Play, and High Seriousness in Chaucer's Poetry', *English Studies* 48 (1967) 16.

23 *A Preface to Chaucer, passim*. See also Bethurum, *Critical Approaches*, and J. MacQueen, *Allegory* (London, 1970). A. L. DeNeef, 'Robertson and the Critics', *Chaucer Review* 2 (1967-8) 205-34, traces the development of Robertson's criticism.

24 Compare similar terminology contrasting inessentials and essentials: *chaf* and *stree* versus *corn*, *MLT*, 701-2; *draf* versus *whete*, *ParProl*, 35-6. The twelfth-century Peter of Riga in the Preface to his *Aurora* (which Chaucer mentions in *BD*) says that he wishes to 'elicit some allegories from the letter, as though the kernel from the nut, the grain from the chaff, the honey from the wax, the fire from the smoke, the meal from the barley, the wine from the grape'. (Quoted by P. E. Beichner, 'The Allegorical Interpretation of Medieval Literature', *PMLA* 82 (1967) 33.)

25 Cf. Donaldson, *Speaking*, p. 173: '*The Parsons Tale* is un-exceptionable in its theological doctrine, but in literary terms it is ill-tempered, bad-mannered, pedantic and joyless.' See also W. W. Lawrence, '*The Tale of Melibeus*', *Essays and Studies in Honour of Carleton Brown* (New York, 1940) pp. 101-9 (reprinted in part in S. Sullivan, *Critics on Chaucer* (London, 1970) pp. 133-7).

26 N. Coghill and C. Tolkien, *The Pardoner's Tale* (London, 1958) p. 21. Another useful edition is that by A. C. Spearing (Cambridge, 1965).

27 R. M. Lumiansky, *Of Sondry Folk* (Austin, 1955) pp. 212, 214.

28 Lumiansky, p. 214.

29 There has been much discussion about the identity of the old man. I think he is best seen as the common allegorical

figure of Elde (Old Age), but his importance is that he is in total contrast to the three rioters: they are young, foolish, impolite and avaricious, while he is old, wise, courteous and contemptuous of the world. See J. M. Steadman, 'Old Age and Contemptus Mundi in *The Pardoner's Tale*', *MÆ* 33 (1964) 121–30.

30 R. W. V. Elliott, 'Our Host's "Triacle"': some Observations on Chaucer's *Pardoner's Tale*', *Review of English Literature* 7 (1966) 61–73; P. E. Beichner, 'Chaucer's Pardoner as Entertainer', *Mediæval Studies* 25 (1963) 160–72.

31 Lumiansky, p. 218.

32 D. Holbrook in *The Age of Chaucer*, ed. B. Ford (Penguin, Harmondsworth, 1954). M. J. Donovan (*JEGP* 52 (1953) 498–508) sees Chanticleer as 'any holy man', the Fox as 'heretic and devil' and the widow as the Church. C. Dahlberg (*JEGP* 53 (1954) 277–90) takes the allegory further and sees in the tale a reflection of the controversy between the secular clergy (Chanticleer) and the friars (the Fox). For a contrary view, see Donaldson in *Critical Approaches* (ed. Bethurum) pp. 16–20 (reprinted in *Speaking*, pp. 134–53).

33 Muscatine, p. 242.

34 H. S. Corsa, *Chaucer: Poet of Mirth and Morality* (Notre Dame, 1964) p. 214.

35 *ParProl*, 31.

Notes to Chapter VI (pp. 195–222)

1 For England, see D. Pearsall, 'The English Chaucerians' in *Chaucer and Chaucerians*, ed. D. S. Brewer (London, 1966) pp. 201–39. For Scotland, C. S. Lewis, *English Literature in the Sixteenth Century, Excluding Drama* (Oxford, 1954) pp. 66–119.

2 R. H. Robbins, 'The Lyrics', Rowland, pp. 313–31.

3 A good introduction to alliterative verse is the chapter by D. J. Williams in *Sphere History*, I, pp. 107–58. See also D. Everett, 'The Alliterative Revival', *Essays in Middle English Literature* (Oxford, 1955) pp. 49–96.

4 S. S. Hussey, *Piers Plowman: Critical Approaches* (London, 1969), Introduction.

5 A. V. C. Schmidt, 'Langland and Scholastic Philosophy', *MÆ* 38 (1969) 150.

6 Quoted above, pp. 25–26.

7 S. S. Hussey, '*Sir Gawain* and Romance Writing', *Studia Neophilologica* 40 (1968) 161–74.

8 ed. R. J. Gates (Philadelphia, 1969).

9 On the ending of *Confessio Amantis*, see C. S. Lewis, *The Allegory of Love*, pp. 217–22.

10 A valuable corrective is C. S. Lewis, *The Discarded Image* (Cambridge, 1964) to which I am indebted in this chapter.

11 For a brief introduction, see C. Wood, 'Chaucer and Astrology' in Rowland, pp. 176–91. Lewis, *Discarded Image*, and W. C. Curry, *Chaucer and the Mediaeval Sciences* (revised ed., New York, 1960) also provide useful background material.

12 M. Rickert, *Painting in Britain: The Middle Ages* (London, 1954). See also J. Evans, *English Art, 1307–1461* (Oxford, 1949).

13 Cf. B. H. Bronson, *In Search of Chaucer* (Toronto, 1960) pp. 16–20; the extract is reprinted in Burrow, pp. 214–18.

14 *Sir Gawain*, 2231; *Piers Plowman*, B xiii 103; *Confessio Amantis* iv 2825.

15 P. F. Baum, *Chaucer: A Critical Appreciation* (Durham, N.C., 1958) p. 124. J. B. Severs ('Appropriateness of Character to Plot in the "Franklin's Tale"', *Studies in Language and Literature in Honour of Margaret Schlauch* (Warsaw, 1966) pp. 385–96) speaks of Dorigen's 'self-centred emotional extravagance'.

16 M. Schlauch, 'Chaucer's Colloquial English: Its Structural Traits', *PMLA* 67 (1953) 1103–16.

17 L. D. Benson, *Art and Tradition in Sir Gawain and the Green Knight* (New Brunswick, 1965) pp. 151–66. This section is reprinted in D. R. Howard and C. K. Zacher, *Critical Studies of Sir Gawain and the Green Knight* (Notre Dame, 1968) pp. 109–24. Cf. the Langland quotation above, pp. 215–16.

Select Bibliography

BIBLIOGRAPHIES

D. D. GRIFFITH, *Bibliography of Chaucer* 1908–53 (Seattle, 1955)
W. R. CRAWFORD, *Bibliography of Chaucer* 1954–63 (Seattle, 1967)
A. C. BAUGH, *Chaucer* (New York, 1968)

EDITIONS

F. N. ROBINSON, *The Complete Works of Geoffrey Chaucer* (2nd ed., Boston, 1957). Used throughout this book.
W. W. SKEAT, *The Complete Works of Geoffrey Chaucer*, 7 vols. (Oxford, 1894–7)
W. W. SKEAT, *Complete Works of Chaucer* (Oxford Standard Authors, Oxford, 1929)
J. M. MANLY AND E. RICKERT, *The Text of the Canterbury Tales*, 8 vols. (Chicago, 1940)
J. M. MANLY, *Canterbury Tales by Geoffrey Chaucer* (New York, 1928)
R. K. ROOT, *The Book of Troilus and Criseyde* (Princeton, 1926)
D. S. BREWER, *The Parlement of Foulys* (London, 1960)

SELECTIONS

A. C. BAUGH, *Chaucer's Major Poetry* (New York, 1963)
E. T. DONALDSON, *Chaucer's Poetry* (New York, 1958)

TEXTS WITH GLOSSES

A. C. CAWLEY, *Geoffrey Chaucer: Canterbury Tales* (London, 1958)
D. COOK, *Troilus and Criseyde by Geoffrey Chaucer* (New York, 1966)

TRANSLATIONS

J. S. P. TATLOCK AND P. MACKAYE, *The Modern Reader's Chaucer* (New York, 1914)

N. COGHILL, *The Canterbury Tales* (Harmondsworth, 1952)

D. WRIGHT, *Geoffrey Chaucer: The Canterbury Tales* (London, 1964)

N. COGHILL, *Troilus and Criseyde* (Harmondsworth, 1971)

G. P. KRAPP, *Troilus and Cressida* (New York, 1956)

AIDS TO STUDY

D. BETHURUM (ed.), *Critical Approaches to Medieval Literature* (New York, 1960)

W. F. BOLTON (ed.), *Sphere History of Literature in the English Language*, I, *The Middle Ages* (London, 1970)

D. S. BREWER, *Chaucer in His Time* (London, 1963)

M. BOWDEN, *A Commentary on the General Prologue to the Canterbury Tales* (2nd ed., New York, 1967)

W. F. BRYAN AND G. DEMPSTER, *Sources and Analogues of The Canterbury Tales* (Chicago, 1941)

M. M. CROW AND C. C. OLSON, *Chaucer Life-Records* (Oxford, 1966)

W. C. CURRY, *Chaucer and the Mediaeval Sciences* (2nd ed., Oxford, 1960)

R. D. FRENCH, *A Chaucer Handbook* (2nd ed., New York, 1947)

R. K. GORDON, *The Story of Troilus* (London, 1934)

F. E. HALLIDAY, *Chaucer and His World* (London, 1968)

M. HUSSEY, A. C. SPEARING AND J. WINNY, *An Introduction to Chaucer* (Cambridge, 1965)

M. HUSSEY, *Chaucer's World* (Cambridge, 1967)

H. KOKERITZ, *A Guide to Chaucer's Pronunciation* (Stockholm, 1954)

C. S. LEWIS, *The Allegory of Love* (Oxford, 1936)

C. S. LEWIS, *The Discarded Image* (Cambridge, 1964)

R. S. LOOMIS, *A Mirror of Chaucer's World* (Princeton, 1965)

M. F. NIMS, (tr.), *The Poetria Nova of Geoffrey of Vinsauf* (Toronto, 1967)

M. MCKISACK, *The Fourteenth Century, 1307–1399* (Oxford, 1959)

D. W. ROBERTSON, *A Preface to Chaucer* (London, 1963)

B. ROWLAND, *Companion to Chaucer Studies* (Toronto, 1968)

J. S. P. TATLOCK AND A. S. KENNEDY, *A Concordance to the Complete Works of Geoffrey Chaucer* (Washington, 1927)

CRITICISM (Books only are listed)

P. F. BAUM, *Chaucer: A Critical Appreciation* (Durham, N.C., 1958)

B. H. BRONSON, *In Search of Chaucer* (Toronto, 1960)

D. S. BREWER, *Chaucer* (London, 1953)

D. S. BREWER, *Chaucer and Chaucerians* (London, 1966)

J. A. BURROW, *Geoffrey Chaucer* (Penguin Critical Anthologies, Harmondsworth, 1969)

W. CLEMEN, *Chaucer's Early Poetry* (London, 1963)

N. COGHILL, *The Poet Chaucer* (2nd ed., London, 1967)

N. COGHILL, *Geoffrey Chaucer*, Writers and Their Work, 79 (London, 1956)

H. S. CORSA, *Chaucer: Poet of Mirth and Morality* (Notre Dame, 1964)

T. W. CRAIK, *The Comic Tales of Chaucer* (London, 1964)

E. T. DONALDSON, *Speaking of Chaucer* (London, 1970)

I. L. GORDON, *The Double Sorrow of Troilus* (Oxford, 1970)

R. M. JORDAN, *Chaucer and the Shape of Creation* (Cambridge, Mass., 1967)

J. LAWLOR, *Chaucer* (London, 1968)

J. L. LOWES, *Geoffrey Chaucer* (Oxford, 1934)

R. M. LUMIANSKY, *Of Sondry Folk* (Austin, 1955)

C. MUSCATINE, *Chaucer and the French Tradition* (Berkeley, 1957)

R. O. PAYNE, *The Key of Remembrance* (London, 1963)

R. PRESTON, *Chaucer* (London, 1952)

P. RUGGIERS, *The Art of the Canterbury Tales* (Madison, 1965)

R. J. SCHOECK AND J. TAYLOR, *Chaucer Criticism*: I, *The*

Canterbury Tales (Notre Dame, 1960; II, *Troilus and Criseyde and The Minor Poems* (Notre Dame, 1961)

A. C. SPEARING, *Criticism and Mediaeval Poetry* (London, 1964)

E. WAGENKNECHT, *Chaucer: Modern Essays in Criticism* (New York, 1959)

T. WHITTOCK, *A Reading of the Canterbury Tales* (Cambridge, 1968)

Index